# Lecture Notes in Computer Science 8914

*Commenced Publication in 1973*
Founding and Former Series Editors:
Gerhard Goos, Juris Hartmanis, and Jan van Leeuwen

More information about this series at http://www.springer.com/series/7411

Jörn Altmann · Kurt Vanmechelen
Omer F. Rana (Eds.)

# Economics of Grids, Clouds, Systems, and Services

11th International Conference, GECON 2014
Cardiff, UK, September 16–18, 2014
Revised Selected Papers

 Springer

*Editors*
Jörn Altmann
Technology, Economics,
  and Policy Program
College of Engineering
Seoul National University
Gwanak-Gu
Seoul
Korea, Republic of (South Korea)

Omer F. Rana
School of Computer Science
Cardiff University
Cardiff
UK

Kurt Vanmechelen
University of Antwerp
Antwerp
Belgium

ISSN 0302-9743        ISSN 1611-3349   (electronic)
Lecture Notes in Computer Science
ISBN 978-3-319-14608-9        ISBN 978-3-319-14609-6   (eBook)
DOI 10.1007/978-3-319-14609-6

Library of Congress Control Number: 2014959176

LNCS Sublibrary: SL5 – Computer Communication Networks and Telecommunications

Springer Cham Heidelberg New York Dordrecht London

Printed on acid-free paper

Springer International Publishing AG Switzerland is part of Springer Science+Business Media
(www.springer.com)

# Preface

The proceedings of the 11th International Conference on the Economics of Grids, Clouds, Systems, and Services (GECON) were held during September 16–18, 2014 in Cardiff, UK. Cloud computing has now become mainstream, whereas in 2003, when this conference was initiated, the general ideas behind Cloud computing were being talked about within the Web Services and Grid computing communities, with a number of (active) researchers also investigating the associated economic models. Whereas Grid computing was initially very much driven by the computational science and engineering communities, with data/computational infrastructure hosted by national laboratories and (generally) research organizations, Cloud computing has, from its beginnings, been promoted by industry. The aim of the GECON conference has been to bring together this technical expertise (e.g., in resource allocation and quality of service management) with economics expertise (focusing on both micro- and macro-economic modeling and analysis) in order to create effective solutions in this space. Many of the models proposed in this event over the years have now materialized, and its widened scope is more relevant than ever considering the recent developments in our service economy with respect to (automated) trading, pricing, and management of services. Eleven years later, GECON remains true to its original objectives and continues to focus on the marriage of these two types of expertise. In line with this combined focus, it is useful to see two different methodological approaches being considered at GECON, one focusing on a technical perspective to problem solving, the other on economic modeling. Authors adopting a more technical focus often use a quantitative approach to validate their findings, whereas those from economic modeling often adopt a mixed methods (qualitative/quantitative) approach. Therefore, a key objective of this conference series is also to promote this multi-perspective, multidisciplinary approach to validate findings and to introduce authors to the use of these ideas in their own research. The review process ensures that both perspectives are considered equally important and relevant.

GECON 2014 took place in Cardiff (the capital of Wales), a city and county borough whose history spans at least 6,000 years. The city has played an important role in the service industry in the UK, with Cardiff being the main port for exports of coal from the surrounding region for many years. To support the service industry, the city grew rapidly in the nineteenth century. Today, Cardiff hosts the National Museum of Wales, the National Assembly of Wales, and Cardiff University where the conference took place.

This year we received a number of high-quality paper submissions. Each submission received at least three reviews by members of an international Program Committee. Our final program consisted of five sessions (two of which are Work-in-Progress sessions). The schedule for the conference this year was structured to encourage discussions and debates – with a round-table session focusing on "Sharing Economy". We believe such discussion sessions are essential to enable more open and informed dialog between presenters and the audience, and to enable the presenters to better position their work for future events and to get an improved understanding of the impact their work is likely to have on the research community. The presentation sessions set up were:

Session 1: Cloud Adoption
Session 2: Work in Progress on Market Dynamics
Session 3: Cost Optimization
Session 4: Work in Progress on Pricing, Contracts, and Service Selection
Session 5: Economic Aspects of Quality of Service

Session 1 started with a paper by Kaufman, Ma, and Yu entitled "A Metrics Suite for Firm-Level Cloud Computing Adoption Readiness" [1], which focused on gauging perceptions of managers and organizations when considering Cloud computing for outsourcing IT infrastructure and data. The authors interviewed a number of companies to better assess the Cloud adoption readiness of these organizations from both a strategy/management and technology/operations perspective. The subsequent paper by Pallas on "An Agency Perspective to Cloud Computing" used a particular economic modeling approach (agency theory) to model potential conflicts (in issues such as security, legal compliance, long-term availability) between users and providers of resources within a Cloud system [2]. Two example scenarios were used to motivate the proposed approach.

Session 2 was a Work-in-Progress session and included two contributions, both focusing on how Cloud provisioning could be supported through aggregating capacity across multiple providers (likely to be of benefit for consumers) compared to accepting and using the capability from a single large provider. Kim, Kang, and Altmann presented their work on "Goliath vs. a Federation of Davids: Survey of Economic Theories on Cloud Federation". It described the benefits and costs of federation for "small" Clouds and how "small" Clouds can compete with larger Cloud providers (with the latter often having an advantage through economies of scale) [3]. This contribution also discussed whether federation of smaller Clouds is economically viable and under what conditions such a federation could compete with larger providers. The contribution by Vega, Meseguer, and Freitag entitled "Analysis of the Social Effort in Multiplex Participatory Networks" investigated how "community Clouds" could be established by pooling together resources from different individual providers ("citizens") in the context of community networks (essentially, networks established over a small geographical area using resources contributed to by citizens) [4]. The authors investigated message exchanges and traffic on forums and mailing lists associated with the Guifi.net community network to understand how a small number of users act as potential "social bridges" between members of the community. The objective of the work was to understand the impact such members have on the community as a whole and the potential for such members to act as hosts of a potential community Cloud.

Session 3 focused on understanding technical metrics associated with Cloud provisioning and how these could be optimized. The contribution by Lučanin et al. entitled "Energy-Aware Cloud Management through Progressive SLA Specification" investigated how virtual machines could be migrated across multiple data centers to provide a particular energy footprint while still maintaining the quality of service targets [5].

The authors considered workload profiles from the Wikipedia and the Grid 5000 projects to validate their work, demonstrating that by offering virtual machines with differing availability and prices they could achieve (on average) 39 % energy saving per virtual machine. The paper "CloudTracker: Using Execution Provenance to Optimize the Cost of Cloud Use" by Douglas et al. discussed how provenance information obtained from executed jobs on Amazon EC2 instances could be used to predict potential cost of execution [6]. The authors also demonstrated how such a job submission system could be integrated with an existing computational science application. The final paper in this session by Me entitled "Migration to Governmental-Cloud Digital Forensics Community: Economics and Methodology" discussed how government agencies (especially crime and policing agencies) could use Cloud computing infrastructure to carry out forensic investigations [7]. The paper compared the cost of using an in-house computational infrastructure with an outsourced, Cloud-based infrastructure for supporting crime investigations. A key focus was on large-scale data analytics and post event, forensic analysis.

Session 4 consisted of three Work-in-Progress papers focusing on pricing and contracts, especially how parameters such as insurance costs and penalties in Service Level Agreements (SLAs) can be characterized. The contribution by O'Loughlin and Gillam entitled "Performance Evaluation for Cost-Efficient Public Infrastructure Cloud Use" investigated performance variation that can be observed when mapping Amazon instances on physical processors [8]. The authors compared the performance of the same Amazon instance using a number of different benchmarks, showing the variability in performance when the instance was requested over different times and within different data centers (using different physical processors to host the instances, e.g., use of Intel vs. AMD). This variability clearly shows the difficulty of developing SLAs when using public Cloud infrastructure. The contribution by Naldi entitled "Balancing Leasing and Insurance Costs to Achieve Total Risk Coverage in Cloud Storage Multi-Homing" focused on characterizing "insurance" costs due to unavailability of a Cloud provider [9]. The author developed a model describing how a penalty value could be associated with unavailability. The contribution by Galati et al. entitled "A WS-Agreement Based SLA Implementation for the CMAC Platform" described how SLAs could be negotiated and monitored based on the "Condition Monitoring on a Cloud" platform [10]. The authors demonstrated their approach using the Cybula engine for large-scale data analysis. The last paper in this session, "A Domain Specific Language and a Pertinent Business Vocabulary for Cloud Service Selection" by Slawik and Küpper [11], described a domain-specific language for describing services and a business vocabulary for supporting selection and brokering of these services. The authors suggest that as additional providers become available, such a vocabulary is necessary to enable comparison across providers.

The final session focused on economic aspects and modeling strategies for supporting quality of service. The first contribution by Tolosana-Calasanz, Bañares, and Colom entitled "Towards Petri Net-Based Economical Analysis for Streaming Applications Executed over Cloud Infrastructures" described how an application deployed over a distributed computing infrastructure (focusing, in this case, on a systolic array-based architecture) could be modeled from both a "functional" and "operational" perspective [12]. The authors used Reference Nets (a type of Petri net) for developing the model and analyzing it with reference to streaming applications. The contribution by Butoi, Stan, and Silaghi entitled "Autonomous Management of Virtual Machine Failures in IaaS Using Fault Tree Analysis" described strategies for supporting VM migration based on predicted failures in the Cloud infrastructure (which can have varying availability and reliability characteristics) [13]. The authors made use of Xen-based fault traces to demonstrate how their approach, based on fault trees, could be used in practice. A key contribution was to determine how a node within such an infrastructure could accept future jobs or delegate jobs to other nodes based on likely availability profiles. The last paper in this session, entitled "How Do Content Delivery Networks Affect the Economy of the Internet and the Network Neutrality Debate?" by Maillé and Tuffin [14], described how economic models could be associated with content delivery networks involving a combination of content providers and Internet service providers (ISPs). The authors described how content provisioning could be shared across multiple ISPs and the associated potential revenue models based on payment by a sender or receiver of the content. The authors also investigated how content should be cached across different providers and how caching benefits ISPs.

In addition to these sessions, we included the paper by Massimo Felici. This paper, which is aligned with Felici's keynote at GECON 2014 [15], discusses the economics of security and investigates how economics may drive operational security and the deployment of security technologies.

Finally, we would like to wholeheartedly thank the reviewers and Program Committee members for completing their reviews on time, and giving insightful and valuable feedback to the authors. Furthermore, we would like to thank Alfred Hofmann of Springer for his support in publishing the proceedings of GECON 2014. The collaboration with Alfred Hofmann and his team has been, as in the past years, efficient and effective.

September 2014                                                    Kurt Vanmechelen
                                                                        Jörn Altmann
                                                                        Omer F. Rana

# References

1. Kauffman, R.J., Ma, D., Yu, M.: A metrics suite for firm-level cloud computing adoption readiness. In: Altmann, J., Vanmechelen, K., Rana, O.F. (eds.) GECON 2014. LNCS, vol. 8914, pp. 19–35. Springer, Heidelberg (2014)
2. Pallas, F.: An agency perspective to cloud computing. In: Altmann, J., Vanmechelen, K., Rana, O.F. (eds.) GECON 2014. LNCS, vol. 8914, pp. 36–51. Springer, Heidelberg (2014)
3. Kim, K., Kang, S., Altmann, J.: Cloud goliath versus a federation of cloud davids: Survey of economic theories on cloud federation. In: Altmann, J., Vanmechelen, K., Rana, O.F. (eds.) GECON 2014. LNCS, vol. 8914, pp. 55–66. Springer, Heidelberg (2014)
4. Vega, D., Meseguer, R., Freitag, F.: Analysis of the social effort in multiplex participatory networks. In: Altmann, J., Vanmechelen, K., Rana, O.F. (eds.) GECON 2014. LNCS, vol. 8914, pp. 67–79. Springer, Heidelberg (2014)
5. Lučanin, D., Jrad, F., Brandic, I., Streit, A.: Energy-aware cloud management through progressive sla specification. In: Altmann, J., Vanmechelen, K., Rana, O.F. (eds.) GECON 2014. LNCS, vol. 8914, pp. 83–98. Springer, Heidelberg (2014)

6. Douglas, G., Drawert, B., Krintz, C., Wolski, R.: CloudTracker: using execution provenance to optimize the cost of cloud use. In: Altmann, J., Vanmechelen, K., Rana, O.F. (eds.) GECON 2014. LNCS, vol. 8914, pp. 99–113. Springer, Heidelberg (2014)

7. Me, G.: Migration to governmental cloud digital forensics community: economics and methodology. In: Altmann, J., Vanmechelen, K., Rana, O.F. (eds.) GECON 2014. LNCS, vol. 8914, pp. 114–129. Springer, Heidelberg (2014)

8. O'Loughlin, J., Gillam, L.: Performance evaluation for cost-efficient public infrastructure cloud use. In: Altmann, J., Vanmechelen, K., Rana, O.F. (eds.) GECON 2014. LNCS, vol. 8914, pp. 133–145. Springer, Heidelberg (2014)

9. Naldi, M.: Balancing leasing and insurance costs to achieve total risk coverage in cloud storage multi-homing. In: Altmann, J., Vanmechelen, K., Rana, O.F. (eds.) GECON 2014. LNCS, vol. 8914, pp. 146–158. Springer, Heidelberg (2014)

10. Galati, A., Djemame, K., Fletcher, M., Jessop, M., Weeks, M., McAvoy, J.: A WS-Agreement based SLA implementation for the CMAC platform. In: Altmann, J., Vanmechelen, K., Rana, O.F. (eds.) GECON 2014. LNCS, vol. 8914, pp. 159–171. Springer, Heidelberg (2014)

11. Slawik, M., Küpper, A.: A domain specific language and a pertinent business vocabulary for cloud service selection. In: Altmann, J., Vanmechelen, K., Rana, O.F., (eds.) GECON 2014. LNCS, vol. 8914, pp. 172–185. Springer, Heidelberg (2014)

12. Tolosana-Calasanz, R., Bañares, J.A., Colom, J.M.: Towards petri net-based economical analysis for streaming applications executed over cloud infrastructures. In: Altmann, J., Vanmechelen, K., Rana, O.F. (eds.) GECON 2014. LNCS, vol. 8914, pp. 189–205. Springer, Heidelberg (2014)

13. Butoi, A., Stan, A., Silaghi, G.C.: Autonomous management of virtual machine failures in iaas using fault tree analysis. In: Altmann, J., Vanmechelen, K., Rana, O.F., (eds.) LNCS, vol. 8914, pp. 206–221. Springer, Heidelberg (2014)

14. Maillé, P., Tuffin, B.: How do content delivery networks affect the economy of the internet and the network neutrality debate? In: Altmann, J., Vanmechelen, K., Rana, O.F. (eds.) GECON 2014. LNCS, vol. 8914, pp. 222–230. Springer, Heidelberg (2014)

15. Felici, M.: Economics, security and innovation. In: Altmann, J., Vanmechelen, K., Rana, O.F. (eds.) GECON 2014. LNCS, vol. 8914, pp. 3–15. Springer, Heidelberg (2014)

# Organization

GECON 2014 was organized by the School of Computer Science of Cardiff University, the Technology Management, Economics, and Policy Program of Seoul National University, and the Department of Mathematics and Computer Science of the University of Antwerp.

## Executive Committee

**Co-chairs**

| | |
|---|---|
| Omer F. Rana | Cardiff University, UK |
| Jörn Altmann | Seoul National University, South Korea |
| Kurt Vanmechelen | University of Antwerp, Belgium |

**Publication Chair**

| | |
|---|---|
| Netsanet Haile | Seoul National University, South Korea |

## Program Committee

| | |
|---|---|
| Rainer Alt | University of Leipzig, Germany |
| Ashraf A. Bany Mohammed | University of Ha'il, Saudi-Arabia |
| Ivona Brandic | Vienna University of Technology, Austria |
| Ivan Breskovic | Vienna University of Technology, Austria |
| Jeremy Cohen | Imperial College London, UK |
| Gheorghe Cosmin Silaghi | Babes-Bolyai University, Romania |
| Costas Courcoubetis | Athens University of Economics and Business, Greece |
| Dang Minh Quan | National Economics University, Vietnam |
| Karim Djemame | University of Leeds, UK |
| Torsten Eymann | University of Bayreuth, Germany |
| Bogdan Franczyk | University of Leipzig, Germany |
| Saurabh Garg | IBM Research, Australia |
| Wolfgang Gentzsch | Ubercloud, Germany |
| Netsanet Haile | Seoul National University, South Korea |
| Thomas Hess | Ludwig-Maximilians-Universität München, Germany |
| Chun-Hsi Huang | University of Connecticut, USA |
| Bahman Javadi | University of Western Sydney, Australia |
| Odej Kao | Technical University of Berlin, Germany |
| Kibae Kim | Seoul National University, South Korea |
| Tobias A. Knoch | Erasmus University, The Netherlands |
| Bastian Koller | HLRS, Germany |

| Harald Kornmayer | Duale Hochschule Baden-Württemberg Mannheim, Germany |
| Dimosthenis Kyriazis | National Technical University of Athens, Greece |
| Hing-Yan Lee | National Cloud Computing Office, Singapore |
| Jysoo Lee | KISTI, South Korea |
| Dan Ma | Singapore Management University, Singapore |
| Richard T.B. Ma | National University of Singapore, Singapore |
| Leandro Navarro | Universitat Politècnica de Catalunya, Spain |
| Dirk Neumann | University of Freiburg, Germany |
| Steven Miller | Singapore Management University, Singapore |
| Karsten Oberle | Alcatel-Lucent Bell Labs, Germany |
| Manish Parashar | Rutgers University, USA |
| Rajiv Ranjan | University of Melbourne, Australia |
| Peter Reichl | Telecommunications Research Center Vienna, Austria |
| Rizos Sakellariou | University of Manchester, UK |
| Satoshi Sekiguchi | AIST, Japan |
| Burkhard Stiller | University of Zurich, Switzerland |
| Johan Tordsson | Umeå University, Sweden |
| Bruno Tuffin | IRISA/Inria, France |
| Gabriele von Voigt | University of Hannover, Germany |
| Stefan Wesner | University of Ulm, Germany |
| Phillip Wieder | GWDG, Germany |
| Ramin Yahyapour | GWDG, Germany |
| Rüdiger Zarnekow | Technical University of Berlin, Germany |
| Wolfgang Ziegler | Fraunhofer Institute SCAI, Germany |

## Steering Committee

| Jörn Altmann | Seoul National University, South Korea |
| José Ángel Bañares | University of Zaragoza, Spain |
| Gheorghe Cosmin Silaghi | Babes-Bolyai University, Romania |
| Steven Miller | Singapore Management University, Singapore |
| Omer F. Rana | Cardiff University, UK |
| Kurt Vanmechelen | University of Antwerp, Belgium |

## Sponsoring Institutions and Companies

Seoul National University, Seoul, South Korea
Cardiff University, Cardiff, UK
University of Antwerp, Antwerp, Belgium
Eysys, Cardiff, UK
Springer LNCS, Heidelberg, Germany

# Contents

## Economic Aspects of Quality of Service

# Keynote

# Economics, Security and Innovation

Massimo Felici[(⊠)]

Security and Cloud Lab, Hewlett-Packard Laboratories, Long Down Avenue,
Bristol BS34 8QZ, UK
massimo.felici@hp.com

**Abstract.** This paper takes into account an economic perspective of security
and innovation. In particular, it discusses aspects of economics that may be
relevant in order to assess and deploy security technologies. At the micro level
of analysis, as an example, this paper highlights discussions on the economics of
security in the cloud. *Do we really understand the economics of security in the
cloud? Are there economic models that capture operational security in the
cloud?* Early work at HP Labs on trust economics underpins a systematic
approach to information security decision-making and risk management. The
results on trust economics highlight how economics may drive operational
security and the deployment of security technologies. At the macro level of
analysis, drawn from ongoing work within the Security and Trust Coordination
and Enhanced Collaboration, this paper links economics to innovation in cyber
security and privacy. Despite the R&D investments in cyber security and privacy, the general perception is that security and privacy technologies are
deployed ineffectively. This paper also presents an integrated framework taking
into account market perspectives that may support identifying suitable R&D
strategies and assessing their impact.

**Keywords:** Economics · Innovation · Cyber security · Privacy

## 1 Introduction

Despite the continuous investment in cyber security and privacy, continuous threats
and attacks remind us that the Internet is a vulnerable ecosystem (or cyberspace). This
section recalls some economic drivers for innovation in cyber security and privacy. In
particular, this section highlights three main perspectives: economics of information
security, economic barriers for information security, and innovation in cyber security
and privacy – *How much does information security cost? How complex is information
security? How to support innovation in cyber security and privacy?*

Recent trends in information security highlight a situation that is no longer sustainable [1]. On the one hand, the spending on information security has been increasing
constantly. On the other hand, the severity and impact of data breaches are getting
bigger too. This somehow exacerbates the economic risk of information security.
Simply, the increasing spending in information security combined with bigger data
breaches make the (economic) risk of information security quite severe.

Further analysis of the economics of security for the Internet points out some
economic barriers to information security [2]. From technical and organisational

© Springer International Publishing Switzerland 2014
J. Altmann et al. (Eds.): GECON 2014, LNCS 8914, pp. 3–15, 2014.
DOI: 10.1007/978-3-319-14609-6_1

viewpoints, two major issues arise: information asymmetry (that is, one party to a transaction has better information than another one) and lack of diversity in platforms and networks. However, these issues also suggest information security as a market differentiator. From an impact viewpoint, externalities are still unclear. Effects (positive or negative) on third parties of economic transactions are often questionable and quite subjective. Future research should advance the understanding of the economic impact of security technologies (breaches). From a legal viewpoint, liability dumping practices and fragmentations of legislation and law enforcement create mistrust. This stresses the need for legal cooperation supporting a free market and trustworthy cyberspace.

Unfortunately, despite the investment in information security the Internet is still vulnerable to various security threats – the perception is of untrustworthiness. A critical analysis of research and development (R&D) activities in cyber security points out that efforts towards innovation have been ineffective in deploying those security mechanisms that are needed for a trustworthy Internet [3]. This problem is characterized by the *"valley of death"*, as shown in Fig. 1, faced by research and development initiatives in cyber security [4]. A critical analysis of such problem points out various issues (e.g. insufficient awareness of complexity of technology transfer, misalignment between market and threat environment) and success factors (e.g. customer and market needs, early involvement, value creation) [4].

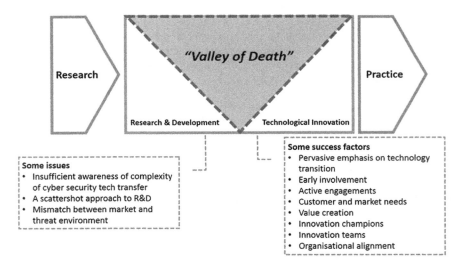

**Fig. 1.** Transitioning cyber security research into practice

This paper is concerned with the economic and market aspects of innovation in cyber security and privacy. It takes into account two perspectives. At the micro level of analysis, it looks at the problem of economics of security in the cloud. Understanding the economics of security (within a specific domain such as the cloud) enables risk-mitigation and deployment strategies for the cloud. At the macro level of analysis, it looks at the problem of road mapping innovation strategies by identifying contingencies between research, technology and market. This paper is structured as follows. Section 2 is concerned with the economics of security in the cloud. It identifies different issues faced by researchers and practitioners. Understanding and addressing such issues would enable risk mitigation and deployment strategies driven by economics. Early work at HP Labs on trust economics underpins a systematic approach to information security decision-making and risk management. Section 3 focuses on innovation in cyber security and privacy. It presents an integrated framework for innovation management. It also discusses some preliminary trends drawn from consultations with stakeholders. Section 4 points out some concluding remarks.

## 2   Economics of Security in the Cloud

This section takes into account a micro perspective of economics. With micro in this case we mean aspects of economics that may be relevant for operational deployment of information and communication technology (ICT). In particular, we analyse the cloud computing domain as one of the most relevant shift in the way ICT is deployed across differ industries. Recent studies forecast *"worldwide public IT cloud services spending to reach nearly $108 billion by 2017 as focus shift from savings to innovation"* [5]. Despite the potential market, further adoptions of cloud computing would require also to take into account also the necessity, hence the cost, of securing the cloud itself [6]. Hereby we are not questioning the benefit of cloud computing or its security, but make sure that the cost associated with securing the cloud is not overlooked (e.g. this may involve various changes in organisational practices too). Cost-benefit analyses are central to the adoption of any technology.

### 2.1   Modelling the Economics of Security

We argue that the better our understanding of the economics of the cloud the better security itself. Unfortunately, despite the research effort in modelling the economics of cyber security, results are yet patchy [7]. Various models have been proposed capturing the economics of cyber security, although they often provide very different analytical results [7]. It is also difficult to assess the validity of modelling results due to a continuous evolving landscape in cyber security (e.g. new threats, new attacks, etc.). Information about cyber security threats and attacks are continuously updated by surveys and new data, which at the same time 'invalidate' (or make irrelevant) previous studies. It is therefore necessary to assess the effectiveness of implemented security measures. Unfortunately, operational information about security measures are seldom available.

Various studies (models) on economics of security provide different account of cyber security. However, in order to benefit from such studies we need first to understand and to compare the underlying economic models of cyber security [7] – *Is the model complete? Is the model consistent? Is the model transparent? Is the model accurate? Is the model conservative? Does the model provide insight?* – Answering such questions is necessary in order to interpret any aspect of economics of security.

We discussed similar points at a dedicated workshop on the Economics of Security in the Cloud (ESC workshop, collocated with the IEEE CloudCom 2013 conference, Bristol, UK). The discussions with presenters and participants at the workshop gave rise to interesting insights:

- **What is the cloud?** There exist, as we know, multiple deployment models and operational scenarios [8]. Unfortunately, most models (on the economics of cyber security) often lack details of different deployments and cloud ecosystems.
- **What are cloud offerings?** There exist different business models (and costs associated with cloud services). However, cloud offerings may look similar, but (technical) details are important too.
- **How do we assess cloud ecosystems?** Cloud computing is a major shift in the way ICT is deployed. Emerging (business) relationships shape the cloud forming cloud ecosystems involving different actors (with different responsibilities). Risk and cost-benefit analyses need to take into account not just individual actors (e.g. the weakest link [9]), but how economics, benefits, risks and security threats propagate throughout the cloud supply chain.
- **How do we address cloud governance?** Adopting the cloud involves a shift in the way ICT is deployed across industries. This also requires new governance models that intend to guarantee compliance with relevant regulatory regimes. Moving to the cloud often involves data transfer from cloud customers to cloud providers [10]. Accountability is emerging among critical requirements in cloud ecosystems. There exist alternative governance models [11] – e.g. centralised, decentralised, delegation of responsibility, third party certification – which are difficult to assess in terms of economics. Economic models (although generic) are then used to characterise alternative governance models, but result difficult to link to operational ones or to transfer into operational environments (e.g. see [12, 13] for examples of economic models concerned with operational aspects of the cloud).
- **Do we understand cost/benefit of security investment?** Despite the effort in assessing security operationally, security metrics tend to be tailored to the specific cases and difficult to generalise. Generally accepted security metrics, across operational domains, are yet a problem requiring further investigations. Moreover, due to the continuous evolving cyberspace, assessing security (and related investments) is like pointing to a moving target (e.g. see [14] for examples of economic models of security investments).
- **Do we understand economic and security models?** The diversity of economic and security models makes their comparison difficult [7]. Unfortunately, they are quite often written for the modellers not for the users of such models. Therefore, they are difficult to adopt and transfer into practice.

These remarks provide critical insights about (modelling) the economics of security in the cloud. Next section discusses briefly how understanding economics may drive operational security and the deployment of security technologies in the cloud.

## 2.2   Cloud Stewardship Economics

As an example, we recall early work at HP Labs on *cloud stewardship economics* [15]. Cloud deployments involve benefits and risks beyond outsourcing [16]. Cloud services are ready-available. Market dynamics (rather than simply commercial agreements) determine the trust in such services and their consumption. Information management in the cloud requires a broader notion than security, specifically a theory for steward-ship. Stakeholders in cloud ecosystems are affected by the choices and actions of others (throughout cloud supply chains). Cloud providers manage data on behalf of cloud customers (or other providers too), who trust and depend on third parties to manage information in the cloud. Beside such responsibilities, there is also a dependence on the robustness, resilience and sustainability of the whole cloud ecosystem. Cloud stew-ardship involves notions of assurance, trust, obligation, incentives, utility, preference, hence *economics*. Cloud stewardship economics, on the one hand, explores the concept of information stewardship in the context of cloud ecosystems, on the other hand, applies economic and mathematical modelling techniques to help stakeholders make strategy and policy decisions. The work conducted by the project on cloud stewardship economics [15] developed system and economic models (based on the utility theory) tailored to the cloud. Simulations of different scenarios (e.g. security and reputation dynamics, information asymmetries, etc.) supported discussions of such models with stakeholders. This helped to validate with stakeholders various behavioural assump-tions about cloud ecosystems as well as to promote a shared understanding of cloud stewardship economics among them. The results on trust economics highlight how economics may drive operational security and the deployment of security technologies. Cloud stewardship economics underpins a systematic approach to information security decision-making and risk management [17, 18].

# 3   Innovation in Cyber Security and Privacy

The economics of security in the cloud, discussed in the previous section, is concerned with analysis of the contingencies between economics and security. This section takes into account different viewpoints of analysis concerned with security research and innovation. Research in security and privacy like other domains faces difficult transi-tion from research into practice [3]. Recent work on cyber security research highlights the main factors (i.e. *"insufficient awareness of the complexity of cyber security transfer"*, *"a scattershot approach to R&D"* and *"mismatch between market and threat environment"* [2]) that jeopardise transferring security technology from research to practice – *"many research investments lead to security technologies that never see the light of the day"* [2]. This difficulty that research outcomes have to transition into real world applications and markets is often depicted as the *"valley of death"* [3].

Research outcomes may fail to have any industry impact. Whilst this usefully serves to filter out poorly conceived propositions, the challenge therein is to identify and support technologies that are valued by the market and of importance to end users [19]. This problem can be analysed from two different viewpoints: *technological* and *contextual*. On the one hand, research outcomes may not be ready or mature enough to be deployed into practice. On the other hand, application domains may not be ready to adopt new technological developments due to low levels of innovation intakes.

From a technological viewpoint of analysis, it is necessary to identify and understand the barriers that inhibit technology transitions to practice, and how to address them [4, 20]. Another technological aspect to be considered is the maturity of developments. The NASA Technology Readiness Levels (TRLs) are often used to assess the maturity of technology to be delivered in operational environments [21, 22]. Moving from one technology readiness level to the next one (and above TRL 3 and TLR 4) requires dealing with a "research and development degree of difficulty" (that is, probability of success of R&D objectives) [23]. Moreover, it also requires a commitment of resources beyond the affordability of many research and development contexts, in particular, of publicly funded research [24, 25]. The assessment by TLRs is now being adapted for use in European Horizon 2020 funded research. This represents a significant shift affecting how funding decisions are reached and post-funding evaluations are carried out. From a contextual viewpoint of analysis, it is necessary to understand whether specific domains are ready to adopt new technologies. Validation processes, collecting evidence to assess the readiness of technology to be deployed in operational environments in order to minimise the risk of innovation, may vary across application domains. At the national level, the innovation index is widely adopted as a measure to assess the level of innovation in different countries [26]. The Global Innovation Index (GII) takes into account composite indicators ranking innovation performances.

The combination of these two perspectives, i.e. technological readiness (that is, how mature technology is) and contextual innovation (that is, how ready the innovation environment is), identifies a readiness-innovation space to discuss strategies to support research impact. It highlights two critical situations: (1) high-readiness of technology and low-innovation context, (2) low-readiness of technology and high-innovation potential context. The former characterises situations where technology has been extensively developed and used, but the deployment context is unable to benefit from innovation for different reasons (e.g. lack of innovation culture, unsuitable supporting mechanisms). The latter characterises situations where technology is under-developed for an innovation ecosystem. These two perspectives have been discussed with industry stakeholders in order to identify *innovation pathways*.

### 3.1 Technological Innovation Pathways

Cyber security and privacy are increasingly important topics for the competiveness of European economy and the current trend of investments in legal, technical or research areas related to these topics illustrate this importance. However, it is also necessary to address emerging and future cyber security and privacy threats and challenges that span multiple organisations, crossing domains and boundaries between companies, sectors, or countries. Unlike other research domains, which also deal with common and global challenges, cyber security and privacy domains are characterised by volatile dynamics – what is secure today might not be tomorrow, what is an unknown threat or vulnerability today might be on the news tomorrow. While threats and challenges are common and global, the solutions and responses are often too fragmented, which yields not only to the waste of resources, but brings also danger of inadequate response.

*Technological innovation pathways* provide a means to identify research and development strategies that will be most effective. Research and development challenges in cyber security and privacy are diverse and ambitious. No single strategy is going to address all emergent issues in cyber security and privacy. Technological innovation pathways take into account challenges of developing and deploying research innovations. Innovation pathways identify alternative research and development strategies. Which may rely on different methodologies, mechanisms and processes. Technological innovation pathways identify those situations faced by research and development activities. Industry stakeholders, we consulted, identified four different types of technological innovation pathways:

- **Demand-driven Innovations:** research and development initiatives focusing on innovations required by clients or sector representatives. This is the case for those technologies and services with existing and recognised markets. Therefore, the relevant topics are identified within such markets focusing on specific clients (end users) and stakeholders (demanding further improvements in existing products and services).
- **Market-shaping Innovations:** research and development activities focusing on new technologies and services that are disruptive to current markets. Innovations that have the potential of creating new market opportunities, but that need the 'multiplication' of the impact in order to create 'hype' or market trend. That is, research and development initiatives that deploy ground-breaking innovations and establish new markets and trends.
- **Cross-fertilisation Innovations:** research and development initiatives supporting cross-fertilisation between different research disciplines as well as industrial sectors (different contexts addressing similar problems in alternative ways, e.g. dependability and security in hardware and software research). This would require acquiring multi-disciplinary skills and thinking programmatically (e.g. like for standardisation initiatives).
- **Grand Challenges:** large scale initiatives bringing Industry and Research in order to address complex problems in cyber security and privacy. This would involve the identification of a list of challenges and the coordination of relevant projects (e.g. clustering initiatives) in order to focus resources strategically.

These technological innovation pathways need to be integrated in and supported by suitable funding mechanisms at the national as well as European level. They point to alternative directions (sometime crossing each other) for innovation requiring different levels of private and public interventions. Moreover, they help us discussing some issues concerned with innovation. In particular, the identification of contingencies between research and development activities (in terms of technological innovation pathways) and issues concerned with technological transfers into industry practice. Figure 2 shows the four technological innovation pathways. Demand-driven innovations require an alignment between markets and users (of technological innovations, e.g. other industries) and consumers' needs, otherwise they may result in users and consumers' dissatisfaction and mistrust in technological innovations. Market-shaping innovations require an understanding of the economics of R&D, otherwise they may result in unclear strategies for investment and decision making (e.g. security technologies often face this type of problem due to a lack of understanding of security economics). Moreover, national and international legal frameworks for innovation shape markets and create the conditions for technological innovations and collaboration (or competition) among stakeholders. Cross-fertilisation innovations are characterised by R&D solutions (already existing in some domains) searching for problems across domains. Grand challenges, like security and privacy, require international cooperation for innovation.

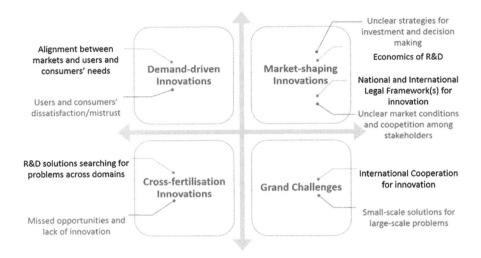

**Fig. 2.** Technological innovation pathways

The technological innovation pathways also supported discussing the barriers to innovation in cyber security and privacy. The aspects of R&D supporting innovation form a basis for an integrated framework for innovation management [27].

## 3.2   Integrated Framework for Innovation Management

This section recalls the integrated framework for innovation management we introduced in [27]. In order to support effectively the transition from publicly funded research to operation environments it is necessary to address different challenges, e.g. human resources, government regulations, deployment issues, and funding cycles [20]. Enhancing the readiness level of technologies requires not only dealing with such challenges but also using the suitable support at the right time. Different mechanisms may be suitable for early research developments but not so effective in supporting transition to operations. Other instruments may support effectively technology transfers and adoption. In order to increase the impact of R&D in cyber security and privacy, different instruments – e.g. research projects, pilot projects, pre-commercial procurements [28, 29] – can support innovation at various stages [30], from R&D initiatives enhancing the maturity and readiness of technology to the adoption of innovative technology. Similar considerations may arise in analysing the risk of technology (new or existing) with respect to market (new or existing) [31]. The European Commission, for instance, is supporting the adoption of pre-commercial procurement in order to deliver innovation in public sectors in Europe [32]. The pre-commercial procurement has been successfully adopted and used across different services [33, 34].

Initial findings from SecCord research combined with insights drawn from critical aspects of R&D, as discussed, highlight three discrete primary areas of investigation [27]: (I) R&D policy and market, (II) technology readiness, and (III) technology transfer (also referred to as transition). Figure 3 illustrates these areas of investigations forming together the integrated framework for innovation management underpinning empirical investigations and roadmaps in cyber security and privacy.

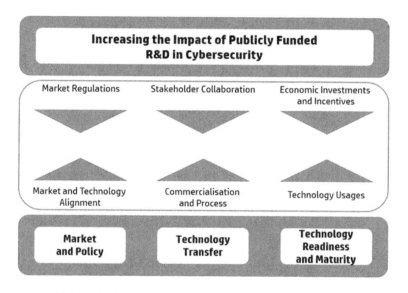

**Fig. 3.** An integrated framework for innovation management

Some stakeholders clearly operate within one particular area of investigation (e.g. regulators and funders within R&D Policy and Market, and Information Communications Technology (ICT) service providers within Technology Transfer), whilst others can provide expert views and experiences across more than one process (e.g. innovators). The integrated framework thus outlines the scope and focus for capturing, integrating and systematically analysing all stakeholder views of cyber security R&D impact. The integrated framework underpins a questionnaire on *Cyber Security and Privacy R&D Impact in Europe* we are using for gathering stakeholders' opinions in order to understand contingencies between different aspects of innovation. Next section discusses some initial indications based on stakeholders' responses.

### 3.3    Ongoing Stakeholder Consultation

The integrated framework identifies three dimensions – i.e. *market and policy, technology transfer, technology readiness and maturity* – influencing the impact of R&D in cyber security and privacy. These dimensions form the basis for a survey we are conducting with stakeholders. For example, Table 1 lists the different statements (and questions) for the dimension concerned with technology readiness and maturity we asked stakeholders to rank (answer) according to their experiences. The other dimensions – i.e. technology transfer, market and policy – are investigated with other relevant statements (questions).

**Table 1.**  Innovation dimension: Technology readiness and maturity

| Technology usages | | |
|---|---|---|
| **Statements** | 1. | Cyber security technologies with a strong business case still lack opportunities to access capital to follow through into application |
| | 2. | Further support mechanisms are needed to help demonstrate utility in large scale systems environments |
| | 3. | Access to actionable test feedback from end users is hard to achieve for new cyber security technologies |
| **Question** | 4. | What factors are critical to the development of competitive business models for new technologies in cyber security and privacy? |
| Economic incentives and investments | | |
| **Statements** | 5. | Industry recognised metrics specific to cyber security and privacy are already widely used in commercial documents to demonstrate the efficacy of new technologies against threats |
| | 6. | Large enterprises should play a greater technical and economic role in supporting new cyber security technology ventures in the wider marketplace |
| | 7. | 3. The effective application of new cyber security technologies is significantly affected by exogenous factors, such as legal frameworks, insurance and taxation |
| **Question** | 8. | What can be done to decrease risk to investments for technologies that have demonstrated potential in laboratory environments? |

We will now discuss some initial indications for each of the dimensions identified by the integrated framework for innovation management (a full study of stakeholder feedback is due once we have completed the survey). The initial indications identified by stakeholders point out insights about R&D in cyber security and privacy.

- **Technology Readiness and Maturity.** Stakeholders indicate the need for further support mechanisms are needed to demonstrate the utility of research and development outcomes in large scale environments. Unfortunately, they also point out that it is difficult to get feedback by end users of security and trust technologies. In terms of economic incentives and investments, stakeholders stress the lack of commonly adopted security (privacy) metrics. Interestingly, despite there is a strong emphasis on measures supporting SMEs, stakeholders recognise that large enterprises should play a leading role in advocating technology innovation.
- **Technology Transfer.** Looking at processes and dynamics of technology transfers, stakeholders indicate that the integration between new security and privacy technologies into current infrastructures presents a significant barrier to technology transfer. This is probably due also to the fact that changes required by integrating new technologies represent often an organisational risk. Moreover, the lack of shared data on security incidents and industry benchmarks is a major obstacle to technology transfers. Another interesting point is that stakeholders recognise the need for effective marketing supporting technology transfers.
- **Market and Policy.** This dimension highlights various contingencies concerned with innovation in cyber security and privacy. In general, these stress the misalignment between the expectations of stakeholders how are responsible for research and development activities (and technology transfers) and the innovation environments (shaped by governmental stakeholders who define relevant policies and economic incentives). Other interesting results point out conflicting views on the effectiveness of publicly-funded research (we will analyse whether or not there are different opinions across stakeholder groups) and well as of stakeholder forums in identifying requirements for security and privacy technologies.

The final results (once analysed in search for statistical correlations and arguments) of the questionnaire we are collecting will inform a road mapping exercise for identifying contingencies in current innovation strategies as well as recommendations for future research and development initiatives.

# 4 Concluding Remarks

This paper has discussed various aspects of economics, security and innovation. The combination of both micro and macro levels of analyses highlights contingencies in the way the economics of security may affect (or, if understood, positively influence) innovation in cyber security and privacy. At the micro level, we discussed the economics of security in the cloud. Although different economic models of security have been proposed, there is still a lack of understanding of the economics of security in the cloud. Future activities intend to understand and discuss further the operational (and pragmatic) aspects of economics of security in cyber security – *What is new in the economics of cyber security and privacy?* At the macro level of analysis, stakeholder indicates various contingencies between innovation dimensions (i.e. technology readiness and maturity, technology transfer, market and policy). This paper discusses various contingencies between economics, security and innovation. Addressing the problem of the "valley of death" faced by R&D in security and privacy would require alignments of technologies, economic incentives and markets. This also would suggest defining innovation in terms of technology investments and deployments by taking into account economics, market opportunities and R&D strategies. In conclusion, economics, security and innovation characterise a complex problem space for R&D in cyber security and privacy – security (privacy) metrics (models) are yet unclear; assessing the economics of security (privacy) is even more complex; innovation in cyber security and privacy without understanding the economics of security (privacy) is probably a utopia.

**Acknowledgements.** I would like to thank colleagues at HP Labs, in particular, Yolanta Beres, Dharm Kapletia, Simon Shiu and Nick Wainwright, who supported me with different materials I further elaborated in this paper. Their work has provided me solid foundations for my research interests. The work on the *'economics of security in the cloud'* and the *'integrated framework for innovation management'* has been partially funded by the Security and Trust Coordination and Enhanced Collaboration (SecCord) – http://www.seccord.eu/ – grant agreement 316622 within the Seventh Framework Programme (FP7) of the European Commission. The section on technological innovation pathways has benefited from feedback by the SecCord's Advisory Focus Group.

# References

1. The Economist: Defending the digital Frontier, Special Report on Cyber-Security (2014)
2. Anderson, R., Boehme, R., Clayton, R., Moore, T.: Security Economics and the Internal Market. ENISA (2008)
3. Maughan, D., Balenson, D., Lindqvist, U., Tudor, Z.: Crossing the valley of death: transitioning cybersecurity research into practice. IEEE Secur. Priv. **11**, 14–23 (2013)
4. Benzel, T.V., Lipner, S.: Crossing the great divide: transferring security technology from research to the market. IEEE Secur. Priv. **11**, 12–13 (2013)
5. IDC: Worldwide and Regional Public IT Cloud Services 2013–2017 Forecast (2013)
6. The Economist: Securing the Cloud (2002)
7. Pfleeger, S.L., Rue, R.: Cybersecurity economic issues: clearing the path to good practice. IEEE Softw. **25**, 35–42 (2008)
8. Mell, P., Grance, T.: The NIST Definition of Cloud Computing, NIST Special Publication 800-145, September 2011
9. Pieters, W.: Defining "The Weakest Link": comparative security in complex systems of systems. In: IEEE International Conference on Cloud Computing Technology and Science (CloudCom 2013), pp. 39–44. IEEE Computer Society (2013)
10. Felici, M., Jaatun, M.G., Kosta, E., Wainwright, N.: Bringing accountability to the cloud: addressing emerging threats and legal perspectives. In: Felici, M. (ed.) CSP EU FORUM 2013. CCIS, vol. 182, pp. 28–40. Springer, Heidelberg (2013)
11. Prüfer, J.: How to govern the cloud? characterizing the optimal enforcement institution that supports accountability in cloud computing. In: IEEE International Conference on Cloud Computing Technology and Science (CloudCom 2013), pp. 33–38. IEEE Computer Society (2013)
12. Díaz-Sánchez, F., Al Zahr, S., Gagnaire, M.: An exact placement approach for optimizing cost and recovery time under faulty multi-cloud environments. In: IEEE International Conference on Cloud Computing Technology and Science (CloudCom 2013), pp. 138–143. IEEE (2013)

13. Johnson, K., Wang, Y., Calinescu, R., Sommerville, I., Baxter, G., Tucker, J.V.: Services2Cloud: a framework for revenue analysis of software-as-a-service provisioning. In: IEEE International Conference on Cloud Computing Technology and Science (CloudCom 2013), pp. 144–151. IEEE Computer Society (2013)
14. Tsalis, N., Theoharidou, M., Gritzalis, D.: Return on security investment for cloud platforms. In: IEEE International Conference on Cloud Computing Technology and Science (CloudCom 2013), pp. 132–137. IEEE Computer Society (2013)
15. HP: Trust Economics: A Systematic Approach to Information Security Decision Making. HP Labs (2011)
16. Catteddu, D., Hogben, G. (eds.): Cloud Computing: Benefits, Risks and Recommendations for Information Security. European Network & Information Security Agency (2009)
17. Baldwin, A., Pym, D., Shiu, S.: Enterprise information risk management: dealing with cloud computing. In: Pearson, S., Yee, G. (eds.) Privacy and Security for Cloud Computing. Computer Communications and Networks, pp. 257–291. Springer, London (2013)
18. Lloyd's: Managing Digital Risk: Trends, Issues and Implications for Business (2010)
19. Auerswald, P.E., Branscomb, L.M.: Valleys of death and darwinian seas: financing the invention to innovation transition in the united states. J. Technol. Transf. **28**(3–4), 227–239 (2003). Kluwer Academic Publishers
20. D'Amico, A., O'Brien, B., Larkin, M.: Building a bridge across the transition chasm. IEEE Secur. Priv. **11**(2), 24–33 (2013)
21. Mankins, J.C.: Technology Readiness Levels: A White Paper. NASA (1995)
22. NASA: HRST Technology Assessments Technology Readiness Levels, Chart (1995)
23. Mankins, J.C.: Research & Development Degree of Difficulty (R&D3). NASA (1998)
24. ENISA: Security Economics & the Internal Market: Evaluation of Stakeholder Replies (2008)
25. ENISA: Security Economics & the Internal Market, Conclusions on Follow-up Activities (2008)
26. INSEAD: The Global Innovation Index 2012: Stronger Innovation Linkages for Global Growth, INSEAD and WIPO (2012)
27. Kapletia, D., Felici, M., Wainwright, N.: An integrated framework for innovation management in cyber security and privacy. In: Cleary, F., Felici, M. (eds.) CSP Forum 2014. CCIS, vol. 470, pp. 135–147. Springer, Heidelberg (2014)
28. ENISA: Activity Report, European Public+Private Partnership for Resilience (2012)
29. ENISA: Work Objectives, European Public+Private Partnership for Resilience (2013)
30. NIST: Between Invention and Innovation: An Analysis of Funding for Early-Stage Technology Development. NIST GCR 02-841, November 2002
31. Hartmann, G.C., Myers, M.B.: Technical risk, product specifications, and market risk. In: Branscomb, L.M., Auerswald, P.E. (eds.) Taking Technical Risks: How Innovators, Executives, and Investors Manage High-Tech Risks. MIT Press, Cambridge (2003)
32. European Commission: Pre-Commercial Procurement: Driving Innovation to Ensure High Public Services in Europe, European Communities (2008)
33. European Commission: Opportunities for Public Technology Procurement in the ICT-related sectors in Europe, Final Report (2008)
34. European Commission: Communication from the Commission to the European Parliament, the Council, the European Economic and Social Committee and the Committee of the Regions, Pre-commercial Procurement: Driving innovation to ensure sustainable high quality public services in Europe, SEC(2007) 1668, COM(2007) 799 final, Brussels (2007)

# Cloud Adoption

# A Metrics Suite for Firm-Level Cloud Computing Adoption Readiness

Robert J. Kauffman, Dan Ma$^{(\boxtimes)}$, and Martin Yu

Singapore Management University, Singapore, Singapore
{rkauffman,madan,martinyu}@smu.edu.sg

**Abstract.** Recent research on cloud computing adoption indicates that there has been a lack of deep understanding of its benefits by managers and organizations. This has been an obstacle for adoption. We report on an initial design for a firm-level cloud computing readiness metrics suite. We propose categories and measures to form a set of metrics to measure adoption readiness and assess the required adjustments in strategy and management, technology and operations, and business policies. We reviewed the relevant interdisciplinary literature and interviewed industry professionals to ground our metrics based on theory and practice knowledge. We identified four relevant categories for firm-level adoption readiness: technological, organizational, economic and environmental factors. We defined sub-categories and measures for each category. We also proposed several propositions to show how the metrics can contribute to business value creation.

**Keywords:** Adoption readiness · Cloud computing · Firm-level · Managerial decision-making · Metrics suite

> *"The agility of [the] cloud enables businesses to get products to market faster by joining up the different parts of the development chain. Sectors such as healthcare and financial services can connect customers and influencers ... to assess market needs and quickly translate this into new ideas and ... new products and services."*

> Rick Wright, Global Cloud Enablement Program Leader, KPMG, 2013

> *"It is not sufficient to consider only the potential value of moving to cloud services. Agencies should make risk-based decisions which carefully consider the readiness of commercial or government providers to fulfill their Federal needs. These can be wide-ranging, but likely will include: security requirements, service and marketplace characteristics, application readiness, government readiness, and program's stage..."*

> Vivek Kundra [2011] CIO of the United States

## 1 Introduction

Cloud computing services offer new technological capabilities that support information technology (IT) services users and enterprise customers, by simplifying IT services acquisition, providing faster implementation, and offering flexibility for the economic consumption of powerful software applications, data management and infrastructure computing support. The U.S. National Institute of Standards and Technology (2013)

© Springer International Publishing Switzerland 2014
J. Altmann et al. (Eds.): GECON 2014, LNCS 8914, pp. 19–35, 2014.
DOI: 10.1007/978-3-319-14609-6_2

defines *cloud computing* as "a model for enabling ubiquitous, convenient, on-demand network access to a shared pool of configurable computing resources that can be rapidly provisioned and released with minimal management effort or service provider interaction." The economic impact of cloud computing is estimated to reach US $1.7 to US$6.2 trillion annually by 2025 (Manyika et al. 2013). As the market develops, diverse and customized services will be available to satisfy sophisticated customers.

In 2012, *InformationWeek* published a commentary that motivated our research: "How should we measure clouds?" (Croll 2013). The author noted: "*[We] need to ... look at the business model. From there, we can derive the relevant metrics ... That's a much more palpable approach to measurement for executives.*" Our approach is different, less operational, and focused on adoption. Managers need to assess cloud computing for how it will support their businesses and create business value. This research emphasizes key issues that need to be addressed to assess what firms will adopt.

Our work is also motivated by the efforts made during the past three or four years by the Asia Cloud Computing Association (ACCA), a non-governmental organization representing the interests of stakeholders in the cloud ecosystem, whose mission is to expand the market in Asia. ACCA (2014) developed a "Cloud Readiness Index" to assess national penetration, for 14 countries in the region, with 10 measures. It categorized countries as "ever-ready leaders," "dedicated improvers," and "steady developers."

In this work, we will present a measurement approach and metrics suite to gauge the extent to which organizations are ready to adopt cloud computing. The metrics also help a firm to measure its adoption readiness and assess the extent that cloud computing will require adjustments to its strategy, management, IT and operations, and business policies. To develop the metrics suite, we ask these questions. (1) What are the major areas that concern business stakeholders the most during adoption decision-making? (2) What are the major facilitators and inhibitors? (3) What does the metrics suite need to consist of to be effective for senior management decision-making use?

Based on a literature review and interviews with industry practitioners, we identified four categories of factors that matter the most, characterize the contexts for clouding computing implementation and value creation well, and are supported by theory and past empirical research. They are: technology issues and cloud computing performance; economic and valuation issues; organizational and strategy issues; and regulation concerns and external business environment issues. These categories for measurement offer a basis for a fuller set of metrics, so it is possible to assess economic issues such as cost-benefit or vendor lock-in risks, or firm issues such as absorptive capacity and senior management support for technology innovation.

Section 2 gives an overview of the literature. Section 3 describes our metrics design approach, and presents our proposed metrics suite for firm-level cloud computing adoption readiness. Section 4 presents our answers to the research questions, and offers propositions about decision-makers' use of the metrics, business and strategy goals.

# 2  Background

To support the development of our metrics suite for cloud adoption readiness, we will begin by reviewing related literature on cloud computing adoption as well as the metrics suite approach.

## 2.1  Technology and Cloud Computing Adoption

There are two main streams of research on cloud computing adoption: theory-oriented works by information systems (IS) researchers, and practice-oriented solution-focused studies by software engineering management researchers.

**Theory.** The literature suggests key categories of variables that push forward or hold back IT adoption. For example, there are a number of works that focus on *technology factors*, such as technological innovations that made cloud computing possible (Armbrust et al. 2010), flexibility, infrastructure and standards (IBM 2009), architecture and systems design (Rimal et al. 2011), and information security (Anthens 2010).

*Organization factors* related to technology adoption are recognized too: the commitment of senior management (Oshri et al. 2010), service quality and partnerships (Grover et al. 1996), the extent to which the firm promotes technological innovation (Hirschheim et al. 2011), the firm's absorptive capacity for new IT projects and new technologies, and the IT governance process (Mani et al. 2006).

*Economic factors* represent another aspect of any explanatory or predictive approach to why firms push forward or hold back adoption. This category includes network effects and client installed base (Rodriguez 2012), lock-in disadvantage and standards (Marston et al. 2011), investment decision-making under uncertainty (Benaroch et al. 2010), value appropriation and return on investments (Alexander and Young and Young 1996), ownership and information sharing (Kim and Moskowitz 2010), and pricing.

A final category is *environmental factors*. They include industry differences and standards (Qu et al. 2011), data privacy and information security (Breuning and Treacy 2008), vendor and technology competition (Ross and Blumenstein 2013), and perceptions in the financial markets (Oh et al. 2006).

**Practice.** There are two groups of practice-oriented studies. One explores the practical reasons for cloud computing adoption. These include the study of adoption and governance (Borgman et al. 2013), opportunities and return-on-investment versus the risks (Merrill and Kang 2014), facilitators versus obstacles (Habib et al. 2012), customer selection of cloud services and vendors, and unexpected market entrants and regulations. Through interviews and questionnaire surveys, various authors have reported critical areas of business practice that are related to cloud adoption decision-making. The other group of studies provides decision-making tools for managers related to technology and cloud adoption. They cover such areas as cost-benefit analysis, technology suitability and economic suitability analysis (Khajeh-Hosseini et al. 2012).

Other industry papers offer suggestions on architectural and IT governance principles for risk control (Cloud Security Alliance 2010), information security (Wright 2004), and implementation effectiveness (Cisco 2014). The reports contain technical details and are vendor-specific, but present the issues that practitioners face, and how cloud readiness metrics can help out.

Firm-level decision-makers can benefit from theory-based explanations of cloud computing adoption and performance, as well as actionable suggestions to help their technology and operations. They also identified the scope for cloud computing readiness. Survey research on IT outsourcing (Ang and Straub 1998) and business process outsourcing (Lacity et al. 2011) involves perceptual scales containing limited technical or economic contents, and are intended to aid in the qualitative aspects of decision-making and strategic planning. Practice-oriented studies tend to focus on specific aspects, such as the technological suitability of cloud computing (The Open Group 2014) or migration guidance (Sutherland and Chetty 2014). Even though they have technical or managerial details, they reflect aspects of cloud computing that are easily understood by senior IT managers and planners. Thus, measures that capture firm changes in cloud adoption readiness must incorporate the strengths and rigor of theory and relevance of practice.

## 2.2  Characteristics and Applications of Measures and Metrics Suite Approaches

**Characteristics.** Individual *measures* are useful to provide basic elements to assess performance in processes and systems, and how technologies will succeed in delivering value. When we bring together measures that represent different aspects of performance, we refer to them as a *metrics suite*. This term is used in engineering, software systems, and business process management contexts. Metrics suites have been used to capture and quantify complex aspects of operational processes, help managers to evaluate business performance, and enable them to make effective adjustments and achieve desirable outcomes. In addition, metrics suites have been used to create measurement approaches to capture quantitative and financial performance, and qualitative and intangible organizational capacities (Kaplan and Norton 1996), measure interdependent aspects of systems design in software development (Chidamber and Kemerer 1994), and simplify financial risks based on a set of numerical measures (Jorion 2000).

Managerial decision-making processes for cloud computing adoption and migration are complicated, and require carefully set targets and effective reviews. Moving to the cloud represents technological changes and also a business model shift for the enterprise. It involves technological, economic, strategic, and business concerns, and considerations about an organization's internal capabilities and its external environment. Senior managers need measures that provide information on this range of issues to evaluate the firm's readiness for cloud computing services. Metrics suites that are based on theory are especially relevant for implementation, since theory is a strong basis for understanding how performance and outcomes arise.

**Applications.** In *software engineering*, metrics suites have been developed to measure the productivity and quality of application designs based on software objects (Briand et al. 1999). Chidamber and Kemerer's (1994) proposed a six-dimension model, including weighted methods per class, depth of inheritance tree, number of children, coupling between object classes, response for a class, and lack of cohesion in methods. These measures can be linked to economic outcomes, such as software productivity and rework effort, which facilitate project planning and control. Empirical evidence has shown that using such metrics in the initial design stage can save 42 % of corrective costs and efforts, and substantially improve final product quality (El Emam et al. 2001).

In *strategic performance management*, researchers and practitioners have designed and developed various metrics to measure process performance and intangible capabilities (Edvinsson and Marlone 1997). These traditionally were ignored by established cost accounting evaluation methods. The Harvard Business School's "Balanced Scorecard" by Kaplan and Norton (Norton 1996) is the most successful metrics suite in performance management. It has been widely used to set management objectives or to plan development and decision-making of new strategic systems (Nørreklit 2000), with 60 % of Fortune 1000 firms in the U.S. having experimented with it (Silk 1998). It integrates quantitative financial outcome measures and non-financial qualitative performance drivers. It assumes there is a causal chain of relationships starting from measures of organizational learning and growth, to internal business processes, then to the customer perspective, and finally to financial performance.

In *financial and accounting risk management*, various metrics such as Stern Stewart's *economic value added* (EVA) and RiskMetrics' *value-at-risk* (VaR) help senior managers to evaluate financial risk and make better investment decisions. EVA is the difference between accounting earnings and the cost of capital used to generate the earnings (Stern et al. 1996). As a metrics suite, it focuses on the measurement of profits that remain after the impacts of debt cost and equity capital on a profit from operations.

In financial risk management, VaR represents the worst expected loss over a given time horizon under normal market conditions at a given level of confidence. It assesses exposure for financial firms for multiple financial instruments, which can be aggregated to assess the firm's composite risk (Jorion 2000). Managers use it to forecast losses that may accrue from shocks to their business. As a consequence, it is viewed as a forward-looking way to measure financial risk. VaR metrics have received wide recognition due to their impacts on financial practice across industries.

## 2.3    On Designing a Cloud Computing Readiness Metrics Suite

Our purpose is to present design ideas for a metrics suite for cloud computing readiness. We have done so with core principles for performance measurement systems design in mind (Dewangan and Godse 2014). Innovation adoption performance metrics should have five characteristics: (1) a stakeholder value orientation; (2) an innovation process orientation; (3) cause-and-effect relationships; (4) multi-dimensional assessments; and (5) easy implementation by people.

**Stakeholder value.** In designing performance metrics suite, how to address the needs of multiple stakeholders has always been an essential issue (Jorion 2000; Kaplan and Norton 1996). A *stakeholder* is an agent who initiates changes or is impacted by changes derived from a technological innovation (Bourne et al. 2000). Cloud computing has the potential to generate beneficial stakeholder impacts, by transforming the use of IT services. Identifying its value as well as the obstacles with multiple stakeholders are fundamental in establishing useful measures for cloud readiness evaluation.

**Innovation process.** Cloud computing adoption will be like adopting a technological innovation which may or may not be perceived as being entirely ready. So a meaningful metrics suite in our context, as Dewangan and Godse (2014) remind us, must also have the built-in capacity to assess cloud computing in a way that technology innovations are assessed – prior to the time they are implemented.

**Cause-and-effect relationships.** A metrics suite must contain identifiable cause- and-effect relationships between the measures that are used and the business goals of the organization (Kaplan and Norton 1996; Stern et al. 1996). Establishing causality will ensure strategy, operations, and technical adjustments can be made to improve cloud readiness, so it will serve organizational goals better and result in more business value. A theoretical basis in the literature and through practitioner interviews helps in identifying useful causal links.

**Multiple measurement categories.** A metrics suite should represent a balanced view of what are under study: financial or non-financial measures, technical or non-technical measures, or internal or external factors. Multiple categories are meaningful, establishing a base for deep managerial insights. This is consistent with the current view of the IT services ecosystem and the cloud computing services context.

**Easy implementation.** An effective metrics suite must be easy for managers to implement. Cloud computing adoption readiness is complex though. Still, it is appropriate to limit the number of measures, and ensure they have a similar level of granularity. Industry reports and input from practitioners helped us to scope and select measures that are aligned with organizational needs (Edvinsson and Marlone 1997).

## 3    A Cloud Computing Adoption Readiness Metrics Suite

When designing the firm-level cloud computing adoption readiness metrics suite, it will be useful to bridge theory and practice, and guide managerial decision-making (Holmstrom et al. 2009; Mohrman et al. 2001). First, we aim to address practical issues in contemporary cloud computing industry settings. This research agenda was developed based on our participation in industry roundtables and workshops hosted by the Asian Cloud Computing Association. Second, we have sought to give equal weight to industry informants as what we were able to learn from the academic literature. Third, we sought to surface practitioners' knowledge to help interpret and understand their views, so as to create an informational base for specifying our metric suite's adoption readiness measures (Nonaka 1994). We communicated with cloud providers, enterprise users, and government planners for cloud computing.

We next present the metrics suite. We will lay out four different measurement categories: technology and performance; organization and strategy; economics and valuation; and regulation and external environment. We will then illustrate the metrics suite.

## 3.1  Technology and Performance

The first category of measures is *technology and performance,* which assesses whether the cloud computing solutions fit the firm's IT and systems. There are two measure sub-categories: self-assessments of compatibility and expected service quality. Managerial decision-makers have to assess technology suitability and understand the expected level of IT service quality to decide whether cloud computing is the right for their organizations Armbrust et al. 2010. This requires fit and compatibility assessment (Low et al. 2011), and information, system and service quality levels that are consistent with the firm's business and IT practices (DeLone and McLean 1992; Tornatzky and Klein 1982). To proxy for compatibility, we selected network access and virtualization. Cloud computing needs high quality network access and virtualization for fast network access and minimal latency (Vouk 2008). Experience with virtualization will reduce the costs for cloud migration (Jamshidi et al. 2013). Security, scalability and availability also are critical quality measures for organizations (Garg et al. 2013).

Cloud computing converts traditional IS, maintenance, and usage into simpler IT services. Service quality – the difference between what the vendor delivers and what the user expects – is critical to firm-level IS success (Pitt et al. 1995). Prior research has addressed the benefits and risks from an IT perspective (Venters and Whitley 2012). In the service quality sub-category, we include three critical measures of quality: security, availability and scalability (Benlian and Hess 2011). Security risks include contractual loopholes, confidentiality, information security, and service outages. Customers expect high availability, the percentage of time a customer can access the service (Garg et al. 2013). Another important aspect of cloud service quality is scalability, which measures customer needs to receive services that scale to demand (Venters and Whitley 2012).

## 3.2  Organization and Strategy

The second category is *organization and strategy*, which assesses whether cloud computing solutions match the firm's strategic orientation and organizational capabilities. The subcategories are self-assessments of these things. Companies with good organizational capabilities and a strategic orientation are more ready to benefit from cloud computing (Buyya et al. 2010). Decision-makers need to recognize the potential impacts of cloud computing use, and prepare for political obstacles (Garrison et al. 2012). In our interviews, some IT executives emphasized that, when moving to cloud services, organizations have to make adjustments in IT governance policy and operating models according to the criticality and sensitivity of their tasks and data. An organization with accumulated experience and managerial capacity will adjust more smoothly (Hsu et al. 2014). The critical capabilities for cloud adoption include absorptive capacity and vendor management experience (Aral and Weill 2007). We use scales for external and internal knowledge acquisition and dissemination to measure an organization's absorptive capacity (Liao et al. 2003), and contractual and relational governance to measure its vendor management capacity (Poppo and Zenger 2002).

Strategy-focused organizations can identify the business value of cloud computing, and match its innovative characteristics with their own internal business needs. For strategic orientation, our metrics suite includes three measures: executive support, innovation inclination, and perceived competitive advantage (Messerschmidt and Hinz 2013). Executive support is critical for creating a supportive climate, with adequate resources and opportunities for cloud adoption (Low et al. 2011). Innovation inclination affects intention to adopt new technologies (Barczak et al. 2007). And perceptions of competitive advantage and business value will affect adoption too (Hsu et al. 2014).

### 3.3    Economics and Valuation

The third category is *economics and valuation*, which assesses the economic suitability and business value of cloud computing. The sub-categories include: service and market valuation, and vendor reputation. Decision-makers need to assess their suitability with an economic perspective. For valuation, we employ a set of measures on the preferred pricing mechanism, estimated cost reduction, and contract flexibility (Truong and Dustdar 2010). When vendors decompose their services into small configurable units, enterprises need to gauge their total execution costs. Flexible contracts will allow clients to balance the trade-offs among cost, benefit, risk, time and resource requirements (Koehler et al. 2010; Li 2011). For example, in the cost calculation for cloud services, operational and hidden costs for IT interoperability need be considered.

The maturity of the cloud market, and market demand and supply will affect the adoption readiness of a firm. Standards, transparency, and reliability for vendor performance are basic market stabilizers (Hauff et al. 2014; ISACA 2012). They help reduce uncertainty. A healthy cloud market will have alternative services and vendors (ISACA 2012). Vendor stability, scale, and reputation are critical for estimating the risk involved in adoption (Pauley 2010). We use three measures for the vendors: financial stability, and technical track records including process maturity and security breaches and outage news.

### 3.4    Regulation and Environment

The final category of the metrics suite is the *external business and regulatory environment constraints* that an enterprise faces, which require an organization's strategic responses. The external business environment creates pressure and obstacles for adopting IT innovations, and can shape the strategic responses of firms that are affected by it (Miles and Snow 1978). According to Walker et al. (2003), the business environment can be viewed as follows: the stage of the relevant product life cycle; extent of market segmentation, competition, and industry concentration; and technological maturity and structure. DeSarbo et al. (2005) suggested three environmental uncertainties: market, competitive and technology. Cloud computing services vendors deliver shared IT resources and capabilities with strong network effects for their clients. Past experience with one vendor's cloud services can generate mimetic and normative pressure on the client's beliefs about adoption (Messerschmidt and Hinz 2013). Thus, we include three business environment measures related to cloud adoption: technology environment uncertainty, pressure to mimic competitors, and normative pressure from alliances.

Regulation constraints constitute the other important environmental factor. Different countries have different legal and regulatory rules regarding data privacy, data sovereignty and how local laws apply to data governance. Many have laws requiring cloud providers to keep customer data and copyrighted material within national boundaries (Armbrust et al. 2010). Such constraints are a bind in multinational business. In our metrics suite, we use new measures for perceived regulatory constraints and data sovereignty issues based on ISACA (2012) and Armbrust et al. (2010).

## 3.5     The Cloud Computing Readiness Metrics Suite

Our metrics suite for cloud computing adoption readiness is shown in Fig. 1. The metrics categories are bold and underlined, and sub-categories are solid bullet points. Hollow bullet points mark the measures, when a category is not also a measure.

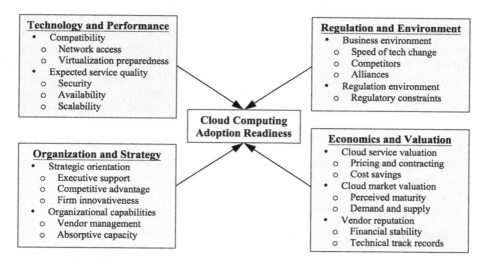

**Fig. 1.** A sketch of the cloud computing adoption readiness metrics suite

Appendix A offers more detailed coverage, as well as the identification of the proxy measures to capture information on the metrics sub-categories. They suggest our sensitivity to the cost and capacity issues for operating cloud services. We comment on the kinds and sources of the measures, and their development. Administration of a related questionnaire will elicit relevant data on adoption for assessment. Then, the information that is obtained can be leveraged to create organizational and technology strategies for adoption and implementation actions based on what the market is able to supply. When management is able to make informed choices to obtain the "right" solutions, they will be able to maximize the business value of cloud computing for the firm.

## 4  Implications for the Business Value of Cloud Computing

We conclude with thoughts about how the metrics suite can be used to create business value. It can be used to support pre-implementation assessment for migrating to cloud. Consulting firms can use it to establish industry adoption benchmarks. Regulators can apply it to investigate the readiness of a sector and assess current policy.

### 4.1  How Use of the Metrics Suite Will Support the Creation of Business Value

We next offer three propositions on the creation of business value that reflect what we have learned so far from businesses and government agencies in Singapore. The propositions are not yet based on deep empirical analysis, which we plan to do later.

Cloud computing is more than just a new IT. It will lead to fundamental changes in how enterprises conduct their IT-related activities. Bringing cloud solutions into a firm makes it necessary to mitigate business risk, and understand the potential for strategic advantage (Iyer and Henderson 2012). The purpose of our metrics suite is to facilitate adoption and help organizations to gauge whether it will create business value. An organization may need to adjust its business model, strategic goals, risk management, and IT governance policy. This is hard: changes and adjustments may need to be made simultaneously. The metrics suite is helpful, since it offers a balanced view of adoption readiness across technology, economic, organizational, and external factors. We assert:

- **Proposition 1 (The Business Value Versus IT Risk Proposition).** *A metrics suite for adoption readiness will help a firm shift focus from the expected level of business value through adoption to balancing value versus risk to support appropriate adjustments in the adoption process.*

The value of cloud computing will be larger when firms are able to make appropriate adjustments. The metrics suite supports managers to identify where changes are needed so they can appropriate the maximum value from cloud computing.

Even as experienced users, some senior managers indicate that their organizations are still learning about the impacts and consequences of cloud computing adoption. Strategic planners want to identify the hidden costs, and then respond accordingly. This is a learning-by-doing process though. The hidden costs and frictions of externally-provided IT services will be revealed only when firms experience them first hand. In addition, role changes that affect IT staff and policy adjustments related to computing resource usage will not be fully understood before migration to the cloud starts.

Our metrics suite emphasizes the role of organizational absorptive capacity, which depicts the path dependence of organizational learning when organizations face new innovations (Cohen and Levinthal 1990). The experience acquired through managing cloud adoption using metrics will help organizations build cumulative knowledge for handling disruptive innovations. Since not everything can be planned in advance, decision-makers need to be open-minded about cloud computing. We suggest:

- **Proposition 2 (The Organizational Learning Proposition).** *A metrics suite will aid decision-makers to view adoption as a learning process. Managers need to identify possible concerns, risks, and costs prior to adoption, apply ongoing adjustments to support value production, and transform the organization's operational and business models after adoption has occurred.*

The metrics suite that we have proposed can be used to evaluate an organization's adoption readiness, regardless of what stage it is in: before adoption has started, during the process, or after it finishes. We encourage decision-makers to plan to learn, to manage unanticipated roadblocks along the way and be effective.

The design of an organization's structure, process, governance and transaction contents create value through the exploitation of business opportunities (Amit and Zott 2001). The paradigm shift resulted from cloud computing allows management decision-makers to redesign these business transaction-making processes to achieve business model innovation (Chesbrough 2010). To make business model innovations, organizations need reliable and informative metrics for continuous monitoring and improvement of their performance. Our metrics suite encourages post-adoption performance measurement. Cloud adoption is not the final goal though: higher revenues and improved stakeholder satisfaction are. So we offer:

- **Proposition 3 (Business Model Innovation Proposition).** *A metrics suite for cloud computing adoption readiness will encourage an organization to implement continuous performance monitoring, which can support cloud-based business model innovation after the adoption process has finished.*

## 4.2 Discussion

To answer the research questions for this work, we developed an initial design of a firm-level cloud computing adoption readiness metrics suite. Enterprise users need reliable measurement tools to support their decision-making process for the costly move to cloud computing. Senior managers from industry, industry organizations, and government motivated us to conduct this research, and we subsequently interviewed them to support our effort to create the metrics suite. To address cloud computing adoption readiness more fully, we have sought to integrate knowledge from industry and university research to reflect the strengths of practice and theory. The initial design of cloud computing adoption readiness metrics suite is the result of this process that led to the definitions of the categories, sub-categories and measures presented in this article.

There are a couple of remaining concerns related to the development and application of our metrics suite. The industry CIOs and CEOs, government agency analysts and policy-makers offered us many useful ideas on how to improve the metrics suite. They also cautioned us about the how much effort will be required to instantiate the knowledge that our metrics suite requires. First, our metrics suite currently has 24 measures, which we expect to distill down to about 12–14, based on the input we obtained. We will only do that based on additional input, and the experience we gain from additional pilot testing. Most of our measures are grounded in theory, a good feature, but pilot testing we already have done led to adjustments to de-emphasize some aspects of our theory that were viewed as being unnecessary by practitioners. We will continue to fine-tune our measurement approach to best suit the intended beneficiaries of this research. We recognize that there is a trade-off between the extraction of appropriate knowledge from our respondents and the cost of its acquisition. They must buy into the results too.

Second, our metrics suite is comprehensive, but we still are seeking more thematic focus. Some respondents suggested that it would be useful to have a survey on the way that regulatory and external issues affect adoption readiness at the firm level. Others told us that economic and business value concerns are paramount. This suggests our research effort will have degrees of freedom for more in-depth exploration.

Finally, the reader should recognize that this is work-in-progress. As a result, we are still learning from the respondents who will make up our final sample. We are fortunate to have support from numerous business, government agency, vendor and consulting organizations, and look forward to reporting new results at GECON 2014.

## Appendix A. Cloud Readiness Metrics Suite: Categories, Sub-categories, Measures, and Measurement-Related Comments

| Categories, Sub-Categories | Sub-Categories, Measures and Proxies | Measurement Comments | Supportive Literature | Related Disciplines |
|---|---|---|---|---|
| **Technology and performance.** Assesses whether the characteristics of cloud computing solutions fit the firm's IT and systems. The measure sub-categories include: *self-assessments of compatibility, expected service quality.* | **Compatibility.** The degree to which cloud computing technology fits with the potential adopter's organizational values, practices and needs. Proxy measures are: *network access* and *virtualization preparedness.*<br>**Cloud computing services quality.** Service quality that a client expects with cloud services. Proxy measures: *security, availability* and *scalability. Security risks* are contract loopholes, data privacy, information security, and service outages. *Availability* refers to the percentage of time a client can access the services. *Scalability* measures a client's desire to consume services that scale to demand. | **Measures.** Perceptual scales adapted from cloud computing. **Validation.** Efficacy and empirical validation are in process via pilot test interviews. | Armbrust et al. 2010<br>Grover et al. 1996<br>Pitt et al. 1995<br>Vouk 2008<br>Garg et al. 2013<br>Jamshidi et al. 2013 | Software engineering<br>Service science<br>Cloud computing |
| **Organization and strategy.** Assesses to what extent cloud computing matches with firm's strategic orientation and organizational capacities. Sub-categories are *self-assessments of strategic orientation and firm capabilities.* | **Strategic orientation.** The degree to which senior managers support technology innovations in the firm. Proxy measures are: *executive support, organizational innovativeness, and perceived strategic value of the cloud.*<br>**Organizational capabilities.** *Absorptive capacity and vendor management capacity. Absorptive capacity: external and internal knowledge acquisition and dissemination. Vendor management capacity: contractual and relational governance.* | **Measures.** Perceptual scales. **Validation.** Also in process. | Buyya et al. 2010<br>Aral and Weill 2007<br>Liao et al. 2003<br>Poppo and Zenger 2002<br>Messerschmidt, Hinz 2013<br>Low et al. 2011<br>Barczak et al. 2007 | Cloud computing<br>Strategic mgmt.<br>Tech. adoption<br>Outsourcing<br>Grid computing |
| **Economics and valuation.** Assesses the economic suitability and business value of cloud computing in cost and benefit terms. The sub-categories include: *cloud services and market valuation, and vendor reputation.* | **Cloud service valuation.** Economic suitability assessment. Proxies include: *vendor pricing mechanism and contract flexibility, as well as the client's expected cost savings.*<br>**Cloud market valuation.** Issues are *market maturity and available supply.* Proxies for market maturity measures are: *availability of performance standards, transparency of the cloud market, and perceived vendor reputation performance at market level,* and *perceived abundance of supply, and availability of alternative services and vendors.*<br>**Vendor's reputation.** Some key risks are the vendor's financial stability, scale economies, and cloud computing service delivery performance. Proxy measures include: *financial stability, and technical track records* pertaining to process maturity and published security breach and outages. | **Measures.** Perceptual, objective. Scales developed or adapted based on research, interviews. **Validation.** Pilot interviews only. Objective measures chosen for clarity and ease of application. Refinement and empirical validation are in process. | Truong and Dustdar 2010<br>Koehler et al. 2010;<br>Li 2011<br>Hauff et al. 2014<br>ISACA 2012<br>Pauley 2010 | Cloud computing<br>IS economics<br>Info security |
| **Regulatory constraints and external environment.** These shape an organization's strategic responses. | **Regulatory environment.** Many countries have laws for cloud vendors to keep customer data within national boundaries. The proxy is a scale for *perceived regulatory constraints.*<br>**External business environment.** Three proxy measures are: *speed of technology change, mimetic pressure from competitors, and normative pressure from alliances.* | **Measures:** Perceptual scales adapted from the literature and self-developed. **Validation:** Refinement and empirical validation in process. | Miles and Snow 1978<br>DeSarbo et al. 2005<br>Walker et al. 2003<br>Messerschmidt, Hinz 2013 | Strategic mgmt.<br>Grid computing |

# References

Alexander, M., Young, D.: Outsourcing: where's the value? Long Range Plan. **29**(5), 728–730 (1996)

Amit, R., Zott, C.: Value creation in e-business. Strateg. Manag. J. **22**(6–7), 493–520 (2001)

Ang, S., Straub, D.: Production and transaction economies and IS outsourcing: a study of the U.S. banking industry. MIS Q. **22**(4), 535–552 (1998)

Anthens, G.: Security in the cloud. Commun. ACM **53**(11), 16–18 (2010)

Aral, S., Weill, P.: IT assets, organizational capabilities, and firm performance. Organ. Sci. **18**(5), 763–780 (2007)

Armbrust, M., et al.: A view of cloud computing. Commun. ACM **53**(4), 50–58 (2010)

Asia Cloud Computing Association: Cloud readiness index 2014. Singapore (2014)

Barczak, G., Sultan, F., Hultink, E.J.: Determinants of IT usage and new product performance. J. Prod. Innov. Manag. **24**(6), 600–613 (2007)

Benaroch, M., Dai, Q., Kauffman, R.J.: Should we go our own way? backsourcing flexibility in IT services contracts. J. Manag. Inf. Syst. **26**(4), 317–358 (2010)

Benlian, A., Hess, T.: Opportunities and risks of software-as-a-service: findings from a survey of IT executives. Decis. Support Syst. **52**(1), 232–246 (2011)

Borgman, H.P., Bahli, B., Heier, H., Schewski, F.: Cloudrise: exploring cloud computing adoption and governance with the TOE framework. In: Proceedings of 46th Hawaii International Conference on System Sciences. ACM Computer Society Press, New York (2013)

Bourne, M.C.S., Mills, J.F., Wilcox, M., Neely, A.D., Platts, K.W.: Designing, implementing and updating performance measurement systems. Int. J. Prod. Oper. Manag. **20**(7), 754–771 (2000)

Briand, L.C., Daly, J.W., Wüst, J.K.: A unified framework for coupling measurement in object-oriented systems. IEEE Trans. Softw. Eng. **25**(1), 91–121 (1999)

Breuning, P.J., Treacy, B.C.: Privacy, security issues raised by cloud computing. Priv. Sec. Law Rep. **8**(10), 1–4 (2008)

Buyya, R., Broberg, J., Goscinski, A.M.: Cloud Computing: Principles and Paradigms, vol. 87. Wiley, New York (2010)

Chesbrough, H.: Business model innovation: opportunities and barriers. Long Range Plan. **43**(2), 354–363 (2010)

Chidamber, S.R., Kemerer, C.F.: A metrics suite for object oriented design. IEEE Trans. Softw. Eng. **20**(6), 476–493 (1994)

Cisco: Implement your cloud computing strategy more easily. San Jose, CA (2014)

Cloud Security Alliance: Cloud Security Alliance unveils governance, risk management and compliance (GRC) stack. Cloud Security Alliance Conference, Orlando, FL (2010)

Cohen, W.M., Levinthal, D.A.: Absorptive capacity: a new perspective on learning and innovation. Adm. Sci. Q. **35**(1), 128–152 (1990)

Croll, A.: How should we measure clouds? InformationWeek, 20 March 2013

DeLone, W.H., McLean, E.: Information systems success: the quest for the dependent variable. Inf. Syst. Res. **3**(1), 60–95 (1992)

Desarbo, W.S., Di Benedetto, C.A., Song, M., Sinha, I.: Revisiting the miles and snow strategic framework: uncovering interrelationships between strategic types, capabilities, environmental uncertainty, and firm performance. Strateg. Manag. J. **26**, 47–74 (2005)

Dewangan, V., Godse, M.: Towards a holistic enterprise innovation performance measurement system. Technovation **34**(9), 536–545 (2014)

Edvinsson, L., Marlone, M.: Intellectual Capital: The Proven Way to Establish Your Company's Real Value by Measuring Its Hidden Values. Piatkus, London (1997)

El Emam, K., Benlarbi, S., Goel, N., Rai, S.N.: The confounding effect of class size on the validity of object-oriented metrics. IEEE Trans. Softw. Eng. **27**(7), 630–650 (2001)

Garg, S.K., Versteeg, S., Buyya, R.: A framework for ranking of cloud computing services. Future Gener. Comput. Syst. **29**(4), 1012–1023 (2013)

Garrison, G., Kim, S., Wakefield, R.L.: Success factors for deploying cloud computing. Commun. ACM **55**(9), 62–68 (2012)

Grover, V., Cheon, M.J., Teng, J.T.C.: The effect of service quality and partnership on the outsourcing of information systems functions. J. Manag. Inf. Syst. **12**(4), 89–116 (1996)

Habib, S.M., Hauke, S., Ries, S., Mühlhäuser, M.: Trust as a facilitator: a survey. J. Cloud Comput. **1**, 1–18 (2012)

Hauff, S., Huntgeburth, J., Veit, D.: Exploring uncertainties in a marketplace for cloud computing: a revelatory case study. J. Bus. Econ. **84**(3), 441–468 (2014)

Hirschheim, R., Heinzl, A., Dibbern, J.: Information Systems Outsourcing: Enduring Themes, Global, 2nd edn. Palgrave MacMillan, Basingstoke (2011)

Holmström, J., Ketokivi, M., Hameri, A.: Bridging practice and theory: a design science approach. Decis. Sci. **40**(1), 65–87 (2009)

Hsu, P.F., Ray, S., Li-Hsieh, Y.: Examining cloud computing adoption intention, pricing mechanism, and deployment model. Int. J. Inf. Manag. **34**, 474–488 (2014)

IBM: Seeding the clouds: key infrastructure elements for cloud computing, Yorktown Heights, NY (2009)

ISACA: Cloud computing market maturity study results (2012). www.isaca.org

Iyer, B., Henderson, J.C.: Business value from clouds: learning from users. MIS Q. Executive **11**(1), 51–60 (2012)

Jamshidi, P., Ahmad, A., Pahl, C.: Cloud migration research: a systematic review. IEEE Trans. Cloud Comput. **1**(2), 142–157 (2013)

Jorion, P.: Value at Risk: The New Benchmark for Managing Financial Risk, 2nd edn. McGraw-Hill, New York (2000)

Kaplan, R.S., Norton, D.P.: Using the balanced scorecard as a strategic management system. Harvard Bus. Rev. **74**(1), 75–85 (1996)

Khajeh-Hosseini, A., Greenwood, D., Smith, J.W., Somerville, I.: The cloud adoption toolkit: supporting cloud adoption decisions in the enterprise. Softw. Pract. Exper. **42**(4), 447–465 (2012)

Kim, A., Moskowitz, S.: Incentivized cloud computing: a principal agent solution to the cloud computing dilemma. Technical report Naval Research Lab, Washington, DC (2010)

Koehler, P., Anandasivam, A., Ma, D., Weinhardt, C.: Customer heterogeneity and tariff biases in cloud computing.In: Proceedings of International Conference on Information System, St. Louis, MO (2010)

Lacity, M.C., Solomon, S., Yan, A., Willcocks, L.P.: Business process outsourcing studies: a critical review and research directions. J. Inf. Technol. **26**, 21–258 (2011)

Li, C.: Cloud computing system management under flat rate pricing. J. Netw. Syst. Manag. **19**(3), 305 (2011)

Liao, J., Welsch, H., Stoica, M.: Organizational absorptive capacity and responsiveness: an empirical investigation of growth-oriented SMEs. Entr. Theory Pract. **28**(1), 63–85 (2003)

Low, C., Chen, Y., Wu, M.: Understanding the determinants of cloud computing adoption. Ind. Manag. Data Syst. **111**(7), 1006–1023 (2011)

Mani, D., Barua, A., Whinston, A.B.: Successfully governing business process outsourcing relationships. MIS Q. **5**(1), 15–29 (2006)

Manyika, J., Chui, M., Bughin, J., Dobbs, R., Bisson, P., Marrs, A.: Disruptive technology: advances that will transform life, business, and the global economy. McKinsey Global Institute, New York (2013)

Marston, S., Li, Z., Bandyopadhyay, S., Ghalasi, A.: Cloud computing: the business perspecrtive. Decis. Support Syst. **51**(1), 176–189 (2011)

Merrill, T., Kang, T.: Cloud computing: is your organization weighing both benefits and risks? ACE USA, New York, (2014)

Messerschmidt, C.M., Hinz, O.: Explaining the adoption of grid computing: An integrated institutional theory and organizational capability approach. J. Strateg. Inf. Syst. **22**, 137–156 (2013)

Miles, R., Snow, C.: Organizational Strategy, Structure, and Process. McGraw-Hill, New York (1978)

Mohrman, S.A., Gibson, C.B., Mohrman, A.M.: Doing research that is useful to practice a model and empirical exploration. Acad. Manag. J. **44**(2), 357–375 (2001)

National Institute of Standards and Technology: NIST Cloud Computing Standards Roadmap. SP 500-291(2), U.S. Department of Commerce, Gaithersburg, MD (2013)

Nonaka, I.: A dynamic theory of organizational knowledge creation. Organ. Sci. **5**(1), 14–37 (1994)

Nørreklit, H.: The balance on the balanced scorecard: a critical analysis of some of its assumptions. Manag. Acc. Res. **11**, 65–88 (2000)

Oh, W., Gallivan, M., Kim, J.W.: The market's perception of the transactional risks of information technology outsourcing announcements. J. Manag. Inf. Syst. **22**(4), 271–303 (2006)

Oshri, I., Kotlarsky, J., Willcocks, L.P.: The Handbook of Global Outsourcing and Offshoring, 2nd edn. Springer, New York (2010)

Qu, W.G., Pinsonneault, A., Oh, W.: Influence of industry characteristics on information technology outsourcing. J. Manag. Inf. Syst. **27**(4), 99–128 (2011)

Pauley, W.A.: Cloud provider transparency: an empirical evaluation. IEEE Secur. Priv. **8**(6), 32–39 (2010)

Pitt, L.F., Watson, R., Kavan, C.B.: Service quality: a measure of information systems effectiveness. MIS Q. **19**(2), 173–187 (1995)

Poppo, L., Zenger, T.: Do formal contracts and relational governance function as substitutes or complements? Strateg. Manag. J. **23**(8), 707–725 (2002)

Rimal, B.P., Jukan, A., Katsaros, D., Goeleven, Y.: Architectural requirements for cloud computing: an enterprise cloud approach. J. Grid Comput. **9**(1), 3–26 (2011)

Rodriguez, T.: The importance of network effects for cloud computing. Enterpr. Cloud (2012)

Ross, P., Blumenstein, M.: Cloud computing: the nexus of strategy and technology. J. Bus. Strategy **34**(4), 39–47 (2013)

Silk, S.: Automating the balanced scorecard. Manag. Acc. **79**(11), 38–44 (1998)

Stern, J.M., Stewart, G.B., Chew, D.H.: EVA: an integrated financial management system. Eur. Financ. Manag. **2**, 223–245 (1996)

Sutherland, S., Chetty, G.: Migration to cloud computing: a sample survey based on a research in progress on the investigation of standard based interoperability protocols for the convergence of cloud computing, servcie oriented architecture and enterprise architecture. Int. J. Inf. Process. Manag. **5**(1), 50–61 (2014)

The Open Group: Cloud computing for business: establishing your cloud vision. San Francisco, CA (2014)

Tornatzky, L.G., Klein, K.J.: Innovation characteristics and innovation adoption-implementation: a meta-analysis of findings. IEEE Trans. Eng. Manag. **29**(1), 28–45 (1982)

Truong, H., Dustdar, S.: composable cost estimation and monitoring for computational applications in cloud computing environments. Proc. Comput. Sci. **1**(1), 2175–2184 (2010)

Venters, W., Whitley, E.A.: A critical review of cloud computing: researching desires and realities. J. Inf. Technol. **27**(3), 179–197 (2012)

Vouk, M.A.: Cloud computing: issues, research and implementations. J. Comput. Inf. Technol. **16**(4), 235–246 (2008)

Walker, O.C., Boyd, H.W., Mullins, J., Larrèchè, J.C.: Marketing Strategy: Planning and Implementation, 4th edn. Irwin/McGraw-Hill, Homewood (2003)

Wright, C.: Top three potential risks with outsourcing information systems. Inf. Syst. Control J. **5**, 1–3 (2004)

# An Agency Perspective to Cloud Computing

Frank Pallas[1,2]([⊠])

[1] Center for Applied Legal Studies, Karlsruhe Institute of Technology,
76131 Karlsruhe, Germany
`frank.pallas@kit.edu`
[2] FZI Forschungszentrum Informatik, 10117 Berlin, Germany

**Abstract.** The field of cloud computing is strongly affected by conflicts of interest between providers and users of resources. A comprehensive and integrative model for representing and analyzing these conflicts on a theoretically well-founded basis is, however, still lacking. Therefore, this paper establishes such a model based on economic agency theory. Employing two realistic example scenarios, we identify representative challenges faced by cloud users and generalize them as typical problems present in agency relations. Based on this conception, we correlate existing practices and strategies from cloud computing with corresponding abstract instruments from agency theory. Finally, we identify approaches that are – even if suggested by economic theory – not practically employed in the cloud domain and discuss the potential to utilize them in future technical and non-technical developments.

**Keywords:** Cloud computing · Agency · Principal-agent · Adverse selection · Moral hazard · Hold-up

## 1 Introduction

Given its paradigmatic differences from traditional IT usage, cloud computing introduces completely novel challenges of technical and non-technical nature. In particular, the relation between the provider and the user of a certain cloud resource deserves specific attention: While the fulfillment of certain requirements can be of crucial importance for the user's decision to employ cloud computing at all, it does in many cases not lie in the interest of the provider. A certain level of physical datacenter security might, for example, be an essential precondition for a potential user to actually consider cloud storage as a viable option. For the provider, however, establishing the required level of physical security raises significant costs which he will usually try to limit to the extent that actually pays off for him. Under certain conditions (which will be laid out in more detail throughout this paper) and without proper countermeasures being used, this would lead a rational provider to not establish the security level aspired by the would-be customer. A potential customer, in turn, can then be assumed to be aware of this fact and therefore to abstain from the use of cloud storage at all.

© Springer International Publishing Switzerland 2014
J. Altmann et al. (Eds.): GECON 2014, LNCS 8914, pp. 36–51, 2014.
DOI: 10.1007/978-3-319-14609-6_3

Comparable problems arise with regard to a multitude of further aspects of cloud computing. Whether in matters of security, legal compliance, long-term availability or many other characteristics: We are always confronted with fundamental conflicts of interest between the user and the provider which, on the large scale, may hinder the broad application of cloud computing in general. There are thus good reasons to search for appropriate strategies and countermeasures for adressing them properly.

Ongoing and ever-increasing research in this field notwithstanding, we do, however, still lack well-established abstract models for representing, understanding and counteracting cloud-specific conflicts of interests between users and providers of resources. It is the aim of this paper to establish such an abstract model which covers the most constitutive factors shaping typical settings of cloud computing. Furthermore, the model shall be applicable across different conflict domains and allow for the development of novel and theoretically well-founded approaches for counteracting the identified conflicts in practice.

For developing our abstract model, we employ economic theory to categorize and understand relevant factors and conflicts arising in the field of cloud computing, thus following an approach of positive economics [8]. In particular, we mainly build upon the well-known agency model as established by [14] and extensively analyzed by [20].[1] Even if the relevance of agency-theory has occasionally been recognized for selective aspects of cloud [9,12], grid [7] and service computing [31] as well as for the closely related domain of IT-outsourcing [3,6,11] before, these considerations have not yet been condensed into an integrative abstract model as established herein. As we will see, however, such a model allows us (1) to better understand and structure the conflicts and challenges arising in the field of cloud computing on an abstract level, (2) to categorize and assess existing concepts for counteracting these conflicts and challenges and (3) to identify possible starting points for necessary extensions to the status quo in matters of technical and non-technical instruments for heightening the broad applicability of cloud computing.

To illustrate our rather conceptional considerations and to demonstrate the broad practical applicability of our abstract model, we use two simple scenarios exemplifying some common materializations of the generic conflicts of interests arising in the context of cloud computing. Of the broadly recognized cloud service models [26], these scenarios mainly comprise infrastructure (IaaS) and platform (PaaS) services, but our considerations and findings are similarly applicable to Software (SaaS) services. Of the various deployment models [26], in turn, we concentrate on settings following a "public-cloud" model and explicitly ignore those where cloud technologies are merely used in-house without involving external providers ("private cloud"). To a certain extent, our findings will also be applicable to intermediate models like "hybrid" and "community clouds", but our primary focus is on "public" offerings.

---

[1] For an overview of agency theory also discussing its different understandings and lines of research, see also [5].

Finally, we explicitly confine our considerations to two-party relations with just one cloud provider and one cloud user involved. Being well aware that practial applications of cloud computing often involve multiple parties with sometimes highly complex interdependencies [15, 21, 27], we consciously do so herein because a sound and scientifically well-founded understanding of the fundamental two-party relation provides an indispensable basis for corresponding future deliberations on rather complex settings.

This being said, the remainder of this paper is structured as follows: In Sect. 2, we sketch our example scenarios that will be used throughout the paper. In Sect. 3, we briefly outline the fundamentals of agency theory and some related concepts from new institutional economics, which together form the theoretical basis of our model. Section 4 then maps these concepts onto the previously sketched example scenarios, establishes our agency perspective to cloud computing and deductively identifies measures that are suggested by theory but not yet broadly applied in practice. Finally, Sect. 5 sums up our findings and points to auspicious strands for future research.

## 2 Example Scenarios

As a first representative example of cloud usage and the conflicts of interests arising in this context, we assume a European medium enterprise wanting to ensure fallback availability of its most important internal systems for the case of large-scale local infrastructure failures. Instead of erecting and maintaining a complete remote site on their own, the enterprise decides to use a model of "cloud standby" [23] for this purpose. In this model, the fallback-infrastructure is held available in the form of virtual machines which are updated to the current state of software and data on a regular basis (e.g. once a day) but which are apart from these update cycles constantly inactive until a disaster actually happens. As opposed to the operation of a complete remote fallback site, this model would provide significant benefits to the company [22] as long as all requirements are met.

Besides fundamental functional properties (e.g. regarding operational capability, performance, etc.), these requirements also include several nonfunctional ones. For example, we can assume that the infrastructure to be replicated also comprises databases holding personal data. As these data must be accessible within the virtualized fallback infrastructure, they cannot be stored in anonymized form, which, in turn, raises several legal restrictions. In our case, these obligate the enterprise to ensure that personal data does not leave the European Union[2], that data

---

[2] In fact, the actual legal regulations are far more sophisticated. For instance, the transfer of personal data beyond the EU can be allowed if the destination country is explicitly recognized as providing an "adequate level of protection" or in case the transfer is covered by instruments like the "safe harbor agreement" or the so-called "standard contractual clauses". This would, however, under certain circumstances (like, e.g., under German legislation) invalidate the legal construct of "processing on behalf of the controller" and thus result in further complications. Without going more into detail and for the sake of clarity, we therefore assume – like it is usually done in practice – a strict "EU-internal" requirement.

are not used (e.g. by the provider) for other purposes than originally collected for, and that certain security procedures are in place to prevent unwanted disclosure. In ensuring compliance with these legal restrictions, the enterprise is obviously dependent on the cloud provider's conduct and will therefore insist upon respective contractual agreements. As soon as the adherence to such agreements can hardly be verified, however, the cloud provider may still have incentives to act against his customer's interest because data replication beyond Europe may be the cheapest way to meet certain availability guarantees, because exploiting the data might provide additional business value or because maintaining certain strong security procedures would raise significant costs. The question is, then, how the medium enterprise can ensure that the cloud provider does not opportunistically serve his own goals.

The same question also arises within our second example. Here, we assume a small startup firm that pursues the strategy of erecting their whole IT infrastructure "in the cloud" from the very beginning in order to ensure strong adaptability to changing requirements (e.g. in matters of sudden growth or highly variable usage patterns) without having to invest substantially into physical infrastructure. Due to their specific use case, the startup firm needs cloud-based resources (1) for running virtual machines with a self-deployed distributed web application, (2) for storing and analyzing large amounts of social media data retrieved from third parties, (3) for storing and handling own datasets (including user data) in a consistent way, and (4) for payments processing. These functionalities are to be realized on the basis of advanced, ready-to-use cloud-based services which are, for reasons of communication performance, to be sourced from one single provider.

Again, this scenario raises basic, functional requirements as well as further, non-functional ones. In particular, we assume the startup firm to have a vital interest in stability and availability of the overall system, in updates, patches, etc. being promtly installed to the virtualization layer by the provider, and in the establishment and proper maintenance of efficient mechanisms for anomaly and intrusion detection. Furthermore, the startup has an interest in a high quality of the fraud detection mechanisms employed in the payment service and, finally, in its core assets – the large amounts of social media data – not being used for own purposes by other parties including the provider himself. Like in the above example, acting in the best interest of his customer is not in the interest of the cloud provider because this would raise costs and efforts for heightening availability, for constant system updates, for the maintenance and enhancement of anomaly, intrusion and fraud detection mechanisms, etc. Again, this implies the question how the startup firm can ensure its requirements to be appropriately met even if this does – a priori – not lie in the interest of the provider.

As we see, the conflicts of interests between the user and the provider of cloud resources can be manifold and originate from various directions including security, legal compliance, quality of results, etc. Instead of – as it is often done – addressing each of these domains directly, we do herein strive for a rather generic, abstract model for representing and analyzing these conflicts on a theoretical basis. This model shall later serve as starting point for the identification of foreseeable obstacles to a broader adoption of cloud computing and for the development of respectice countermeasures. Economic agency theory matches this aim and the basic setting with user and provider facing a goal divergence quite well and will, supplemented by further concepts from new institutional economics, therefore serve as the theoretical basis of our model. Its foundations shall thus be outlined in brief before applying it to our exemplary scenarios in Sect. 4.

## 3   The General Agency Model

Basically, the general agency model consists of two parties interacting with each other – the principal and the agent. Both are assumed to be opportunistic utility maximizers and thus to primarily serve their own individual goals. Under these givens, the "principal engages the agent to perform some service on his behalf, and to facilitate the achievement of the activity, he delegates some decision-making authority to the agent" [10, p. 162]. Furthermore, the model assumes that information is "asymmetric in the sense that (1) the agent's action is not directly observable by the principal [...] or (2) the agent has made some observation that the principal has not made [where] in the first case, one speaks of hidden action, in the second of hidden information" [10, p. 162]. These givens lead to the first problem present in principal-agent relationships: Moral hazard.

### 3.1   Moral Hazard

Basically, the above-mentioned information asymmetries suggest an opportunistic agent to not always act in the best interest of the principal but to primarily serve his own goals instead. Being aware of the principal's hidden action problem, for example, an agent can put low effort at carrying out the task delegated to him while the fact of hidden information allows him to attribute poor outcomes of his efforts to adverse situational conditions instead of, say, to the fact of having been negligent. In order to counteract this so-called moral hazard problem, different countermeasures can be employed:

- *Monitoring* refers to the principal's activities for reducing the information asymmetries between him and the agent during service provision. In particular, monitoring can refer to agent behavior (adressing hidden action) as well as to situational givens (adressing hidden information). While more comprehensive monitoring reduces the expectable divergence between actual agent behavior and the principal's interest, it also raises costs by itself. These must be weighed against the accomplished reduction of moral hazard.
- *Bonding*, in turn, is a strategy where the agent makes efforts or expenditures in order to guarantee that he will not act opportunistically against the principal's interest. A typical example for this strategy are bonds deposited with the principal which are "forfeited if the agent is caught cheating" [25, p. 195]. Like monitoring, bonding mechanisms raise costs by themselves and their extent must be weighed against the achieved reduction of moral hazard.

Due to the costs induced by monitoring and bonding mechanisms, it is usually rational for the principal to accept a certain level of opportunistic agent behavior, which is referred to as "residual loss". Together, monitoring costs, bonding costs and residual loss make up the overall "agency costs" a principal has to accept in the course of delegating a task to an agent instead of performing it himself.

Besides the moral hazard problem (and the respective costs) occuring *during* the provision of a delegated service, agency relations are characterized by further challenges. Even if not being part of agency theory's core, the problems of "adverse selection" and "hold-up" apply to many agency relationships and shall therefore also be included in the following analysis.

## 3.2 Adverse Selection

Adverse selection refers to the principal's initial selection of an agent: While the agent is very well aware of his characteristics and, thus, of the expectable quality of a certain service delivered by him, the principal cannot perfectly assess these characteristics beforehand. Without additional countermeasures being taken, this would lead to a so-called "lemons-market" [1] where high-quality agents cannot achieve appropriate payments and therefore leave the market while low-quality agents stay in. The principal can then only choose between different low-quality agents providing inferior service quality. Again, different strategies can be employed to prevent such unwanted outcomes:

- *Screening* is conducted by the principal and encompasses all activities of examination aimed at directly increasing the principal's knowledge about the agent's actual quality. A typical example of screening are assessment centers in the employment market.
- *Signaling* is basically conducted by the agent and refers to certificates, references and other evidence that shall demonstrate the agent's quality. In order to be meaningful, it must be ensured that such signals are less expensive to emit for high-quality agents than for low-quality ones [28] – like it is, for example, the case for university degrees.
- *Self-Selection*, in turn, refers to models with different contracts being offered to agents, featuring characteristics that make high-quality agents choose other options than low-quality ones. Typical examples of such mechanisms include insurance contracts with different deductibles or employment contracts for salespersons with different commission rates. For this scheme to work properly, it must be ensured that the facts determining the agents outcome (e.g., the sales volume) can easily and doubtlessly be ascertained.

## 3.3 Hold-Up

Hold-up situations, in turn, emerge from specific, non-recoverable investments being made in preparation of or within an agency relation by one party, thereby providing a certain possibility of opportunistic exploitation – e.g. through demanding price reductions or other detrimental condition changes – to the other [16, pp. 310ff]. In agency relations, hold-up problems share some characteristics of moral hazard but can apply to both, principal and agent, depending on the concrete setting and the specific investments having to be done. Whoever makes a significant investment specific to his counterpart will be at disadvantage and face the risk of his "locked in" position being exploited. Beyond those already mentioned above for counteracting moral hazard in general (esp. bonding), economic theory suggests several countermeasures to address such hold-up situations:

- *Long-term contracts* can, if they are sufficiently complete and easily enforceable, mitigate the hold-up problem through eliminating the risk of ex-post condition changes demanded by one party. On the other hand, long term contracts may also introduce new, "inverted" hold-up situations because of the formerly strong party now being bound to a single contractor, for example [16, pp. 308f].
- *Non-contractual long-term relations* based on mutual trust, reputation and anticipated future rewards are another way for dealing with the risk of hold-up [13, pp. 80ff].
- *Multiple, substitutable counterparties* ensure that there are always alternatives which can be employed in case of one partner trying to exploit a hold-up situation. Thereby the risk of such opportunistic behavior can be limited [13, pp. 80ff]. On the other hand, this also implies that a highly specific investment must be done multiple times – either by one party having to adopt to the specifics of multiple partners or by the different partners each adopting to the same specifics of their common counterparty.
- *Vertical Integration*, finally, also is a possible strategy for dealing with the need to make specific investments. Instead of trying to manage the hold-up problem, the involved parties are simply merged into one entity. Especially in case of "extensive hold-up problems", vertical integration can prove advantageous over remaining with a two-party agency relation [13, p. 74].

After having laid out the fundamentals of agency theory and strongly related problems from new institutional economics in general, we will now show how these abstract concepts can be mapped to our exemplary scenarios and what we can learn from this mapping with regard to well-known concrete challenges of cloud computing.

## 4    An Agency Model of Cloud Computing

Given the above-mentioned fundamental characteristics of agency relations, the application of agency-theory to cloud-based settings seems promising. In the following, we will therefore demonstrate how abstract concepts from agency theory on the one and concrete problems and approaches from the field of cloud computing on the other hand can be mapped onto each other by interpreting the cloud user (in our example scenarios, this is the medium enterprise or the startup firm, respectively) as the principal and the cloud provider as the agent.

For each of the main challenges – adverse selection, moral hazard and hold-up – we will furthermore demonstrate in brief how agency theory can be employed to deduce starting points for the development of novel or enhanced approaches for diminishing uncertainties and risks currently hampering a broader adoption of cloud computing in general.

### 4.1   Adverse Selection in Cloud Computing

Like any agency relation, every use of cloud computing begins with the selection of an appropriate provider. In the example of cloud standby, for instance, this means that the medium enterprise has to find a provider that offers the required functionalities (operational capability, performance, etc.) and at the same time provides sufficient certainty that the enterprise can still comply with its legal obligations regarding the handling of personal data replicated to the cloud.

While the fulfillment of basic functional requirements can easily be estimated in advance through test installations, benchmarks, or provider-independent comparisons based on long-term measurements[3], this is not the case for non-functional ones. In particular, it is basically unknown to the potential cloud user what security precautions a certain provider has in place and of what quality the provider's security competences are in general. While the ex-ante information asymmetries seem manageable with regard to functional requirements, they are thus significant in matters of characteristics like security [9].

Faced with this uncertainty (and in the absence of any measures for counteracting it), the enterprise having to select a provider would for any potential choice have to assume a medium level of security and thus a medium probability of being able to meet its legal obligations. This, in turn, would imply a medium willingness to pay, drive those providers out of the market that invest considerable efforts in the provision of high security and, in the end, lead to a "lemons market" for security [2] where a rational customer would have to expect none of the remaining providers to offer sufficient security for complying with his legal obligations. In this case, the enterprise would certainly abstain from employing a cloud-standby model at all. The same effect could also be expected for the second example of a startup firm pursuing an all-encompassing cloud strategy from the very beginning. Beyond the above security-related considerations, the adverse selection effect could here also be expected for the quality of the fraud and misuse detection mechanisms employed in the payment service, for example.

In order to counteract this adverse selection effect, agency theory suggests screening, signaling and self-selection as potential strategies. These can be mapped to different measures commonly used in or at least proposed for the practice of cloud computing.

- *Screening:* Conducting in-depth security audits, for example, would from the agency perspective represent a screening activity and could in fact reduce ex-ante uncertainty about the provider's security-related capabilities.

---

[3] Like, e.g., CloudHarmony – https://www.cloudharmony.com/.

Unfortunately, such audits would raise significant screening costs as compared to the expectable overall volume of most cloud contracts, rendering it an unfeasible option for most cases.[4] Technologies providing trustworthy information about provider-internal givens to external parties [4,17,30] might, however, also be harnessed for assessing the capabilities of different providers and therefore be employed as screening tools for diminishing the risk of adverse selection.

– *Signaling:* Audit certificates issued by third parties are an instrument often referred to with regard to cloud computing [29]. Even if chronically misunderstood as proving certain assured facts about actual givens and conduct currently present on the provider's side, such certificates rather have to be considered as credible signals about the provider's capabilities in the respective domain. For instance, a security certificate issued a year ago only confirms that a provider demonstrated *his ability* to establish a certain level of security to the auditing third party that one year ago. It does, however, say nothing about whether the provider still makes the same effort of maintaining a certain level of security today or about whether he opportunistically exploits his customer's data for own purposes. Nonetheless, and perfectly in line with agency theory, certificates can still be an effective measure for counteracting the adverse selection problem faced by cloud users as they help to distinguish between providers with strong and those with weak capabilities in the respective domain.[5]

– *Self-Selection:* Contract schemes employing self-selection to make the provider reveal information about his capabilities, in turn, are currently not broadly established on the cloud market. They might, however, provide an interesting option for future arrangements. Strictly following the abstract concept of self-selection laid out above, this would require a menu of contracts being offered by the cloud user which contains options more interesting to high-quality providers on the one and other options preferred by low-quality providers on the other hand, while the facts that determine the provider's ultimate outcome must be easily ascertainable. For our example cases, one could, for instance, think of different contract options obligating the provider to pay different penalties in case a breach of data becomes publicly known. A provider with poor security capabilities would then tend to choose the option with the lowest penalty even if this implies a lower base price while a high-quality provider would rather choose an option with a higher possible compensation in exchange for a higher base price. Of course, more complex contract menus could also be thought of but it should even from this simple example become clear that self-selection schemes offer interesting options for counteracting ex-ante information asymmetries and the resulting problem of adverse selction

---

[4] High-volume contracts concluded by government agencies or large, multinational corporations might be the exception here.

[5] In order to actually provide this functionality, it is a necessary (but not sufficient) condition that receiving the certificate is more expensive for less capable providers than for strong ones. This can, however, be assumed for typical certification schemes.

in cloud computing scenarios. This would, however, require that cloud users actually have the necessary bargaining power and are not, as it is mostly the case today, simply facing "take it or leave it" offers from providers.

## 4.2   Moral Hazard in Cloud Computing

Moral hazard problems are probably the most decisive obstacles for a further development of the cloud market today. As delineated above, they emanate from information asymmetries between the principal and the agent regarding agent behavior (hidden action) and the circumstances of this behavior (hidden information).

Mapped to our cloud standby example, this moral hazard problem would particularly emerge with regard to the cloud provider's data handling, as the cloud user cannot know whether the provider actually transfers personal data beyond the European Union, whether he exploits the data for own purposes, or what efforts he actually spends in order to maintain security procedures preventing unintended disclosure of the data. Being aware of the user's nescience, the provider then has a clear incentive to act opportunistically: Whenever secretly transferring data beyond the EU, exploiting the data, or cutting down on security-related efforts would provide a benefit, he could – as long as no countermeasures are in place – be assumed to do so, even if he is contractually bound to abstain from such conduct. A well-informed user would be aware of this fact and thus know that he cannot ensure his legal obligations to be met. In the end, he would not employ the model of cloud standby at all.

For our startup example, the situation would be quite similar. The startup firm also cannot know whether security patches are promtply installed, whether intrusion and fraud detection mechanisms are constantly developed further, or whether the provider exploits the massive social media data for his own purposes to generate additional income. Regarding the requirements for maximum stability and availability, in turn, one could think that the provider's efforts are very well observable for the user through external monitoring of the efforts' outcome [12, p. 448]. This does, however, raise the problem of hidden information: For instance, the provider could explain that observed downtimes or crashes are not caused by his inappropriate conduct but rather by unforeseeable adverse exogenous conditions like a massive DDoS-attack or self-propagating large-scale glitches that lay beyond his influence. Without knowledge about such circumstances, the user could not assess the appropriateness of the provider's conduct, which, again, results in possibilities for the provider to engage in opportunistic shirking instead of acting in the interest of his customer. In order to prevent such outcomes, agency theory suggests monitoring and bonding.

– *Monitoring:* As laid out above, monitoring refers to all activities of the cloud user aimed at reducing the information asymmetries about the provider's actual conduct as well as about the circumstances the conduct took place in. Random auditing, for instance, is often suggested to cloud users in order to ensure appropriate provider behavior [12, p. 448]. This approach does, however, seem hardly valuable in practice, as it would repeatedly induce considerable monitoring costs for the user which would hardly be justified by the expectable reduction in opportunistic shirking. Technologies for providing trustworthy event logging [17] or "digital evidence" [4,30], in contrast, also help the cloud user to assess the provider's actual conduct albeit featuring a much better ratio between monitoring costs and reduction of opportunistic provider behavior. For our first scenario, we can, for instance, expect any technology providing the cloud user with trustworthy information about storage location, data access or on the provider's security-related effort to be highly welcome by the medium enterprise because this would significantly lower the risk of his data being handled illegitimately, thereby making cloud standby a considerable option at all. For the startup example, this also extends to contextual information. With trustworthy information revealing whether, for instance, a DDoS-attack actually took place, the cloud provider could be prevented from attributing good outcomes to his own efforts while blaming external conditions for bad ones.

- *Bonding:* Like the strongly related concept of self-selection for addressing adverse selection, bonding mechanisms suggested by agency theory for counteracting moral hazard are not yet established in the domain of cloud computing. Their implementation would, however, be quite straight forward: Through depositing a certain (e.g. monetary) bond with the cloud user or a commonly trusted third party, the provider could convince his customer that he will refrain from opportunistically exploiting the cloud user's data, from cutting down on security-related efforts, etc. As soon as the detection of shirking behavior is sufficiently probable (where monitoring plays an important role again), such bonding schemes could thus represent a valuable measure for cloud providers to prove their willingness not to act opportunistically against their customers.

Together, such bonding schemes and technologies reducing monitoring costs for cloud users could thus significantly limit the omnipresent moral hazard problem in cloud computing and thereby play a crucial role for the further establishment of the cloud market.

### 4.3   Hold-Ups in Cloud Computing

Vendor lock-in is the most important kind of hold-up situation that can be expected in the context of cloud computing. Basically, such a vendor lock-in emerges whenever specific and non-recoverable investments are made by one party of the agency relation. As switching to another partner would be prohibitively expensive for the investing party once the investment is done, it then faces the hold-up risk of his counterparty demanding detrimental conditions. Consistently with the theoretical concept outlined above, research has shown that potential customers are very well aware of this risk [12, p. 456], constituting a significant obstacle for them to adopt cloud computing at all.

Within our cloud standby example, such specific investments could, for instance, refer to the establishment of the fallback infrastructure and the respective update procedures on the basis of the virtualization environment and the management services (orchestration etc.) made available by the cloud provider. As soon as a once-established infrastructure and the respective automated processes cannot be easily migrated from one cloud provider to another, the medium enterprise faces switching costs which result in a vendor lock-in [19, p. 33]. Finally, this leads to a hold-up situation allowing the provider to, for example, stay with the once-established rates and performance points while the rest of the market follows the usual IT-cycles of price reductions or performance increases.

In the startup example, the hold-up risks are even more significant as the cloud user heavily relies on advanced, ready-to-use services. The specific investments in this case refer to all development activities utilizing the advanced services' programming interfaces and following their predetermined programming paradigms. Especially for advanced services like the massive data storage and analysis service or the payment service assumed in our example, these interfaces and paradigms usually are highly provider-specific and the implementations based upon them are thus hardly transferable. The more our assumed startup firm thus ties itself to the advanced services of a given provider, the higher are the obstacles for switching to another provider and the higher is the risk of this hold-up situation being exploited by the provider through, e.g., inappropriate prices or lowered availability commitments.

Again, agency theory suggests several strategies and instruments for counteracting hold-up risks in the context of cloud computing:

- *Long-Term Contracts:* Of the four strategies suggested by agency theory for counteracting hold-ups, long-term contracts could reduce such risks through ex-ante agreements on periodic price reductions or performance increases. Due to the requirement of such long-term-contracts to be complete and easily enforceable, their application seems, however, at least questionable with regard to the foreseeability of every potential source of hold-up risks as well as in matters of covering security-related and other aspects which are hard to ascertain and which are therefore also subject to the moral hazard problem (see above).
- *Availability of Alternatives:* Ensuring the availability of alternatives which could easily be switched to whenever a provider tries to exploit a hold-up possibility would therefore seem highly worthwhile for both of our assumed example users. This would, however, require them to always adopt their solutions to the specific givens of at least two different providers, thus causing significant additional costs. In this regard, technologies abstracting from provider-specific programming interfaces and thus allowing to realize the respective implementations in a provider-independent way[6] play an important role as they significantly reduce the costs of maintaining different options in parallel. Such technologies are, however, currently only available for rather foundational, generic resources like storage or the management and execution of complete virtual machines. More specific, higher-level functionalities like those provided

---

[6] Like, e.g., the Apache toolkits jclouds (https://jclouds.apache.org/) and libcloud (https://libcloud.apache.org/).

by the data analysis and the payment service assumed in the startup-scenario are, at least currently, not covered by established abstraction frameworks and it is questionable to what extent such abstractions are realistic and reasonable at all for higher-level services implementing rather specific functionalities [19, pp. 34f].[7] For those cases not covered by abstraction technologies, maintaining multiple provider alternatives would thus require to constantly adopt implementations to the specifics of the respective alternatives, thus causing significant costs.

- *Non-Contractual Long-Term Relationships:* Especially for our second example massively employing such higher-level services, the third option of countervailing hold-up risks through long-term relationships based on reputation and trust is thus to be considered. Given the limited feasibility and establishedness of the two strategies discussed above, it could very well be argued that reputation and trust are actually the most relevant mechanisms currently keeping the cloud market running at all. Their general role for the cloud market is, however, not yet well-understood [18] and requires further examination. In particular, this also includes the question to what extent the intrinsically informal processes around reputation and trust can actually be formalized and proceduralized [24] for the domain of cloud computing.

In any case, countermeasures for diminishing hold-up risks will be of crucial relevance for the further development of the cloud market in general because only with effectual mechanisms available, it will in the long run be rational for a potential cloud user to not fall back on the fourth option suggested by agency theory: *vertical integration.* For the context of cloud computing, this would basically imply to *not* make use of external providers at all but rather stay with the traditional model of providing the respective resources in-house. The availability of effective mechanisms for countering hold-up risks is therefore clearly in the very interest of cloud providers, too.

## 5   Conclusion and Research Implications

As we have demonstrated, agency theory is highly suitable for representing, understanding and analyzing the conflicts of interests arising between providers and users of cloud resources on a theoretically well-founded basis. While isolated aspects of agency theory have been applied to cloud computing before, the integrative perspective developed herein provides a comprehensive mapping of agency theory to cloud computing. This, in turn, allows us to evaluate concrete existing instruments like auditing or certifications in the light of corresponding abstract concepts and, in particular, to identify strategies suggested by agency theory which have no or only dysfunctional practical equivalents yet.

In particular, the fact of audit certificates being chronically misunderstood as proving facts while rather representing credible *signals* on his capabilities

---

[7] The same arguments do, of course, also apply to initiatives for cloud-related standardization which are basically also aimed at reducing the hold-up risk by establishing provider substitutability.

sent out by the provider has only briefly been addressed above and should in the future be investigated in more detail. Furthermore, agency-specific contract schemes are – except, maybe, for high-volume customers like governments or multinational corporations – not broadly established in the cloud market. Nonetheless, we showed that such advanced contract schemes are suggested by agency theory for countering *adverse selection, moral hazard* and *hold-ups* and that the respective abstract concepts could very well be transferred to the concrete domain of cloud computing. Further research on such advanced contract schemes for cloud computing thus seems highly valuable. As such contract schemes require the customer to be in a sufficiently strong bargaining position, this research should comprise policy aspects, too.

Regarding the further development of technology, we demonstrated that mechanisms providing credible information on the provider's capabilities and actual conduct could significantly reduce *screening* and *monitoring* costs and thus lead to more efficient outcomes or make cloud computing a viable option at all. In order to prevent a cloud provider from incorrectly attributing bad outcomes to detrimental external conditions, agency theory suggests these mechanisms to cover the externally given conditions of provider conduct, too. As such instruments would address the core problem of information asymmetries directly and at comparatively low operating costs, we see much potential for counteracting agency-related inefficiencies here. The whole field of providing credible digital evidence to the cloud user is thus a domain that we will explicitly focus our future research on – not only from the technical perspective but also regarding its legal and regulatory dimension.

As intended, however, the main result of this paper is the establishment of an agency perspective to cloud computing itself. Due to its theoretical well-foundedness and its broad practical applicability, this perspective opens up the whole field of agency-related research for application to the cloud computing domain. Certainly, this is not limited to the development of further novel approaches for counteracting well-recognized practical problems as exemplarily done herein. Instead, the abstract perspective established throughout this paper will also serve the prospective analysis of ongoing technological developments and thereby help to better foresee upcoming but yet unrecognized conflicts and challenges in the cloud market. This, in turn, will prove highly valuable from the perspective of policymaking, too.

**Acknowledgements.** The research presented in this paper has been partially funded by the European Commission in the context of the Research Framework Program Seven (FP7) project SECCRIT (Grant Agreement No. 312758, https://seccrit.eu).

# References

1. Akerlof, G.A.: The market for "Lemons": quality uncertainty and the market mechanism. Q. J. Econ. **84**(3), 488–500 (1970)
2. Anderson, R., Moore, T.: The economics of information security. Science **314**(5799), 610–613 (2006)

3. Aubert, B.A., Patry, M., Rivard, S.: Assessing the risk of IT outsourcing. In: Proceedings of 31st HICSS, vol. 6, pp. 685–692 (1998)
4. Bless, R., Flittner, M.: Towards corporate confidentiality preserving auditing mechanisms for clouds. In: Proceedings of 3rd International Conference on Cloud Networking (CloudNet), (2014). doi:10.1109/CloudNet.2014.6969025
5. Eisenhardt, K.M.: Agency theory: an assessment and review. Acad. Manag. Rev. **14**(1), 57–74 (1989)
6. Elitzur, R., Gavious, A., Wensley, A.K.: Information systems outsourcing projects as a double moral hazard problem. Omega **40**(3), 379–389 (2012)
7. Eymann, T., Knig, S., Matros, R.: A framework for trust and reputation in grid environments. J. Grid Comput. **6**(3), 225–237 (2008)
8. Friedman, M.: The methodology of positive economics. In: Hausman, D.M. (ed.) The Philosophy of Economics - An Anthology, 2nd edn, pp. 180–213. Cambridge University Press, Cambridge (1994)
9. Friedman, A.A., West, D.M.: Privacy and Security in Cloud Computing. Center for Technology Innovation at Brookings (2010)
10. Furubotn, E.G., Richter, R.: Institutions & Economic Theory: The Contribution of the New Institutional Economics, 2nd edn. The University of Michigan Press, Ann Arbor (2005)
11. Hamlen, K.W., Thuraisingham, B.: Data security services, solutions and standards for outsourcing. Comput. Stand. Interfaces **35**(1), 1–5 (2013)
12. Hauff, S., Huntgeburth, J., Veit, D.: Exploring uncertainties in a marketplace for cloud computing: a revelatory case study. J. Bus. Econ. **84**(3), 441–468 (2014)
13. Holmström, B., Roberts, J.: The boundaries of the firm revisited. J. Econ. Perspect. **12**(4), 73–94 (1998)
14. Jensen, M.C., Meckling, W.H.: Theory of the firm: managerial behavior, agency costs and ownership structure. J. Financ. Econ. **3**(4), 305–360 (1976)
15. Kim, K., Altmann, J.: Evolution of the software-as-a-service innovation system through collective intelligence. Int. J. Coop. Inf. Syst. **22**(3), 1340006 (2013)
16. Klein, B., Crawford, R.G., Alchian, A.A.: Vertical integration, appropriable rents, and the competitive contracting process. J. Law Econ. **21**, 297–326 (1978)
17. Ko, R.K.L., Lee, B.S., Pearson, S.: Towards achieving accountability, auditability and trust in cloud computing. In: Abraham, A., Mauri, J.L., Buford, J.F., Suzuki, J., Thampi, S.M. (eds.) ACC 2011, Part IV. CCIS, vol. 193, pp. 432–444. Springer, Heidelberg (2011)
18. Kshetri, N.: Privacy and security issues in cloud computing: the role of institutions and institutional evolution. Telecommun. Policy **37**(4), 372–386 (2013)
19. Kurze, T., Klems, M., Bermbach, D., Lenk, A., Tai, S., Kunze, M.: Cloud federation. In: Proceedings of Second International Conference on Cloud Computing, GRIDs, and Virtualization, pp. 32–38 (2011)
20. Laffont, J.J., Martimort, D.: The Theory of Incentives - The Principal-Agent Model. Princeton University Press, Princeton (2002)
21. Leimeister, S., Böhm, M., Riedl, C., Krcmar, H.: The business perspective of cloud computing: actors, roles and value networks. In: Proceedings of ECIS 2010, Paper 56 (2010)
22. Lenk, A., Pallas, F.: Modeling quality attributes of cloud-standby-systems. In: Lau, K.-K., Lamersdorf, W., Pimentel, E. (eds.) ESOCC 2013. LNCS, vol. 8135, pp. 49–63. Springer, Heidelberg (2013)
23. Lenk, A., Tai, S.: Cloud standby: disaster recovery of distributed systems in the cloud. In: Villari, M., Zimmermann, W., Lau, K.-K. (eds.) ESOCC 2014. LNCS, vol. 8745, pp. 32–46. Springer, Heidelberg (2014)

24. Macías, M., Guitart, J.: Cheat-proof trust model for cloud computing markets. In: Vanmechelen, K., Altmann, J., Rana, O.F. (eds.) GECON 2012. LNCS, vol. 7714, pp. 154–168. Springer, Heidelberg (2012)
25. Milgrom, P., Roberts, J.: Economics, Organization & Management. Prentice Hall, Englewood Cliffs (1992)
26. National Institute of Standards and Technology (NIST): Special Publication 800–145 - The NIST Definition of Cloud Computing (2011). http://csrc.nist.gov/publications/nistpubs/800-145/SP800-145.pdf
27. National Institute of Standards and Technology (NIST): Special Publication 500–292 - NIST Cloud Computing Reference Architecture (2011). http://www.nist.gov/customcf/get_pdf.cfm?pub_id=909505
28. Spence, M.: Job market signaling. Q. J. Econ. **87**(3), 355–374 (1973)
29. Sunyaev, A., Schneider, S.: Cloud services certification. Commun. ACM **56**(2), 33–36 (2013)
30. Taylor, M., Haggerty, J., Gresty, D., Hegarty, R.: Digital evidence in cloud computing systems. Comput. Law Secur. Rev. **26**(3), 304–308 (2010)
31. Vykoukal, J., Wolf, M., Beck, R.: Services grids in industry - on-demand provisioning and allocation of grid-based business services. Bus. Inf. Syst. Eng. **1**(2), 177–184 (2009)

# Work in Progress on Market Dynamics

# Cloud Goliath Versus a Federation of Cloud Davids

## Survey of Economic Theories on Cloud Federation

Kibae Kim, Songhee Kang, and Jörn Altmann[✉]

Technology Management, Economics and Policy Program College
of Engineering, Seoul National University, Gwanak-Ro 1, Gwanak-Gu,
Seoul 151-742, South Korea
kibae36@snu.ac.kr, soyedda@gmail.com,
jorn.altmann@acm.org

**Abstract.** Cloud computing, which can be described as a technology for provisioning computing infrastructure as a service, runtime platform as a service, and software as a service, is considered as a keystone for innovation in the IT area. However, a limiting factor to innovation through cloud computing could be the economies of scale and network externalities that give more benefits to larger cloud providers. Due to the economies of scale and network externalities in an oligopolistic environment, a giant cloud provider can offer resources at lower cost than smaller providers. To overcome the disadvantage of small clouds, some research proposes architectures, in which small clouds can federate through common virtual interfaces. Therefore, academy and industry ask whether the federation of small cloud providers is economically feasible and can compete with a giant cloud provider. However, it is hard to solve those problems because the specifications of a cloud federation and the conditions of cloud market are unclear. To fill this gap, in this paper, we survey the conceptual background of cloud computing and the federation of small cloud providers. The results of this paper are expected to guide how to define the economic problems on cloud federation and provide constraints to the problems.

**Keywords:** Cloud computing · Economic analysis · Infrastructure-as-a-Service · Platform-as-a-Service · Software-as-a-Service · Service ecosystem · Economies of scale · Cloud federation

## 1 Introduction

Cloud is a new paradigm of computing that replaces the paradigm of localized computing and server client architecture [1]. In this paradigm, a cloud provider manages hardware and software to provide clients with an infrastructure as a service, platform as a service, and software as a service through an interface [2]. A client can resolve its scalability problem by paying for using cloud systems of providers on demand [3, 37].

© Springer International Publishing Switzerland 2014
J. Altmann et al. (Eds.): GECON 2014, LNCS 8914, pp. 55–66, 2014.
DOI: 10.1007/978-3-319-14609-6_4

Due to the benefit of scalability, cloud has substituted the conventional computing paradigm (i.e., data centers and software products).

The key to cloud computing is that a cloud provider achieves economies of scale to reduce its operating cost and enhance the elasticity of services [3]. Besides, a cloud provider gains benefit from the clients, whose utility show network externalities, so that two-sided market strategies work [4, 38, 41]. Economies of scale and network externalities make larger cloud providers to be even stronger. A giant cloud vendor can offer low-priced services and the large size of the provider attracts even more clients as the risk of large providers to go bankrupt is low. The revenue from those clients can be used by the provider to upgrade its facility. In addition to this, it is hard for small cloud providers to compete with a giant vendor [41]. For this reason, the concept of cloud federation emerges in academy and in the market. Cloud federation means to "federate disparate data centers or cloud providers, including those owned by separate organizations to enable a seemingly infinite service computing utility" [5, 37]. In the federation, small cloud vendors share their resources and clients to achieve the economies of scale, enabling them to compete better with a giant cloud vendor [2]. Therefore, both academy and industry requires a framework that explains the economic feasibility of the cloud federation to answer the question whether small cloud vendors can survive in the market with the relevant technologies. However, it is still unclear what the market conditions for a successful deployment of cloud federation are and in what way the cloud provider business models change through the federation of small cloud vendors.

In this paper, we survey the conceptual background of cloud computing and the federation of small cloud vendors from an economic perspective. In particular, we discuss the economic forces that emerge if federation is introduced to the cloud market. The research questions are: First, what conditions govern the industry of cloud computing, and what business models need to be executed by a cloud provider? Second, how does federation change the business models of the cloud industry? Third, what economic issues arise through the introduction of federation in the cloud industry?

To answer these questions, we depict the technological concepts of cloud federation and their economic implications. In particular, we survey economic theories relevant to issues of cloud federation (i.e., theories on the economies of scale and two-sided market theories), and we discuss the interrelations of cloud computing, federation of clouds, and market environments.

The remainder of this paper is organized as follows. In the next section, we introduce the conceptual background of cloud computing and cloud federation. In Sect. 3, we introduce the economic theories relevant to the cloud federation. In Sect. 4, we describe the details for designing an economic model of cloud federation. Finally, Sect. 5 concludes our paper with a discussion of the implications of our findings.

## 2   Conceptual Background

### 2.1   Basic Concept of Cloud Computing

Cloud computing is a new paradigm of computing [37]. The National Institute of Standards and Technology (NIST) defines it as a "a model for enabling convenient,

on-demand network access to a shared pool of configurable computing resources …
that can be rapidly provisioned and released with minimal management effort or service
provider interaction" [6]. A cloud provider integrates servers into a cluster, and manages multiple virtual operating systems on a physical system through a hyperviser [7].
With the help of virtualization and clusterization technologies, the workload is distributed into cheap small computing units efficiently. Therefore, a cloud provider can
operate its cloud at low operating cost, so that it provides service developers and end
users can obtain computing on demand at low prices [1].

The delivery models of cloud computing vary [45] and, recently, the cloud community simply refers to them as "XaaS" [8]. The major delivery models of cloud
computing are Infrastructure-as-a-service (IaaS), Platform-as-a-service (PaaS), and
Software-as-a-service (SaaS). In brief, IaaS providers package computing resources into
virtual machines and cloud communications, while PaaS providers deliver computing
platforms, which application developers can use without dealing with different underlying system layers. SaaS providers provide access to applications and databases and
manage the underlying infrastructures and platforms [8]. Due to the XaaS delivery
models, cloud computing re-organizes the market of IT services forming a cloud ecosystem [41]. It makes computing a utility, as electricity did in the early 20th century [9].

## 2.2    Federation of Cloud Davids

It has not been discussed in the cloud computing community yet that the factors making
cloud computing successful can also threaten the market structure. The number of cloud
users determines the potential revenue of a cloud provider through the levying of fees for
computing [37]. Economies of scale gives a large cloud provider potentially more
revenue through cost savings than a smaller cloud provider [10]. Therefore, a large cloud
provider, which entered the market of cloud computing, has an absolute advantage in the
competition with its rivals. This situation can be the reason for a cloud provider to lock in
its users by slightly deviating its interfaces and protocols from standards [7]. In line with
this lock-in behavior, small cloud providers face the difficulty to fulfill users' adoption
criteria for operating their cloud ecosystem (e.g., high viability of cloud vendor [38]).
Without having many users adopting the cloud though, economies of scale, which are
necessary to survive in the cloud computing market, cannot be achieved.

To address this problem, computer science approaches suggest to share resources
among cloud providers through a framework with standardized interfaces and standardized goods [11, 39, 40]. Sharing computing resources across cloud providers
requires the same framework with standardized interfaces for each participating cloud
provider [11]. For example, Cisco designs an architecture (Application Centric Infrastructure (ACI) [13] ) for federating clouds. Another approach for federation is to insert
a meta-framework among clouds that provides all interfaces that exists in other cloud
frameworks [12]. In addition to this, the cloud providers can organize themselves by
finding the best standardized good [39, 40].

Through these efforts, cloud users, accustomed to one cloud service vendor, can
also utilize other cloud service vendors without spending large effort on migrating their
resources to another cloud. In this environment, cloud vendors are free from the strong

effect of the number of users and the economies of scale, as they share the computing resources with each other. They do not need to captivate users in their own systems, and they can focus on enhancing their quality of service and reducing their service prices on the basis of shared cloud resources [12, 39, 40].

The federation idea is mainly developed for competing with large cloud vendors like Amazon, Microsoft, and Google [13]. It is also for sure that federation gives more benefit to smaller cloud providers (Davids) than a larger one (Goliath). If a small cloud provider decides to cooperate with its competitors in a federation, it can compete in the market governed by an existing giant cloud provider with which they could not compete without federation owing to the behavior of cloud vendors as described earlier. This strategic cooperation among competitors is called "co-opetition" [14]. However, it is not clear whether the interoperability between clouds that the current technologies enable is economically feasible. Therefore, the cloud computing community needs discussions on the economic feasibility of cloud federation.

In particular, the federation at different levels of the cloud architecture needs to be discussed. Federation at the IaaS level means that VMs of one provider can be executed on the infrastructure of another provider. Federation at the PaaS level means that the management functions on different platforms are identical and can be accessed via the same interface. Federation at the SaaS level means that the data input and output of interfaces are clearly defined and that all interfaces that have ever been offered are supported until the end of the lifetime of the software. This is extremely difficult. For example, a Microsoft Word document can be opened in LibreOffice, but the text style might be broken due to a slight incompatibility.

## 3   Relevant Economic Theories

### 3.1   Economies of Scale

Previous literature designates economies of scale as the property that makes cloud computing attractive [3, 7, 15]. Economies of scale describes the economic characteristic that the long-term average cost decreases as the number of products increases in a fixed factor production environment [16]. It is to be noted that the short-term average cost, which is not considered for the economies of scale, might increase due to the inefficiency of using large quantities of input. In this case, the short term average cost shows a U-shaped curve [17].

In case of cloud computing, a large vendor invests a large amount of initial capital on establishing a computing infrastructure, and operates the infrastructure with inexpensive electricity and a small number of system administrators [7]. That is, the fixed cost for providing cloud computing is large compared to the variable cost [37, 43]. Therefore, economies of scale work strongly for cloud computing.

The effect of economies of scale has been shown empirically in a variety of industries that require a huge amount of investment on infrastructure [17–19]. They investigated the effect of economies of scale by measuring the indicator that is defined as the ratio of the difference of cost to the difference of output. The analysis results provide the rationale for merging industries or companies. For example, the integration between TV and radio industries in Japan saved 12 % of cost compared to those provided separately [18]. The integration of Danish hospitals also yielded cost savings [19]. However, the increase in scale does not always result in a company benefit. The water infrastructure industry of the UK showed that the cost efficiency increased when the water industry was separated from the sewerage industry [20].

In theoretical studies, the economies-of-scale property is considered as a linearly decreasing factor price. The total cost is expressed as the sum of quadratic factor costs [21, 22], which are different from cost functions that were assumed in earlier studies. In those earlier studies, factor functions increased linearly according to the factor quantity. The nonlinearity of the cost function of recent studies makes the cost minimization problem complex and the profit maximization problem hard to solve. Therefore, Bayon et al. (2012) introduced infimal convolution to the firm's optimization problem, if the economies of scale is at work [22]. In this method, the smallest cost function is chosen among several cost functions for each segment of the amount of output, and the profit is calculated for each segment on the basis of the chosen cost function.

While the economies-of-scale property is considered as one of the most significant properties of cloud computing, it has not been analyzed in the cloud computing industry. Economic studies on cloud computing simply assume that economies-of-scale benefits a cloud provider. They do not prove the economic origin of this property. They only investigate the effect of the assumed economies-of-scale property on the economic performance. For example, assuming economies-of-scale, a theoretical study proved the model that leasing computational resources from clouds saves cost compared to using on premise computers [23, 24].

## 3.2  Network Externalities

Cloud computing providers offers a new platform, on which a number of technology components complement each other. These platforms exist on the infrastructure level, virtual machine management level, and the software level [4]. A cloud provider allows third party agents to utilize its computing resources according to its business model. Then, the third party agents "create value" with partners and "share the value" through putting their own service model on top of an existing one or an combination of existing service models [25]. In this service ecosystem, the role of each company is flexible. Companies can compete or collaborate with one another, while providing users with complementary service. Their decisions are based on their own interests (i.e., profit in case of private companies). Therefore, the platform of cloud computing forms an ecosystem of business entities that is different from previous business ecosystems, in which companies needed to develop all new technologies within the company to compete with its rivals [25, 26].

Previous studies in economics and management science approached the platform issues from the perspective of two-sided markets, which was prompted by two economic articles [27, 28]: Rochet and Tirole (2003) designed an economic model, in which a platform mediates two sides of economic agents to gain its profit from transactions between the two sides, and the demand of one side responds positively to the number of agents on the opposite side [28]. Similarly, Caillaud and Jullien (2003) assumed in their two-sided market model that the utility of an agent on one side depends on the size of the opposite side as well as on the registration and transaction fees levied by a platform provider [27]. With the two sided model above, they showed that there is an equilibrium in the market mediated by platforms and the equilibrium depends on the registration and transaction fees, users' price elasticity of demand, and regulatory conditions. The results imply the feasibility that a few platform providers can dominate the market and that multiple platforms can compete in a market.

The essence of the two-sided market models is that network effect works across sides in the market and that a platform provider needs to enable it to make the ecosystem on its platform work [38, 41].

Network effect means that the utility of an agent depends on the number of agents using the same technology (direct network effect) or the number of complementary technologies (indirect network effect) [29, 41]. It governs the market organization and evolution [29, 30]. To promote the agents on both sides of a platform, a platform provider should determine the "subsidy side" and the "money side" and charge the users of both sides strategically according to their sensitivity to price or quality for harnessing the network effect [31]. The two-sided market approach was applied to a variety of cases including operating systems [32], information products [15, 31, 32], the Internet [33], and advertisements [34].

A platform provider provisions its resources to users such that sellers can gain benefits from the population of users. In general, finding the money-generating side is complicated [42, 44]. For example, Google Maps provides a service to users and charges fees to developers, who utilize the Google Maps professionally (i.e., the traffic from the services of the developers exceeds a threshold). Salesforce.com, however, charges customers for using its platform, levies fee from an application developer when it sells its application to customers [35]. Salesforce.com does not charge for transactions of applications that are offered free-of-charge to users by developers. Sometimes, platform providers have also to decide whether to share its platform with rivals, considering its position with respect to multi-homing costs and differentiation [31].

## 4 Specifications of Cloud Federation

### 4.1 Industry Architecture

The key to the newly rearranged computing ecosystem is that cloud clients outsource computing for providing their services. This way they can concentrate their effort on their own services, while the former software ecosystem required the computing facility to be in-house.

The mechanisms applied vary according to the delivery models of cloud services, (i.e., software-as-a-service, infrastructure-as-a-service, and platform-as-a-service). In case of software-as-a-service, a client builds up a business relationship with a cloud provider to utilize the software service provisioned by the cloud provider. In case of infrastructure-as-a-service, a cloud provider builds a business relationship with any third party agents to sell its computing resources. The third party agents could be service providers or simply clients. In many cases, a cloud provider establishes a specific contract with the third-party agent, if the third-party agent uses the computing resources for business. In case of personal use, the cloud provider publishes a listed pricing system and customer agreements (e.g., customer agreement of Amazon AWS]. The mechanism in the model of platform-as-a-service is similar to the one of infra-structure-as-a-service but more complicated. Clients can be businesses as well as service users.

Figure 1(a) describes the competition between two cloud providers in the cloud ecosystem. Each cloud provider provisions its computation service to clients through its specific interface in return for their payment. An interesting characteristic of the cloud market is that a few cloud providers account for the majority of the global market share. For example, about 24 % of IaaS and PaaS services were provided by Amazon. Amazon, Salesforce, Microsoft, IBM, and Google together provided about 51 % of the IaaS and PaaS services in the $2^{nd}$ quarter of 2014 [46]. In this environment, any new (small) cloud provider needs to compete with these large cloud providers. The challenge of the small cloud provider is that the economies of scale and network externalities support the large cloud providers.

Figure 1(b) describes the software ecosystem developed by a federation of cloud providers. The key to cloud federation is a common interface, through which cloud providers and cloud clients can access the resources of all cloud providers. With such a common interface, a third-party agent involved in one cloud platform can utilize the computing resources of another cloud platform without changing any technical set up. By doing so, a federation gives benefits not only to cloud providers but also to third-party agents. From a cloud providers' point of view, computing resources are not shared through the common interface as the provider gets compensated for any resource usage. From an ecosystem perspective, however, clients and service providers can share resources without investing further capital or changing their business models. This extension of computing resources and users enhances the economies of scale of the providers in the federation. The overload of one cloud provider can be moved to another cloud provider with ease. From the clients' point of view, they gain the guarantee of the quality of service without writing additional contracts with multiple

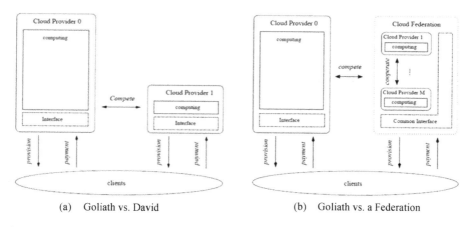

(a)   Goliath vs. David                    (b)   Goliath vs. a Federation

**Fig. 1.** (a) Competition between a Cloud Goliath and Cloud David. (b) Competition between a Cloud Goliath and a federation of Cloud Davids.

cloud providers. The clients might not even recognize that their request to its cloud provider has been fulfilled by another cloud provider. Like clients of a giant cloud, clients of a federation can utilize the computation resources provided by their cloud federation by paying a service fee.

However, the profits of cloud providers within the cloud federation change. A cloud provider within the federation saves cost due to the economies-of-scale by sharing its computing resources and cloud users with other cloud providers of the federation. As the formation of a federation incurs cost for cloud providers through investments in the development of a common interface, making contracts with other cloud providers in the federation on sharing benefits, and establishing procedures on resolving collaboration issues between providers, joining a cloud federation requires a strategic decision of cloud providers considering the benefits and costs.

## 4.2    Economic Issues

Through the formation of a federation, cloud providers can share their computing resources (IaaS), platforms (PaaS), or software services (SaaS) [5, 36]. To investigate whether cloud federation is a useful effort of small cloud providers to compete with a giant cloud providers (e.g., Amazon), we discuss three delivery models: IaaS, PaaS, and SaaS. While IaaS has to consider resource allocation, PaaS and SaaS do not.

Table 1 summarizes the analysis result for three delivery models (i.e., IaaS, PaaS, and SaaS) and two economic mechanisms that govern the federation of clouds. In detail, it describes how the economic property changes due to the federation from the

**Table 1.** Motivations for cloud federation considering two delivery models (IaaS, PaaS)

| Delivery Model | Economies of Scale | Network Externalities |
|---|---|---|
| IaaS | • A cloud provider can reduce the cost of maintaining scalability of its service, if a federation is formed. <br> • A cloud provider can improve the resource utilization through cloud federation. <br> • The cost of each cloud provider for managing the computation resources does not decrease, although they form a federation. | • The utility of a client does not change, although the client population increases due to the federation of cloud providers. |
| PaaS | • A cloud provider does not save the cost of provisioning its service, although the cloud provider participates in a federation. | • The utility of a service developer increases, as a cloud federation increases the client population. |
| SaaS | • A cloud provider does not save the cost of provisioning its service, although the cloud provider participates in a federation. | • The utility of clients and a service developers increase, as federated clouds increase the enhanced service variety and the client population. |

perspectives of economies-of-scale and network externalities. Our focus is on the rationale according to which a cloud provider should form a federation despite of spending money on the cooperation with its competitors.

In case of IaaS, forming a federation enables a cloud provider to utilize the computation resources of its partner in the federation. Due to this cooperation, a cloud provider can reduce the risk of service failure. The federation enhances the scalability without investments in the infrastructure. That is, a cloud provider can reduce the cost to maintaining the scalability of its service, as it participates in a cloud federation. At the same time, the federation can achieve a better utilization of the resources across all providers in the federation. The cost reduction gives the cloud provider the advantage in price, so that it is competitive to a large cloud provider. However, the federation does not reduce the cost of maintaining the computation resources of a cloud provider. A cloud provider manages its own computation resources independently, even if it is involved in a federation. Therefore, the scale of resources that a company manages does not change. Moreover, the utility of a client is invariant though the client population increases due to the cloud federation. Instead, the utility of a client changes through the decrease in price, which is due to the cost reduction as we can see in the discourse of economies of scale.

In case of PaaS and SaaS, the cloud provider's benefit of forming a federation is different from the one for IaaS. Economies-of-scale do not work in these delivery models, as a cloud provider does not save the cost of provisioning its PaaS and SaaS services within a federation. Therefore, the scalability is expected not to increase through the formation of a federation. Moreover, the cost of managing computational resources is invariant like in the case of IaaS. The cost of managing the software does not change through federation as well. On the other hand, PaaS and SaaS cloud providers gain benefits by forming a federation due to the network externalities on two sides. The utility of a service developer depends on the client population that it can sell its service to. Therefore, the utility of a service developer increases according to the increase in the client population, which comes with forming a federation in the PaaS and SaaS delivery model. In addition to this, in the SaaS delivery model, a client and a developer obtain utility through service variety and service quality. Therefore, forming a federation, which extends the service variety, increases the utility.

## 5   Discussion and Conclusion

We discussed the rationales that cloud providers form a federation on the basis of two economic properties: economies of scale and network externalities. The benefit that a cloud provider can gain from forming a federation varies over the service delivery model. This is a new result compared to the assumptions made in literature so far.

In case of IaaS, forming a federation is beneficial in terms of the economies of scale. A cloud provider can reduce the cost to maintaining the scalability of its services. In case of PaaS and SaaS, on the other hand, a federation enhances the network externalities because sharing the clients and, for SaaS, sharing the software resources between the cloud providers involved in the federation increases the utility of service developers and the service clients.

Our research is expected to contribute to academia. That is, our results guide designing economic models for cloud federation to analyze their sustainability. Prior research has emphasized economies of scale [7, 10, 41], scalability [3, 8, 38], and network externalities [4, 41] as the keys to cloud computing. However, prior research did not analyze empirically and theoretically whether these properties give benefit to cloud providers, cloud clients, and service developers and how much if they do. For example, a prior study considered economies of scale in its model, just assuming that economies of scale is a valid economic factor [24]. With our study, we filled the gap by analyzing the economic feasibility of cloud federation on the basis of the theories on economies of scale and network externalities. Furthermore, prior research on cloud federation mainly focused on engineering instead of economics, probably assuming that a federation among cloud providers will give benefit for sure. However, as the results of our study showed that the benefit of an advanced technology needs to be analyzed in detail and verified before they can be assumed in models. Our results showed significant differences between SaaS, PaaS, and IaaS cloud services.

In the future, we will extend our work by considering further economic properties that might be at play within cloud federations.

**Acknowledgements.** This work has been funded by the Korea Institute for Advancement of Technology (grant no. ITEA2 10014) as part of the ITEA2 project EASI-CLOUDS.

# References

1. Hayes, B.: Cloud computing. Commun. ACM **51**, 9–11 (2008)
2. Vaquero, L.M., Rodero-Merino, L., Caceres, J., Lindner, M.: A break in the clouds: towards a cloud definition. SIGCOMM Comput. Commun. Rev. **39**, 50–55 (2008)
3. Armbrust, M., Stoica, I., Zaharia, M., Fox, A., Griffith, R., Joseph, A.D., Katz, R., Konwinski, A., Lee, G., Patterson, D., Rabkin, A.: A view of cloud computing. Commun. ACM **53**, 50 (2010)
4. Cusumano, M.: Cloud computing and saas as new computing platforms. Commun. ACM **53**, 27–29 (2010)
5. Yang, X., Nasser, B., Surridge, M., Middleton, S.: A business-oriented cloud federation model for real-time applications. Future Gener. Comput. Syst. **28**, 1158–1167 (2012)
6. Mell, P.M., Grance, T.: SP 800-145. The NIST Definition of Cloud Computing. National Institute of Standards & Technology, Gaithersburg, MD, United States (2011)
7. Babcock, C.: Management Strategies for the Cloud Revolution: How Cloud Computing Is Transforming Business and Why You Can't Afford to Be Left Behind. McGraw-Hill, New York (2010)
8. Garrison, G., Kim, S., Wakefield, R.L.: Success factors for deploying cloud computing. Commun. ACM **55**, 62 (2012)
9. Brynjolfsson, E., Hofmann, P., Jordan, J.: Cloud computing and electricity: beyond the utility model. Commun. ACM **53**, 32 (2010)
10. Weinman, J.: Cloudonomics, + Website: The Business Value of Cloud Computing. Wiley, Hoboken (2012)
11. Bermbach, D., Kurze, T., Tai, S.: Cloud federation: effects of federated compute resources on quality of service and cost. In: 2013 IEEE International Conference on Cloud Engineering (IC2E), pp. 31–37 (2013)

12. Falasi, A.A., Serhani, M.A., Elnaffar, S.: The sky: a social approach to clouds federation. Procedia Comput. Sci. **19**, 131–138 (2013)
13. Bent, K., Burke, S.: Cisco Embraces Amazon, Microsoft With InterCloud Infrastructure Software. http://www.crn.com/news/networking/240165714/cisco-embraces-amazon-microsoft-with-intercloud-infrastructure-software.htm/pgno/0/1
14. Nalebuff, B.J.: Co-Opetition. Currency Doubleday, New York (1997)
15. Evans, D.S., Schmalensee, R.: The industrial organization of markets with two-sided platforms. Compet. Policy Int. **3**, 151–179 (2005)
16. Varian, H.R.: Microeconomic Analysis, 3rd edn. W. W. Norton & Company, New York (1992)
17. Nam, C., Kwon, Y., Kim, S., Lee, H.: Estimating scale economies of the wireless telecommunications industry using EVA data. Telecommun. Policy **33**, 29–40 (2009)
18. Asai, S.: Scale economies and scope economies in the Japanese broadcasting market. Inf. Econ. Policy **18**, 321–331 (2006)
19. Kristensen, T., Olsen, K.R., Kilsmark, J., Lauridsen, J.T., Pedersen, K.M.: Economies of scale and scope in the Danish hospital sector prior to radical restructuring plans. Health Policy Amst. Neth. **106**, 120–126 (2012)
20. Pollitt, M.G., Steer, S.J.: Economies of scale and scope in network industries: Lessons for the UK water and sewerage sectors. Util. Policy. **21**, 17–31 (2012)
21. Floudas, C.A., Visweswaran, V.: Quadratic Optimization. In: Horst, R., Pardalos, P.M. (eds.) Handbook of Global Optimization, pp. 217–269. Springer, US (1995)
22. Bayón, L., Otero, J.A., Ruiz, M.M., Suárez, P.M., Tasis, C.: The profit maximization problem in economies of scale. J. Comput. Appl. Math. **236**, 3065–3072 (2012)
23. Brumec, S., Vrček, N.: Cost effectiveness of commercial computing clouds. Inf. Syst. **38**, 495–508 (2013)
24. Künsemöller, J., Karl, H.: A game-theoretic approach to the financial benefits of infrastructure-as-a-service. Future Gener. Comput. Syst.
25. Iansiti, M., Levien, R.: Strategy as ecology. Harv. Bus. Rev. **82**(68–78), 126 (2004)
26. Gawer, A., Cusumano, M.A.: Platform Leadership: How Intel, Microsoft, and Cisco Drive Industry Innovation. Harvard Business Review Press, Boston (2002)
27. Caillaud, B., Jullien, B.: Chicken and egg: competition among intermediation service providers. Rand J. Econ. **34**, 309–329 (2003)
28. Rochet, J.-C., Tirole, J.: Platform Competition in Two-Sided Markets. J. Eur. Econ. Assoc. **1**, 990–1029 (2003)
29. Katz, M.L., Shapiro, C.: Network externalities, competition, and compatibility. Am. Econ. Rev. **75**, 424–440 (1985)
30. Farrell, J., Saloner, G.: Installed base and compatibility: innovation, product preannouncements, and predation. Am. Econ. Rev. **76**, 940–955 (1986)
31. Eisenmann, T., Parker, G., Alstyne, M.W.V.: Strategies for two-sided markets. Harv. Bus. Rev. (2006)
32. Economides, N., Katsamakas, E.: Two-sided competition of proprietary vs. open source technology platforms and the implications for the software industry. Manag. Sci. **52**, 1057–1071 (2006)
33. Economides, N., Tåg, J.: Network neutrality on the internet: A two-sided market analysis. Inf. Econ. Policy **24**, 91–104 (2012)
34. Reisinger, M.: Platform competition for advertisers and users in media markets. Int. J. Ind. Organ. **30**, 243–252 (2012)
35. Baek, S., Kim, K., Altmann, J.: Role of platform providers in service networks: The case of Salesforce.com AppExchange. In: Presented at the, Proceedings of the IEEE Conference of Business Informatics 14 July 2014

36. Rochwerger, B., Breitgand, D., Epstein, A., Hadas, D., Loy, I., Nagin, K., Tordsson, J., Ragusa, C., Villari, M., Clayman, S., Levy, E., Maraschini, A., Massonet, P., Muñoz, H., Tofetti, G.: Reservoir - When One Cloud Is Not Enough. Computer **44**, 44–51 (2011)
37. Altmann, J., Kashef, M.M.: Cost model based service placement in federated hybrid clouds, future generation computer systems. Int. J. Grid Comput. eSci. (2014). doi:10.1016/j.future. 2014.08.014
38. Haile, N., Altmann, J.: Estimating the value obtained from using a software service platform. In: Altmann, J., Vanmechelen, K., Rana, O.F. (eds.) GECON 2013. LNCS, vol. 8193, pp. 244–255. Springer, Heidelberg (2013)
39. Breskovic, I., Brandic, I., Altmann, J.: Maximizing Liquidity in Cloud Markets through Standardization of Computational Resources. SOSE 2013, International Symposium on Service-Oriented System Engineering, San Jose, USA (2013)
40. Breskovic, I., Altmann, J., Brandic, I.: Creating standardized products for electronic markets. future generation computer systems. Int. J. Grid Comput. eSci. **29**(4), 1000–1011 (2013). (Elsevier. ISSN: 0167-739X)
41. Haile, N., Altmann, J.: Value creation in it service platforms through two-sided network effects. In: Vanmechelen, K., Altmann, J., Rana, O.F. (eds.) GECON 2012. LNCS, vol. 7714, pp. 139–153. Springer, Heidelberg (2012)
42. Rohitratana, J., Altmann, J.: Impact of pricing schemes on a market for software-as-a-service and perpetual software. Future Generation Comput. Syst. Int. J. Grid Comput. eSci. **28**(8), 1328–1339 (2012). doi:10.1016/j.future.2012.03.019. Elsevier
43. Kashef, M.M., Altmann, J.: A cost model for hybrid clouds. In: Vanmechelen, K., Altmann, J., Rana, O.F. (eds.) GECON 2011. LNCS, vol. 7150, pp. 46–60. Springer, Heidelberg (2012)
44. Rohitratana, J., Altmann, J.: Agent-based simulations of the software market under different pricing schemes for software-as-a-service and perpetual software. In: Altmann, J., Rana, O.F. (eds.) GECON 2010. LNCS, vol. 6296, pp. 62–77. Springer, Heidelberg (2010)
45. Mohammed, B.A., Altmann, J., Hwang, J.: Cloud computing value chains: understanding business and value creation in the cloud. In: Neumann, D., Baker, M., Altmann, J., Rana, O. (eds.) Economic Models and Algorithms for Distributed Systems. Autonomic Systems book series. Springer, Birkhäuser (2009)
46. Synergy Research Group. http://www.srgresearch.com. Accessed 18 July 2014

# Analysis of the Social Effort in Multiplex Participatory Networks

Davide Vega$^{(\boxtimes)}$, Roc Meseguer, and Felix Freitag

Computer Architecture Department,
Universitat Politecnica de Catalunya - BarcelonaTech, Barcelona, Spain
{dvega,meseguer,felix}@ac.upc.edu

**Abstract.** Community networks are participatory connectivity solutions for citizens where all the resources are owned, managed and controlled by the participants. As a natural evolution, in recent years some initiatives have flourished to provide higher level services based on volunteer computing and resource sharing paradigms. A fundamental aspect of these paradigms is user participation. In this work, we apply some social mining techniques aiming to identify the roles of the individuals in the social network behind a community network, here Guifi.net, and to measure the participatory involvement in the community network from 2003 to 2014. We observed that community network participants generally dedicate their time and effort to a single participatory forum, generating several types of community structures. We analyzed such structures using a multiplex network formed by mailing list in Guifi.net and a relationship graph built pairwise of users that share a physical wireless link. We were able to distinguish between non-hierarchical participatory forums, where almost all users are part of the same big community and two-tier participatory forums leaded by a small number of users that act as social bridges between their members. Finally, by testing the impact of community leaders in all participatory layers, we profiled the utility of the members' effort to the whole wireless community network.

**Keywords:** Social Effort · Multiplex · Collectives

## 1 Introduction

Community networks are growing fast as a sustainable model for self-provisioned computer networking infrastructures [6], alternative to other service offerings. This has been accelerated by the reduction of the costs of WiFi and optic networking equipment, combined with the growing popularity of wireless devices, and the lower complexity of network setup. In recent years, a plethora of non-profit initiatives have flourished to create community networks providing, among other services, Internet access. A few examples are Guifi.net [2] and FunkFeuer [1].

A characteristic of these initiatives is that the network topology grows organically, without a planned deployment or any consideration other than connecting devices from new participants or locations by linking them to an existing one

© Springer International Publishing Switzerland 2014
J. Altmann et al. (Eds.): GECON 2014, LNCS 8914, pp. 67–79, 2014.
DOI: 10.1007/978-3-319-14609-6_5

or improving the network service. Typically the deployment and management tasks are performed by the community network members, mostly volunteers. Avonts et al. [3] reported that community networks members considered finding and keeping volunteers the largest organizational challenge, next to funding and finding devices maintainers the most second important challenge.

Beyond Internet access provision, the community networks' physical infrastructure is sometimes used by some members to provide applications (e.g. web servers, monitoring systems). As a natural evolution, some community networks are looking for ways to implement higher level applications [13], which would require mechanisms to regulate and normalize how their members interact with the computational resources [16]. The feasibility of implementing such contributory systems is highly dependent on the network participants' ability to rank and evaluate members' participation.

User participation can be measured in multiple ways and it is not limited to deploy and maintain physical devices or links. Community networks usually have other participatory forums where users can contribute to the growth and improvement of the network. Some community networks maintain online discussion forums while others use mailing lists or organize face-to-face meeting activities. These forums help users to organize and give support to new members to integrate into the network.

Figure 1 shows the empirical cumulative distribution function (ECDF) plotted as the Lorenz curve, of users participation in Guifi.net, the largest community network to the best of our knowledge. The participation is measured separately as the number of new devices created by users and the number of messages exchanged in one of its participatory mailing list. The Gini coefficient [8], measured as the area between the line of equality and each of the curves, is close to the absolute inequality in both participatory forums – 0.8358 in the devices creation and 0.8320 in the message exchange. The Lorenz distribution function also suggests that network members behave differently in terms of participation in the examined forums.

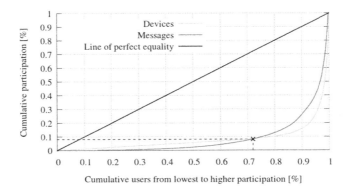

**Fig. 1.** Gini coefficient of two participatory forums in Guifi.net.

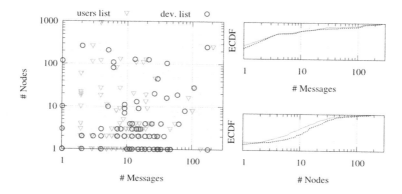

**Fig. 2.** Guifi.net users participation measured as the number of messages posted in the mailing lists users-list and dev-list, and the number of new communication devices.

As an example of individual different participatory involvement, we consider the number of messages and devices created by each user identified in both participatory forums in Fig. 2. We observe that most of the users are selective and choose to collaborate only in one of the participatory forums, contributing with little or nothing to the other. For example, there is a high concentration of users participating in the development mailing list, but these are users which contributed only with one or two devices to the physical communication network.

In this work we measure the level of user involvement in a wireless community network by applying social mining techniques to understand the differences observed among users of several participatory forums. We gather and process information from 13,407 registered users in the community network with more than 36,629 active communication devices, and a total of 10,045 threads and 49,355 messages in their most active mailing lists. We then study the evolution of participation and observe that participatory forums are currently in a mature state, which according to [10] suggests a relationship and subgroups analysis. Therefore, we conduct the analysis of interactions and community structure in each participatory forum separately. We find evidences of hierarchical community structures in the network's mailing lists with strong ties among their members and poor communication with other communities. We also observe a lack of structure in the communication network. Finally, we measure the significance of the members in each participatory layer to the community network as a global entity. Our methodology is inspired by [9], which conducted work on a multiplex and multi-layer analysis of online and offline users' interaction, where the authors discuss the existence of weak and strong ties among community members.

The contributions made in this work can be summarized as follows:

– We describe the evolution of members' activities since the creation of the network until 2014 (Sect. 3). We observed that the network is currently in a mature stage and therefore the community and relationship analysis applies. Additionally we found evidence of seasonal participative patterns.

- We identify different community structures on each participatory layer, and observed that weak relations arise more in the communication layer, while strong relations are more common among members of the small communities that govern the mailing lists (Sect. 4.1).
- We measure the participants' social value as individuals using centrality measures, and observed that only a small portion of the participants can be considered of having a high social value (Sect. 4.2).
- In terms of their impact on other layers, we simulate the robustness of the network against the disappearance of important members (Sect. 4.3), and found that their activities in each participatory forum should be measured differently, since their impact on the community network is also different.

## 2    Experimental Framework

In this section we present our framework for the analysis of the social interactions and the estimation of the users' effort in Guifi.net. We first introduce the Guifi.net wireless community network. Then, we describe the current participatory forums and how we aggregate their data to build our analysis graphs. Finally, we explain the assembly process used to build the multiplex graph.

### 2.1    Guifi.net Network and Information Gathering

The Guifi.net network started in 2004 and in 2014 it has reached more than 24,000 operational devices, most of them in Catalonia and nearly all of them in the Iberian peninsula. In 2008 their members created the Guifi.net Foundation, a non-profit organisation responsible to coordinate the volunteers and provide deployment support to its users. The Guifi.net foundation encourages the deployment of the network, but does not control it. Therefore, virtually all the decisions concerning the network growth and maintenance are up to the users.

**Physical nodes and communication layer representation:** The network consists of a set of nodes interconnected through mostly wireless equipment that users must install and maintain, typically on building rooftops. The network grows driven by the needs of individuals. New links only appears based on the needs for connectivity by their owners or indirect beneficiaries (e.g. users of a community network crowd-funded by municipalities). Deploying a new node, or improving the connectivity for an existing one, is difficult without the cooperation of the owner/manager of the communication device to connect with. The communication layer intends to capture such interaction between participants in a graph structure to ease the analysis.

Using the topological graph built previously [16] and a dump of the Guifi.net web database, we relate each owner with their active devices as we show in Fig. 3. Then, we build an undirected graph where vertices represent the members of the network and edges represent a link in the topology graph that connects two nodes owned or modified by one of the users. Additionally, the weight of the vertices represents the number of nodes created, while the weight of the edges stands for the number of links between users.

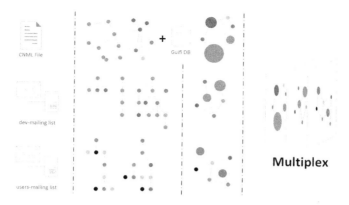

**Fig. 3.** The initial set of data gathered and the multiplex graph generation process.

**Mailing lists and social layer representation:** Social participation in Guifi.net changed during the community network lifetime. Nowadays, mailing lists are the only online and social participatory forums left. The Guifi.net Foundation maintains two general-purpose mailing lists to coordinate users and developers since 2006. The first of them, *users-list*, is mainly used to discuss general topics, issues on coordinating physical infrastructure creation and maintenance and to help new users. The other one, *dev-list*, serves as a communication channel between some of the most active members in Guifi.net, most of them developers. Each mailing list is currently managed independently and contains only a small subset of the users registered in the web page – i.e. the dev-list reports 401 different users registered, while the Guifi.net webpage reports 13,407.

We used web scraping to gather information from the mailings lists dump published on the Guifi.net web site. Following the same methodology proposed by [7], for each mailing list we built a tree for each thread (see Fig. 3). Then, we used the sender email information to build a participants directed graph that includes as vertices the users in the mailing lists. While in the original framework the authors considered that connections between participants are reciprocal, we instead considered them directional. Therefore, in our graph an arc from user $v$ to $u$, represents an answer from $v$ to a message previously sent by $u$ in the same thread, while arc's weight stands for the amount of messages ever sent by $v$ to $u$. We use vertices weight to keep track of the threads created by each user.

## 2.2 Homonymous Detection

Homonymy is a characteristic of most distributed systems, like Peer-to-Peer applications, which implies the existence of users with multiple identifiers in the network [15]. Guifi.net anonymous exists because authentication is based on the email address of the participants and because the authentication for each participatory forum is independent. Homonymy was detected using the email similarity rule suggested by Bird et al. [4], which is based on the Levenshtein

**Table 1.** Summary of the basic properties of the graph layers

| Network layer | Type | Nodes | Edges | Degree (max, min, avg.) | Components | Average distance | Diameter | Clustering coefficient |
|---|---|---|---|---|---|---|---|---|
| Communication | undirected | 1919 | 3201 | 384, 0, 3.3361 | 250 | 3.238 | 7 | 0.1520 |
| Users | directed | 538 | 4607 | 521, 0, 17.1264 | 19 | 1.9675 | 2 | 0.751 |
| Development | directed | 401 | 3926 | 202, 0, 19.5810 | 13 | 2.3247 | 4 | 0.5614 |

edit distance between email address bases. Being as conservative as possible, we tag two identities as homonymous only if they have a distance of 1 or below.

### 2.3   Communities Detection

Social relations in a group of participants can form a community if they are more willing to interact among them than with other members of the network. This is a well-known phenomena – called communities structure – that arises in most complex networks. The community's size, structure or even members' interactions outside and inside the communities are a good source of information to study the roles of the network users.

The community detection problem has been studied for a long time, and there are different algorithms and methods that can be applied, depending on the properties of the network and the properties of the targeted communities. In this work we apply two different methods, the *clique percolation method* [14] and the *Louvain method* [5] to detect two different community structures, and discuss the differences and the role of their members. In practical terms, the difference is that while the percolation method is based on the detection and aggregation of k-clique disjoints sets inside the graph – which will have maximum connectivity among their members –, the Louvain method is an optimized algorithm to find partitions providing that the modularity (the relationship between average degrees inside the community and intra communities) is minimized.

**Multiplex graph:** multiplex or multi-level graphs are abstract data structures which assemble the information of several graphs in such a way that each original graph is represented by a separated layer, meaning that each layer holds their original connectivity matrix [11]. The basic properties of each layer are summarized in Table 1. The structure of the multiplex enables to relate nodes with the same identifier between them. We built a 3-layer multiplex graph as the assemble of the participation layers (see Fig. 3). We use it to discuss the impact of the most active members of each layer in the whole network.

## 3   Network Evolution

In this section we study the activity performed by individuals on each participatory forum since the creation of the network. We analyze the activity of users by measuring the number of new physical communication devices registered in the network and the number of messages and threads sent in both mailing lists. Group activities are compared with the individual's interest, which lead us to

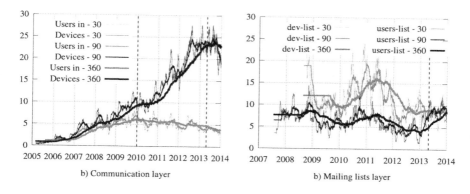

b) Communication layer             b) Mailing lists layer

**Fig. 4.** Evolution of members' participation in each participatory layer.

the conclusion that Guifi.net is in a mature state with evidence of lack of interest by non-members.

## 3.1 Network State Detection

Figure 4 shows the activities done day by day by network participants in each participatory layer as the simple moving average at intervals of approximately one month (30), quarter of a year (90) and one year (360). We observe that users' participation switches from long periods of high activity to short periods of less activity. We identify the periods of lower activity, as those that correspond to the last quarter of every year – Spanish winter season.

The last cycle of less activity has been extended in the communication layer after a long period of increasing activity which lasted for 77 months. This change of trend was predictable as the number of new registered users have been decreasing the past 4 years. Nowadays only 20 % of the new working devices are installed and managed by users registered 62 days before or less.

Regarding the activity in both mailing lists, it is not comparable because the number of members is quite different (25.46 % difference according Table 1). However we can observe that, on average, the participation by user in the development list used to outnumber the participation in the users list (see Fig. 4).

## 3.2 Interest Generated

Users' habits have changed over the time. While the interest in the communication network decreases since 2010, the users interest in the discussions and information exchange prevailed one year and a half after. Nowadays, while developers activities are decreasing, the rest of the users contribute to the increase of the users mailing list (see Fig. 4).

We conclude that voluntarism – measured as participation in the three layers – is stable in the network, and nowadays is concentrated around the senior members of the network. The network is still in a mature state, but is attracting fewer new users every day.

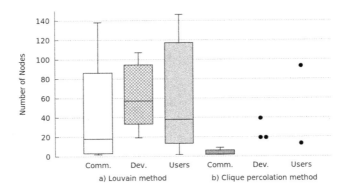

**Fig. 5.** Number of nodes by community. Comm., Dev. and Users refer to the communication, dev-list and users-list layers.

## 4    Communities and Multiplex Analysis

From the examination of the structure of the participatory forums in Guifi.net, we can consider the network mature enough to be subject of a community and interaction analysis. First, we focus on detecting possible independent communities which will capture the preferential interactions among members. Then, we address the detection of key actors in such communities to understand if there is some hierarchy. Finally, we address the multiplex analysis by understanding the role of layer authorities and well-connected members in the network.

### 4.1    Community Structure

Community structure is a common characteristic shown by most complex networks, which allows us to discuss common properties among their members. We analyse the existence or not of community structures in the most important participatory forums, as a function of members interactions. Each boxplot in the Fig. 5 summarises the nodes composition of communities detected in our layers when the 2 different detection techniques are applied (see Sect. 2.3). Members of a layer which do not belong to any community are not represented.

We find that it is possible to divide all layers into several disjoint communities, where 75 % of them have between 2 and 147 users. The communities median size detected in the communication layer represents less than 1 % of the users, while in the case of the development and users mailing lists it represents 14.4 % and 7.11 %, respectively, of the users.

In the communication layer 74.38 % of the links are internal – between two members of the same community – and only 25.62 % of the interactions are between members of two different communities, as shows the Fig. 6, resulting in a two-tier structure with users geographically close showing high participation among them. Participants in the mailing lists, however, show no preference in answering to members of their community or members of other communities.

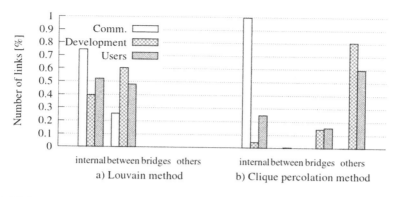

**Fig. 6.** Links distribution between communities. Bridges are links between two participants, both members of the same community, but one of them member of another community, too. Others are links to nodes which do not belong to any community.

The analysis of the participatory layers using the *clique percolation method* (see Sect. 2.3) reveals another community structure, enclosed by a core group of members. While the core group in the mailing list is formed by a small portion of users – from 17.28 % in the users layer to 9.97 % in the development layer, the core group of members 86.24 % of the participants in the communication layer with 86.24 % of the participants represents almost the entire network.

In contrast, the social layers show less ties among members of their communities than with other participants in the layer, as shown in Fig. 6, where communities are detected using cliques. Communities are connected only through bridges, suggesting that both social layers face a two-tier structure with several cores coordinated by some of the members. Finally, it is interesting to observe a stronger connectivity in the users mailing lists' communities, which suggests a large gap of involvement between core community members and the other members of the participatory forum.

## 4.2 Individual Participation and Social Value

We have seen so far that in the participatory forums of Guifi.net, 72 % of the members generate more than 91.2 % of the contributions. Nevertheless, the social value of a community member for the whole network depends more on its connectivity and position towards the rest of the participants than on his or her individual contributions. For instance, if somebody sends a lot of messages to a single person, it does not imply that he or she is generating any social value.

We measured the individual impact of the users inside the network as their *closeness centrality, HITS authorities* and *hubs.* Closeness centrality for a connected graph is defined as the inverse of the average distance to all other nodes. In our case, the distance is measured as the sum of the weights of the nodes managed for the communication layer and of the messages answered in the mailing lists layers of each link it has to traverse.

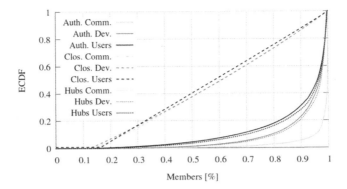

**Fig. 7.** Empirical Cumulative Distribution Function (ECDF) of members' centrality scores.

HITS [12] is a ranking algorithm used in the past to exploit the web's hyperlink structure. As a result, we obtain two measures for each node, the authority and hubs. The first one is a measure of individuals as a source of information, while the second one ranks higher those nodes with high quality out-links. In order to apply the HITS algorithm directly to our mailing lists graphs, we transform them to undirected graphs.

Figure 7 shows as we expected the same distribution for both HITS values in the communication layer due to the fact that the graph is undirected. Indeed, the social graphs present small differences between the authorities and hubs distributions. It is important to note that the authorities distribution shows that only a small portion of the users are of high value because their messages generate more replies from others.

Individuals' analysis revealed that there are only two users in common on all layers among the 10 higher ranked members, which are identified as the network founders. There are also two members in common in the mailing list which do not appear as top ranked in the communication layer. It highlights the higher affinity between members of the social participation layers compared with the communication layer.

### 4.3   Global Impact of Participation

In the previous section we discussed the social value generated by members in their own participatory layer. In this section, we turn our interest to understand their impact on the whole network by studying what happens when top layer authorities decide to leave the network. To this end, we firstly ordered the members of each participatory layer by the authorities score. Then, we proceeded recursively removing the top ranked node of the remaining ones and measuring the size of the largest component on each other layer in the multiplex.

Figure 8 shows the robustness of each participatory layer when the authority members are recursively removed in the multiplex. Ideally, when an authority

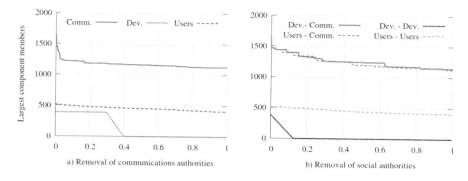

a) Removal of communications authorities          b) Removal of social authorities

**Fig. 8.** Multiplex layers robustness.

is removed, we expect that the size of each layer to be reduced only by one member – the authority itself. However, if the authority removed is essential to maintain the connectivity, we expect some other members getting disconnected – and the size of the layer's biggest component reduced.

In examining the multiplex robustness in case of the disappearance of members from any layer, we observe a huge impact on the dev-list layer, and a moderate impact on the communication layer. However, the graph structure of the users-list layer makes it indifferent to these removals, even of their authorities. Thus, we can argue that the communication and dev-list layers show a higher dependence on the particular contributors.

## 5     Conclusions and Discussion

### 5.1     Summary of Contributions

This work makes several contributions to the analysis of member participation in a community network. Using the historical data from users' activities in the participatory forums, we explained why the communities' structure and multiplex analysis are relevant to measure members' participation, by showing that our target network is in a mature state. Therefore, our findings could be applicable to other community networks in the same life-cycle stage.

We show that the analysed community structures indicate the existence of a hierarchical structure in the governance of the on-line participatory layers. This structure is leaded by a small set of members who only have contact with the rest of the subscribers through a few bridges. These bridge members are ranked highly as the most valuable members of the participatory layers. The asymmetry in participation found in the community network makes these members unique and essential for the communication network survival. Furthermore, the communication layer is structured in a weak way as an effect of the demographic distribution of their members.

## 5.2  Limitation of the Analysis

Studying participation in the context of building new devices is relevant for measuring the effort dedicated to increase and improve the communication network, and as we have observed in this work, not all users dedicate the same effort to this task. However, there exist other ways to improve or to help building the physical network that were not captured by our model, because they require a very deep understanding of users' choices, and which could be more community network specific.

In general, the analysis of the social participatory forums allows detecting communities and users' roles. In our work, we conducted the study using the two most important mailing lists in Guifi.net network. However, many other social interactions occur through other ways, like the general face-to-face assembly of the Guifi.net foundation, sporadic physical encounters among members, or region specific mailing lists. Including the data from other mailing lists would lead us to understand in more detail the heterogeneity of the network and to detect more relevant communities in such regions. Nevertheless, with our current analysis we were able to detect clusters of users, whose actions and connections have a high impact on the whole community network.

## 5.3  Implications of the Analysis

Most previous works have addressed the resource sharing or service regulation problem in various scenarios and measure the users' participation with physical resources. In a cooperative complex ecosystem like community networks, the effort dedicated to maintain and improve the network must be taken into account, too.

The social value analysis in Sect. 4.2 is a first step to measure the effort dedicated by community network members through their contributions. However, it does not capture the utility of members' contributions. A more precise measure should include the interest of the members in participating with users from different clusters or communities, avoiding the rise of closed communities.

Contributory systems designers can take advantage of the results shown in Sect. 4.3 in order to design their regulation mechanisms, and adapt the effort evaluation of each member to the participatory layer robustness.

**Acknowledgments.** This work was partially supported by the European Community through the projects Community Networks Testbed for the Future Internet (CONFINE): FP7-288535, A Community Networking Cloud in a Box (CLOMMUNITY): FP7-317879, and also by the Spanish government under contract TIN2013-47245-C2-1-R.

## References

1. FunkFeuer free net, http://www.funkfeuer.at
2. Guifi.net: Open, Free and Neutral Network Internet for everybody. http://guifi.net/en

3. Avonts, J., Braem, B., Blondia, C.: A questionnaire based examination of community networks. In: Wireless and Mobile Computing, Networking and Communications (WiMob), pp. 8–15. IEEE (2013)
4. Bird, C., Gourley, A., Devanbu, P., Gertz, M., Swaminathan, A.: Mining email social networks. In: Mining Software Repositories, pp. 137–143. ACM (2006)
5. Blondel, V.D., Guillaume, J.L., Lambiotte, R., Lefebvre, E.: Fast unfolding of communities in large networks. J. Stat. Mech.: Theory Exp. **2008**(10), P10008 (2008)
6. Braem, B., Baig Viñas, R., Kaplan, A.L., Neumann, A., et al.: A case for research with and on community networks. ACM SIGCOMM Comput. Commun. Rev. **43**(3), 68–73 (2013)
7. Dorat, R., Latapy, M., Conein, B., Auray, N.: Multi-level analysis of an interaction network between individuals in a mailing-list. Ann. Telecommun. **62**(3–4), 325–349 (2007)
8. Gini, C.: On the Measure of Concentration with Espacial Reference to Income and Wealth. Cowles Commission (1936)
9. Hristova, D., Musolesi, M., Mascolo, C.: Keep your friends close and your facebook friends closer: a multiplex network approach to the analysis of offline and online social ties. In: Weblogs and Social Media (2014)
10. Iriberri, A., Leroy, G.: A life-cycle perspective on online community success. ACM Comput. Surv. **41**(2), 11:1–11:29 (2009)
11. Kivelä, M., Arenas, A., Barthelemy, M., Gleeson, J.P., Moreno, Y., Porter, M.A.: Multilayer networks. CoRR abs/1309.7233 (2013)
12. Kleinberg, J.M.: Hubs, authorities, and communities. ACM Comput. Surv. **31**(4es), 5 (1999)
13. Marinos, A., Briscoe, G.: Community cloud computing. In: Jaatun, M.G., Zhao, G., Rong, C. (eds.) Cloud Computing. LNCS, vol. 5931, pp. 472–484. Springer, Heidelberg (2009)
14. Palla, G., Derényi, I., Farkas, I., Vicsek, T.: Uncovering the overlapping community structure of complex networks in nature and society. Nature **435**(7043), 814–818 (2005)
15. Pfitzmann, A., Köhntopp, M.: Anonymity, unobservability, and pseudonymity - a proposal for terminology. In: Federrath, H. (ed.) Designing Privacy Enhancing Technologies. LNCS, vol. 2009, pp. 1–9. Springer, Heidelberg (2001)
16. Vega, D., Meseguer, R., Ochoa, S., Pino, J., Freitag, F., et al.: Sharing hardware resources in heterogeneous computer-supported collaboration scenarios. Integr. Comput.-Aided Eng. **20**(1), 59–77 (2013)

# Cost Optimization

# Energy-Aware Cloud Management Through Progressive SLA Specification

Dražen Lučanin[1]([⊠]), Foued Jrad[2], Ivona Brandic[1], and Achim Streit[2]

[1] Vienna University of Technology, Vienna, Austria
{drazen,ivona}@infosys.tuwien.ac.at
[2] Karlsruhe Institute of Technology, Karlsruhe, Germany
{foued.jrad,achim.streit}@kit.edu

**Abstract.** Novel energy-aware cloud management methods dynamically reallocate computation across geographically distributed data centers to leverage regional electricity price and temperature differences. As a result, a managed virtual machine (VM) may suffer occasional downtimes. Current cloud providers only offer high availability VMs, without enough flexibility to apply such energy-aware management. In this paper we show how to analyse past traces of dynamic cloud management actions based on electricity prices and temperatures to estimate VM availability and price values. We propose a novel service level agreement (SLA) specification approach for offering VMs with different availability and price values guaranteed over multiple SLAs to enable flexible energy-aware cloud management. We determine the optimal number of such SLAs as well as their availability and price guaranteed values. We evaluate our approach in a user SLA selection simulation using Wikipedia and Grid'5000 workloads. The results show higher customer conversion and 39% average energy savings per VM.

**Keywords:** Cloud computing · SLA · Pricing · Energy efficiency

## 1 Introduction

Energy consumption of data centers accounts for 1.5 % of global electricity usage [11] and annual electricity bills of $40M for large cloud providers [18]. In an effort to reduce energy demand, new energy-aware cloud management methods leverage geographical data center distribution along with location- and time-dependent factors such as electricity prices [21] and cooling efficiency [23] that we call *geotemporal inputs*. By dynamically reallocating computation based on geotemporal inputs, promising cost savings can be achieved [18].

Energy-aware cloud management may reduce VM availability, because certain management actions like VM migrations cause temporary downtimes [14]. As long as the resulting availability is higher than the value guaranteed in the SLA, cloud providers can benefit from the cost savings. However, current cloud providers only offer high availability SLAs, e.g. 99.95 % in case of Google and Amazon. Such SLAs do not leave enough flexibility to apply energy-aware cloud management or result in SLA violations.

© Springer International Publishing Switzerland 2014
J. Altmann et al. (Eds.): GECON 2014, LNCS 8914, pp. 83–98, 2014.
DOI: 10.1007/978-3-319-14609-6_6

Alternative SLA approaches exist, such as auction-based price negotiation in Amazon spot instances [6] or calculating costs per resource utilisation [5]. However, estimating availability and price values that can be guaranteed in SLAs for VMs managed based on geotemporal inputs is still an open research issue. This problem is challenging, because exact VM availability and energy costs depend on electricity markets, weather conditions, application memory access patterns and other volatile factors.

In this paper, we propose a novel approach for estimating the optimal number of SLAs, as well as their availability and price values under energy-aware cloud management. Specifically, we present a method to analyse past traces of dynamic cloud management actions based on geotemporal inputs to estimate VM availability and price values that can be guaranteed in an SLA. Furthermore, we propose a progressive SLA specification where a VM can belong to one of multiple treatment categories, where a treatment category defines the type of energy-aware management actions that can be applied. An SLA is generated for each treatment category using our availability and price estimation method.

We evaluate our method by estimating availability and price values for SLAs of VMs managed by two energy-aware cloud management schedulers – the live migration scheduler adapted for clouds from [3,15] and the peak pauser scheduler [16]. We evaluate the SLA specification in a user SLA selection simulation based on multi-auction theory [10] using Wikipedia and Grid'5000 workloads to represent multiple user types. Our results show that more users with different requirements and payment willingness can find a matching SLA using our specification, compared to existing high availability SLAs. Average energy savings of 39% per VM can be achieved due to the extra flexibility of lower availability SLAs. Furthermore, we determine the optimal number of offered SLAs based on customer conversion.

## 2  Related Work

The related work consists of: (1) energy-aware distributed system management methods and (2) alternative VM pricing models suited for energy-aware cloud management.

Qureshi et al. simulate gains from temporally- and geographically-aware content delivery networks in [18], with predicted electricity cost savings of up to 45 %. Lin et al. [13] analyse a scenario with temporal variations in electricity prices and renewable energy availability for computation consolidation. Liu et al. [15] define an algorithm for power demand shifting according to renewable power availability and cooling efficiency. A job scheduling algorithm for geographically-distributed data centers with temperature-dependent cooling efficiency is given in [22]. A method for using migrations across geographically distributed data centers based on cooling efficiency is shown in [12]. These approaches, however, do not consider the implications of energy-aware cloud management on quality of service (QoS) and costs in the SLA specification.

The disadvantages of current VM pricing models relying on constant rates have been shown by Berndt et al. [5]. A new charging model for platform as a service (PaaS) providers, where variable-time requests can be specified by the users, is developed in [20]. Ibrahim et al. applied machine learning to compensate interferences between VMs for a pay-as-you-consume pricing scheme [9]. Though related, Amazon spot instances [6] permanently terminate VMs that get outbidden, hence requiring fault-resilient application architectures. Aside from this, they perform exactly like other Amazon instances, again not allowing temporary downtimes necessary every day for energy-aware cloud management. Amazon spot instances do show that end users are willing to accept a more complex pricing model to lower their costs for certain applications, indicating the feasibility of such approaches in real cloud deployments. None of the mentioned pricing approaches consider energy-aware cloud management based on geotemporal inputs or the accompanying QoS and energy cost uncertainty, which is the focus of our work.

## 3   Progressive SLA Specification

To be able to reason about energy-aware cloud management in terms of SLA specification, we analyse two concrete schedulers: (1) migration scheduler (adapted for clouds from [3,15]) – applies a genetic algorithm to dynamically migrate VMs, such that energy costs based on geotemporal inputs are minimised, while also minimising the number of migrations per VM to retain high availability. (2) peak pauser scheduler [16] – pauses the managed VMs for a predefined duration every day, choosing the hours of the day that are statistically most likely to have the highest energy cost, thus reducing VM availability, but also the average energy cost. To illustrate the inputs affecting scheduling decisions, a three-day graph of real-time electricity prices and temperatures in four US cities is shown in Fig. 1 (we describe the source dataset in the following section). Rapid changes in electricity prices can be seen on the 13th of January, and very small changes the following day. Subsequently, the migration scheduler would trigger more frequent VM migrations on the first day, As we cannot predict future geotemporal inputs with 100 % accuracy, we can also only estimate future scheduling actions.

With such energy-aware cloud management methods in mind, we propose a progressive SLA specification, where services are divided among multiple treatment categories, each under a different SLA with different availability and price

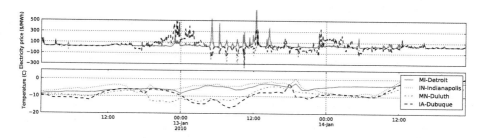

**Fig. 1.** Real-time electricity prices and temperatures in four US cities over three days

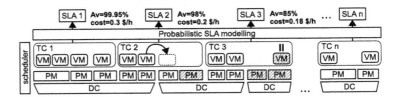

**Fig. 2.** Progressive SLA specification

values. Hence, different schedulers can be used for VMs in different treatment categories (or the same scheduler with different QoS constraint parameters). The goal of this approach is to allow different levels of energy-aware cloud management and thus achieve higher energy savings on VMs with lower availability requirements. What is given, therefore, are the schedulers for each treatment category, and the historical traces of generated schedules. What we have to find are the availability and price values that can be guaranteed in the SLAs for each treatment category and the optimal number of such SLAs to balance SLA flexibility and search difficulty for users.

We illustrate this approach in Fig. 2. A cloud provider operates a number of VMs, each hosted on a physical machine (PM) located in one of the geographically-distributed data centers (DC). Each VM belongs to a treatment category (TC) that determines the type of scheduling that can be applied to it. For example, TC 1 is a high availability category where no actions are applied on running VMs. TC 2 is a category for moderate cloud management actions, such as live VM migrations (marked by an arrow) which result in short downtimes. TC 3 is a more aggressive category where VMs can be paused (marked as hatched with two vertical lines above it) for longer downtimes. Other TCs can be defined using other scheduling algorithms or by varying parameters, e.g. the maximum pause duration. The optimal number of TCs (and therefore also SLAs) $n$ is determined by analysing user SLA selection to have enough variety to satisfy most user types, yet not make the search too difficult, which we explore in Sect. 6. Aside from selecting the number of SLAs, another task is setting availability and price values for every SLA. As energy-aware cloud management that depends on geotemporal inputs introduces a degree of randomness into the resulting availability and price values of a VM, we can only estimate the values that can be guaranteed. We do this using a *probabilistic SLA modelling* method for analysing historical cloud management action traces to calculate the most likely worst-case availability and average energy cost for a VM in a TC. For the example in Fig. 2, sample values are given for the SLAs. SLA 1 might have an availability (Av) of 99.95 % and a high cost of 0.3 \$/h due to no energy-aware management, SLA 2 might have slightly lower values due to live migrations being applied on VMs in TC 2, SLA 3 might have even lower values due to longer downtimes caused by VM pausing... In the following section, we will show how to actually estimate availability and price values for the SLAs using probabilistic SLA modelling.

## 4    Probabilistic SLA Modelling

To estimate availability and price values that can be guaranteed in an SLA using probabilistic modelling for a certain TC, we require historical cloud management traces. Cloud management traces can be obtained through monitoring, but for evaluation purposes we simulate different scheduling algorithm behaviour.

VM price is estimated by accounting for the average energy costs. To calculate VM availability, we analyse the factors that cause VM downtime. While the downtime duration of the peak pauser scheduler can be specified beforehand, the total downtime caused by the migration scheduler depends on VM migration duration and rate as dictated by geotemporal inputs, so we individually analyse both factors.

### 4.1    Cloud Management Simulation

Our modelling method can be applied to different scheduling algorithms and cloud environments. To generate a concrete SLA offering for evaluation purposes, we consider a use case of a cloud consisting of six geographically distributed data centers. We use a dataset of electricity prices described in [4] and temperatures from the Forecast web service [1]. We represent a deployment with world-wide data center distribution shown in Fig. 3. Indianapolis and Detroit were used as US locations. Due to limited data availability[1], we modified data for Mankato and Duluth to resemble Asian locations and Alton and Madison to resemble European locations (using inter-continent differences in time zones and annual mean values). The effects of the migration and peak pauser scheduler are determined in a simulation using the Philharmonic cloud simulator we developed [7]. The cloud simulation parameters are summarised in Table 1. We illustrate the application of the presented methods with this use case as a running example.

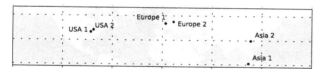

**Table 1.** Cloud simulation

| Duration | DCs | PMs | VMs |
| --- | --- | --- | --- |
| 3 months | 6 | 20 | 80 |

**Fig. 3.** Simulated world-wide data centers

### 4.2    Migration Duration

Even a live VM migration incurs a temporary downtime, in the stop-and-copy phase of VM memory transferring. A very accurate model, with less than 7% estimation errors, for calculating this downtime overhead is presented in [14]. The total VM downtime during a single live migration $T_{down}$ is a function of the

---

[1] US-only electricity price source and a limit of free API requests for temperatures.

VM's memory $V_{mem}$, data transmission rate $R$, memory dirtying rate $D$, pre-copying termination threshold $V_{thd}$ and $T_{resume}$, the time necessary to resume a VM.

$$T_{down} = \frac{V_{mem}D^n}{R^{n+1}} + T_{resume} \quad , \text{where} \quad n = \left\lceil log_{\frac{D}{R}} \frac{V_{thd}}{V_{mem}} \right\rceil \tag{1}$$

All of the parameters can be determined beforehand by the cloud provider, except for $R$ and $D$ which depend on the dynamic network conditions and application-specific characteristics. Based on historical data, it is possible to reason about the range of these variables. In our running example, we assume a historical range from low to high values. $R$ values in the 10–1000 Mbit/s range were taken based on an independent benchmark of Amazon EC2 instance band-widths. $D$ values from 1 kbit/s (to represent almost no memory dirtying) to 1 Gbit/s were taken (the maximum is not important, as will be shown). We assumed constant $V_{mem} = 4$ GB, $V_{thd} = 1$ GB, $T_{resume} = 5$ s, as these values do not affect the order of magnitude of $T_{down}$. We show how $T_{down}$ changes for different $R$ and $D$ in Fig. 4. Looking at the graph, we can see that higher $R$ and $D$ values result in convergence towards negligible downtime durations and the only area of concern is the peak happening when $R$ and $D$ are both very low. This happens, because close $R$ and $D$ values lead to a small number of pre-copying rounds and copying the whole VM under slow speeds leads to long downtimes. $T_{down}$ is under 400 s in the worst-case scenario, which will be our SLA estimation as suggested in [5].

### 4.3 Migration Rate

Aside from understanding migration effects, we need to analyse how often they occur, i.e. the migration rate. We present a method to analyse migration traces obtained from the cloud manager's past operation. A histogram of migration rates for the migration traces from our running example described in Sect. 4.1 can be seen in Fig. 5. The two plots show different zoom levels, as there are few hours with higher migration rates. Most of

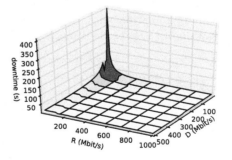

**Fig. 4.** VM downtime during a live migration

the time, no migrations are scheduled, with one migration per hour happening about 3 % of the time.

The idea is to group migrations per VM and process them in a function that aggregates migrations in intervals meaningful to the user. We consider an aggregation interval of 24 h. The *aggregated worst-case* function counts the migrations per VM per day and selects the highest migration count among all the VMs in every interval. The output time series is shown in Fig. 6. There is one or zero

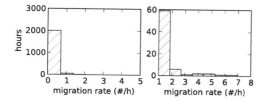

**Fig. 5.** Hourly migration rate histogram

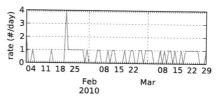

**Fig. 6.** Aggregated worst-case migration rate

migrations per VM most of the time, with an occasional case with a higher rate, such as the peak in January. Such peaks can occur due to more turbulent geotemporal input changes.

Given that this data is highly dependent of the scheduling algorithm used and the actual environmental parameters, fitting one specific statistical distribution to the data to get the desired percentile value would be hard to generalise for different use cases and might require manual modelling. Instead, we propose applying the distribution-independent bootstrap confidence interval method [8] to predict the maximum aggregated migration rate. For our migration dataset, the 95 % confidence interval for the worst-case migration rate is from three to four migrations per day.

### 4.4   SLA Options

By combining the migration rate and duration analyses, we can estimate the upper bound for the total VM downtime and, therefore, the availability that can be warranted in the SLA. We define availability $(Av)$ of a VM as:

$$Av = 1 - \frac{\text{total VM downtime}}{\text{total VM lease time}} \qquad (2)$$

For our migration dataset and the previously discussed migration duration and rate, we estimate the total downtime of a VM controlled by the migration scheduler to be 27 min per day in the worst case, meaning we can guarantee an availability of 98.12%. We can precisely control the availability of the VMs managed by the peak pauser.

The average energy savings $(en\_savings)$ for a VM running in a treatment category $TC_i$ can be calculated by comparing it to the high availability $TC_1$. From the already described simulation, we calculate $en\_cost$, the average cost of energy consumed by a VM based on real-time electricity prices and temperatures. We divide the energy costs equally among VMs within a TC. This is an approximation, but serves as an estimation of the energy saving differences between TCs. We calculate energy savings as:

$$en\_savings(VM_{TC_i}) = 1 - \frac{en\_cost(VM_{TC_i})}{en\_cost(VM_{TC_1})} \qquad (3)$$

where $en\_cost(VM_{TC_1})$ is the average energy cost for a VM in $TC_1$ with no actions applied and $en\_cost(VM_{TC_i})$ is the average energy cost for a VM in the target $TC_i$.

The VM cost consists of several components. Aside from $en\_cost$, $service\_cost$ groups other VM upkeep costs (manpower, hardware amortization, profit margin etc.) during a charge unit (typically one hour in infrastructure as a service (IaaS) clouds). We assume the service component to be charged linearly to the VM's availability.

$$cost = en\_cost + Av \cdot service\_cost \qquad (4)$$

To generate the complete SLA offering we consider an Amazon m3.xlarge instance which costs 0.280 \$/h (Table 2) as a base VM with no energy-aware scheduling. Base instances with different resource values (e.g. RAM, number of cores) can be used, but this is orthogonal to the QoS requirements of availability that we consider and would not influence the energy-aware cloud management potential. Similarly, Amazon spot instances were not considered specially as they perform exactly the same as normal instances while running, as we explained in Sect. 2. We assumed the service component to be 0.1 \$/h, about a third of the VM's price. The prices of VMs controlled by the two energy-efficient schedulers were derived from it, applying $en\_savings$ obtained in the cloud simulation. The resulting SLAs are shown in Fig. 7. SLA 1 is the base VM. SLA 2 is the VM controlled by the migration scheduler. The remaining SLAs are VMs controlled by the peak pauser scheduler with downtimes uniformly distributed from 12.5% to 66.67% to represent a wide spectrum of options. We chose eight SLAs to analyse how SLA selection changes from the user perspective. We later show that this number is in the 95 % confidence interval for being the optimal number of SLAs based on our simulation. We analyse a wider range of 1–60 offered SLAs and how they impact customer conversion from the cloud provider's perspective in Sect. 6. The lines in the background illustrate value progression. $Av$ decreases only slightly for the migration SLA, yet the energy savings are significant due to dynamic VM consolidation and PM suspension. For peak pauser SLAs, availability and costs decrease linearly, from high to low values. The $en\_savings$ values are at first lower than those attainable with the migration scheduler, as the peak pauser scheduler cannot migrate VMs to a fewer number of PMs, but can only pause them for a certain time. With lower availability requirements, however, the peak pauser can achieve higher $en\_savings$ and lower prices, which could not be reached by VM migrations alone.

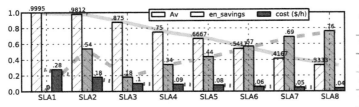

**Fig. 7.** SLAs generated for different TCs

**Table 2.** Base VM

| Type | m3.xlarge |
|---|---|
| Av | 99.95 % |
| Cost | 0.28 \$/h |
| Service | 0.1 \$/h |

# 5   User Modelling

Knowing the SLA offering, the next step is to model user SLA selection in order to analyse the benefits of our progressive SLA specification. We first describe how we derive user requirements and then the utility model used to simulate user SLA selection based on their requirements.

## 5.1   User Requirements Model

To model user requirements, we use real traces of web and high-performance computing (HPC) workload, since I/O-bound web and CPU-bound HPC applications represent two major usage patterns of cloud computing. As we do not have data on availability requirements of website owners, we generate this dataset based on the frequency of end user HTTP requests directed at different websites and counting missed requests, similarly to how reliability is determined from the mean time between failures [17]. A public dataset of HTTP requests made to Wikipedia [19] is used. To obtain data for different websites, we consider Wikipedia in each language as an individual website, because of its unique group of end users (different in number and usage pattern). In this scenario we consider a website owner to be the user of an IaaS service (not to be confused with the end user, a website visitor). The number of HTTP requests for a small subset of four websites (German, French, Italian and Croatian Wikipedia denoted by their two-letter country codes) is visualised in Fig. 8(a) for illustration purposes (we use the whole dataset with 38 websites for actual requirements modelling). The data exemplifies significant differences in amplitudes. Users of the German Wikipedia send between 1 k and 2 k requests per minute, while the Italian and Croatian Wikipedia have less than 300 requests per minute. Due to this variability, we assume that different Wikipedia websites represent diverse requirements of website owners. We model availability requirements by applying a heuristic – a website's required availability is the minimum necessary to keep the number of missed requests below a constant threshold (we assume 100 requests per hour). Using this heuristic, we built an availability requirements dataset for the web user type from 5.6 million requests divided among 38 Wikipedia language subdomains. The resulting availability requirement histogram can be seen in Fig. 8(b). It follows an exponential distribution (marked in red). There is a high concentration of sites that need almost full availability, with a long tail of sites that need less (0.85–1.0).

For HPC workload, we use a dataset of job submissions made to Grid'5000 (G5k) [2], a distributed job submission platform spread across 9 locations in France. The number of jobs submitted by a small subset of users is visualised in Fig. 9(a). While some users submit jobs over a wide period (*user109*), others only submit jobs in small bursts (*user1, user107*), but the load is not nearly as constant as the web requests from the Wikipedia trace. To model HPC users' availability requirements, where jobs have variable duration as well as rate (unlike web requests, which typically have a very short duration), we use another heuristic. Every user's availability requirement is mapped between

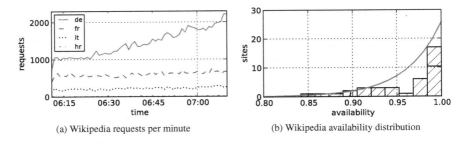

(a) Wikipedia requests per minute                (b) Wikipedia availability distribution

**Fig. 8.** Web user modelling (Color figure online)

a constant minimum availability (we assume 0.5) and full availability using *mean_duration · mean_rate*, which stands for mean job duration and mean job submission rate per user. Using this heuristic, we built a dataset of availability requirements for the HPC user type from jobs submitted over 2.5 years by 481 G5k users. The resulting availability requirement distribution (normalised such that the area is 1) can be seen in Fig. 9(b). The distribution marked red again follows an exponential distribution (the first bin, cut off due to the zoom level, shows a density of 100), but with the tail facing the opposite direction than the web requirements. HPC users submit smaller and less frequent jobs most of the time, with a long tail of longer and/or more frequent jobs (from 0.5 to 0.75).

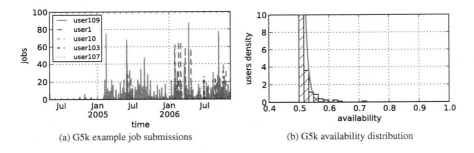

(a) G5k example job submissions                (b) G5k availability distribution

**Fig. 9.** HPC user modelling

Every user's willingness to pay (WTP) is derived by multiplying his/her availability requirement with the base VM price and adding Gaussian noise $\mathcal{N}(0, 0.05^2)$ to express subjective value perception. We selected the noise standard deviation to get positive WTP values considering the availability model. The resulting WTP histogram is shown in Fig. 10. It can be seen that HPC users have lower WTP values, but there is also an overlap area with web users who have similar requirements.

## 5.2   Utility Model

The utility-based model is used to simulate how users select services based on their requirements. We use a quasi-linear utility function adopted from multi-attribute auction theory [10] to quantify the user's preference for a provided SLA. The utility is calculated by multiplying the user's SLA satisfaction score with WTP and subtracting the VM cost charged by the provider. The utility for user $i$ from selecting a VM instance type $t$ with availability $Av_t$ is calculated as:

$$U_i(VM_t) = WTP_i \cdot f_i(Av_t) - cost(VM_t) \tag{5}$$

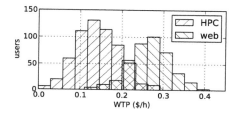

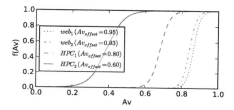

**Fig. 10.** WTP histogram            **Fig. 11.** SLA satisfaction function

where $f_i(Av_t)$ is the user's satisfaction with the offered VM's availability. We model it using a mapping function $f_i : [0,1] \rightarrow [0,1]$, extended from [10] with variable slopes:

$$f_i(Av_t) = \frac{\gamma}{\gamma + \beta e^{Av_{offset_i}^2 \alpha(Av_{offset_i} - Av_t)}} \tag{6}$$

where $Av_{offset_i}$ is the required availability specific to each user, which we select based on the exponential models of Wikipedia and G5k data presented earlier. $\alpha$, $\beta$ and $\gamma$ are positive constants common for all users, which we set to 60, 0.01 and 0.99 respectively. These values were chosen for a satisfaction of close to 1 for the desired availability value and a steep descent towards 0 for lower values, similar to earlier applications of this satisfaction function [10]. The slope of the function also depends on $Av_{offset_i}$, to model that users who require a lower availability have a wider range of acceptable values. The mapping function is visualised in Fig. 11 for a small sample of two HPC and two web users. We can see that for the two web users, the slope is almost the same and very steep (at 0.93 their satisfaction is close to 1 and at 0.8 it is almost 0). The $HPC_1$ user is similar to the web users, only with lower availability requirements and a slightly wider slope. The $HPC_2$ user has low requirements and a wide slope from an availability of 0.2–0.6. Later in our evaluation, we generate 1000 users, each with different mapping functions, distributed according to the user requirements model.

User $i$ chooses a VM instance type $VM_{selected}$ offering the best utility value:

$$U_i(VM_{selected}) = \max_{\forall t} \; U_i(VM_t) \tag{7}$$

Unless all types result in a negative utility, in which case the user selects none. Additionally, we model search difficulty by defining $P_{stop}$, a probability that a user will give up the search after an SLA has been examined. We model this probability as increasing after every new SLA check, by having $P_{stop_j} = j \cdot check\_cost$, where $j$ is the number of checks already performed and $check\_cost$ is a constant parameter standing for the probability of stopping after the first check. Based on every user's requirements and the SLA offering, $min\_checks$ is the minimum number of checks necessary to reach a VM type that yields a positive $U_i(VM)$. We define $P_{quit}$ to be the total probability that a user will quit the search before reaching a positive-utility SLA. By applying the chain probability rule, we can calculate $P_{quit}$ as:

$$P_{quit} = \sum_{j=1}^{min\_checks-1} P_{stop_j} \prod_{k=1}^{j-1}(1 - P_{stop_k}) \tag{8}$$

The outer sum is the joint distribution of all possible stop events that may occur for a user and the inner product stands for all event outcomes when searching continued until the $j$-th event was realised as stopping. We use this expression in the evaluation as a measure of difficulty for users to find a matching SLA.

## 6    Evaluation

In this section we describe the simulation of the proposed progressive SLA specification using user models based on real data traces and analyse the results.

### 6.1    Simulation Environment

The simulation parameters are summarised in Table 3. The first step of the simulation is to generate a population of web and HPC users based on the requirement models derived from the Wikipedia and Grid'5000 datasets, respectively. We simulated 1000 users to represent a population with enough variety to explore different WTP and availability requirements. We assume the ratio between web and HPC users of 1:1.5, based on an anlysis of a real system performed in [15]. We determine each user's WTP from the desired availability with Gaussian noise, as already explained in the previous section. The SLA offering was derived from the migration and peak pauser scheduler using the probabilistic modelling technique (Sect. 4). For the examination of SLA selection from the user's perspective, the eight SLAs we already defined in Sect. 4.4 were used. To examine the cloud provider's perspective, we evaluated 1–60 SLAs, doing 100 simulation runs per offering to calculate the most likely optimal number of SLAs. A $check\_cost$ of 0.015 is selected to initially start with a low chance of the user quitting and then subsequently increase it for every SLA check per Eq. 8. The same $\alpha$, $\beta$, $\gamma$ values that we already explained in the previous section were set that result in a utility of 1 for the required availability and a gradual decline towards a utility of 0 for lower availabilities. The core of the simulation is to determine each user's SLA selection (if any) based on the utility model (Sect. 5).

**Table 3.** Simulation settings

| Parameter | Users | Web:HPC | #SLAs | Runs | $check\_cost$ | $\alpha$ | $\beta$ | $\gamma$ |
|-----------|-------|---------|-------|------|--------------|----------|---------|----------|
| Value | 1000 | 1:1.5 | 1–60 | 100 | 0.015 | 60 | 0.01 | 0.99 |

## 6.2  User Benefits

Simulation results showing the distribution of users among the eight offered SLAs from Sect. 4.4 are presented in Fig. 12. Different colours are used for web and HPC users types. It can be seen that most of the users successfully found a service that matches their requirements, with less than 5 % of unmatched requests. The majority of HPC users are distributed between SLA 7 and 8 offering 42 % and 33 % availability, respectively. The majority of web users selected SLA 2, the migration scheduler TC, due to its high availability comparable to a full availability service, but a more affordable price due to the energy cost savings. 26 % of web users opted for SLA 3, the peak pauser instance which still offers a high availability (87.5 %), but at almost half the price of SLA 2.

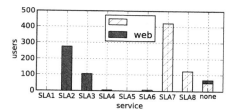

**Fig. 12.** Simulated service selection

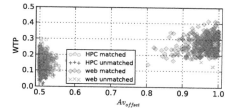

**Fig. 13.** Matched and unmatched users

The distribution of unmatched users who did not select any of the offered services (where utility was negative for all SLAs) is shown alongside the matched users in Fig. 13, showing their $Av_{offset}$ and WTP values. We can see that unmatched users have low WTP values, the cause of them not being able to find a suitable service option.

## 6.3  Cloud Provider Benefits

Customer conversion means the number of users who looked at the SLA offering and found an SLA that matches their needs. This metric is an indicator of the provider's economic success. To compare the multiple treatment category system with the traditional way of only having a full availability option, we simulated different SLA offerings. Figure 14 shows customer conversion with colour indicating the selection distribution for different offering combinations of the eight previously examined SLAs. Customer conversion growth can be seen with more service types, due to users having a higher chance of finding a category that matches their requirements. With SLAs 1–2 offered, only SLA 2 was selected, as it still offers a high-enough availability to satisfy user requirements and the price is lower than in SLA 1. As we widen the offering, more SLAs get selected, but the majority of users choose among two SLAs that best suit the two user types that we modelled. Still, a small number of users select other SLAs (SLA 3 and, if offered, SLA 8) which better suit their needs. SLA 5 is never selected due to user requirements and in real clouds such SLAs should be removed to simplify selection.

The introduced service types can be managed in a more energy efficient manner. The average energy savings weighted based on the lease time per VM for the SLA 1–8 offering, compared to the current 99.95 % availability Amazon instances represented by SLA 1, are 39%. Full annual lease time was assumed for web users (as web applications are typically running all the time) and was varied based on job runtime and frequency for HPC users (we assume that a VM is provisioned just to perform the submitted job). This shows that more energy efficient management is possible if users declare the QoS levels they require through SLA selection. For the SLA 1–8 scenario, where 5.89× more users can be converted and the annual lease times explained above, a 43% revenue increase is calculated from the service component of the selected VMs. Exact numbers depend on the user type ratio that will vary between cloud providers.

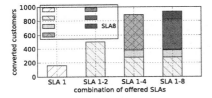

**Fig. 14.** Matched users per SLA combination

**Fig. 15.** Users and $\overline{P}_{quit}$ per SLA number

To find the optimal number of offered SLAs, we performed a simulation where we explore customer conversion for a higher number of SLAs. The extra SLAs were generated for the peak pauser scheduler, which allows for arbitrary control of VM availability and price. The peak pauser SLAs were uniformly interpolated between full and no availability to avoid duplicates. Figure 15 shows how the number of offered SLAs affects the user conversion count and $\overline{P}_{quit}$, the mean $P_{quit}$ value over all the users (including unmatched ones). After an initial linear growth, we can see that the number of users begins to stagnate and slowly decrease. Once a sufficient offering to satisfy the majority of users is achieved, adding extra SLA options only increases search difficulty. This is seen from the steadily increasing $\overline{P}_{quit}$, the probability that a user will quit the search before finding a positive-utility SLA. For our scenario, the optimal number of converted customers is achieved between 6 and 14 SLAs, depending on the $P_{quit}$ random variable realisations. By applying the bootstrap confidence interval method, we calculate the 95 % confidence interval (CI) for the optimal number of SLAs to be between 8 and 10.

# 7   Conclusion

We presented a novel progressive SLA specification suitable for energy-aware cloud management. We obtained cloud management traces from two schedulers optimised for real-time electricity prices and temperature-dependent cooling efficiency. The SLAs are derived using a method for a posteriori probabilistic modelling of cloud management data to estimate upper bounds for VM availability, energy savings and the resulting VM prices. The SLA specification is evaluated in a utility-based user SLA selection simulation using realistic workload traces from Wikipedia and Grid'5000. Results show mean energy savings per VM of up to 39% due to applying more aggressive energy preservation actions on users with lower QoS requirements. Furthermore, a wider spectrum of user types with requirements not matched by the traditional high availability VMs can be reached, increasing customer conversion.

In the future, we plan on expanding the probabilistic model with time series forecasting for more accurate SLA metrics. Additional TCs could be added to represent other cloud management methods, such as the kill-and-restart pattern used on stateless application containers in modern web application architectures. We also plan to explore SLA violation detection and how it could be integrated into our SLA specification. Furthermore, as predictions change based on day-night and seasonal changes, exploring time-changing SLAs in the manner of stocks and bonds to match the volatile geotemporal inputs would be feasible.

**Acknowledgements.** The work described in this paper has been funded through the Haley project (Holistic Energy Efficient Hybrid Clouds) as part of the TU Vienna Distinguished Young Scientist Award 2011.

# References

1. Forecast. http://forecast.io/
2. GWA-t-2 grid5000. http://gwa.ewi.tudelft.nl/datasets/gwa-t-2-grid5000
3. Abbasi, Z., Mukherjee, T., Varsamopoulos, G., Gupta, S.K.S.: Dynamichosting management of web based applications over clouds. In: 2011 18th International Conference on High Performance Computing (HiPC), pp. 1–10, December 2011
4. Alfeld, S., Barford, C., Barford, P.: Toward an analytic framework for the electrical power grid. In: Proceedings of the 3rd International Conference on Future Energy Systems: Where Energy, Computing and Communication Meet. e-Energy '12, , pp. 9:1–9:4. ACM, New York (2012)
5. Berndt, P., Maier, A.: Towards sustainable IaaS pricing. In: Altmann, J., Vanmechelen, K., Rana, O.F. (eds.) GECON 2013. LNCS, vol. 8193, pp. 173–184. Springer, Heidelberg (2013)
6. Chen, J., Wang, C., Zhou, B.B., Sun, L., Lee, Y.C., Zomaya, A.Y.: Tradeoffs between profit and customer satisfaction for service provisioning in the cloud. In: Proceedings of the 20th International Symposium on High Performance Distributed Computing, HPDC '11, pp. 229–238. ACM, New York (2011)
7. Dražen Lučanin: Philharmonic (2014). https://philharmonic.github.io/

8. Efron, B., Tibshirani, R.J.: An Introduction to the Bootstrap. CRC Press, Boca Raton (1994)

9. Ibrahim, S., He, B., Jin, H.: Towards pay-as-you-consume cloud computing. In: 2011 IEEE International Conference on Services Computing (SCC), pp. 370–377, July 2011

10. Jrad, F., Tao, J., Knapper, R., Flath, C.M., Streit, A.: A utility-based approach for customised cloud service selection. Int. J. Comput. Sci. Eng. (forthcoming)

11. Koomey, J.G.: Worldwide electricity used in data centers. Environ. Res. Lett. **3**, 034008 (2008)

12. Le, K., Bianchini, R., Zhang, J., Jaluria, Y., Meng, J., Nguyen, T.D.: Reducing electricity cost through virtual machine placement in high performance computing clouds. In: Proceedings of 2011 International Conference for High Performance Computing, Networking, Storage and Analysis, SC '11, pp. 22:1–22:12. ACM, New York (2011)

13. Lin, M., Liu, Z., Wierman, A., Andrew, L.: Online algorithms for geographical load balancing. In: 2012 International Green Computing Conference (IGCC), pp. 1–10, June 2012

14. Liu, H., Xu, C.Z., Jin, H., Gong, J., Liao, X.: Performance and energy modeling for live migration of virtual machines. In: Proceedings of the 20th International Symposium on High Performance Distributed Computing, pp. 171–182 (2011)

15. Liu, Z., Chen, Y., Bash, C., Wierman, A., Gmach, D., Wang, Z., Marwah, M., Hyser, C.: Renewable and cooling aware workload management for sustainable data centers. In: Proceedings of the 12th ACM SIGMETRICS/PERFORMANCE Joint International Conference on Measurement and Modeling of Computer Systems, SIGMETRICS '12, pp. 175–186. ACM, New York (2012)

16. Lučanin, D., Brandic, I.: Take a break: cloud scheduling optimized for real-time electricity pricing. In: 2013 Third International Conference on Cloud and Green Computing (CGC), pp. 113–120. IEEE (2013)

17. O'Connor, P., Kleyner, A.: Practical Reliability Engineering. Wiley, Oxford (2011)

18. Qureshi, A., Weber, R., Balakrishnan, H., Guttag, J., Maggs, B.: Cutting the electric bill for internet-scale systems. SIGCOMM Comput. Commun. Rev. **39**(4), 123–134 (2009)

19. Urdaneta, G., Pierre, G., van Steen, M.: Wikipedia workload analysis for decentralized hosting. Elsevier Comput. Netw. **53**(11), 1830–1845 (2009)

20. Vieira, C.C.A., Bittencourt, L.F., Madeira, E.R.M.: Towards a PaaS architecture for resource allocation in IaaS providers considering different charging models. In: Altmann, J., Vanmechelen, K., Rana, O.F. (eds.) GECON 2013. LNCS, vol. 8193, pp. 185–196. Springer, Heidelberg (2013)

21. Weron, R.: Modeling and Forecasting Electricity Loads and Prices: A Statistical Approach, 1st edn. Wiley, Chichester (2006)

22. Xu, H., Feng, C., Li, B.: Temperature aware workload management in geo-distributed datacenters. In: Presented as part of the 10th International Conference on Autonomic Computing, pp. 303–314. USENIX, Berkeley (2013)

23. Zhou, R., Wang, Z., McReynolds, A., Bash, C.E., Christian, T.W., Shih, R.: Optimization and control of cooling microgrids for data centers. In: 2012 13th IEEE Intersociety Conference on Thermal and Thermomechanical Phenomena in Electronic Systems (ITherm), pp. 338–343. IEEE (2012)

# CloudTracker: Using Execution Provenance to Optimize the Cost of Cloud Use

Geoffrey Douglas, Brian Drawert, Chandra Krintz$^{(\boxtimes)}$, and Rich Wolski

Computer Science Department, University of California, Santa Barbara, USA
ckrintz@cs.ucsb.edu

**Abstract.** In this work, we investigate tools that enable dollar cost optimization of scientific simulations using commercial clouds. We present a framework, called CLOUDTRACKER, that transparently records information from a simulation that is executed in a commercial cloud so that it may be "replayed" exactly to reproduce its results. Using the automated CLOUDTRACKER provenance and replay facilities, scientists can choose either to store the results of a simulation or to reproduce it on-demand – whichever is more cost efficient in terms of the dollar cost charged for storage and computing by the commercial cloud provider. We present a prototype implementation of CLOUDTRACKER for the Amazon AWS commercial cloud and the StochSS stochastic simulation system. Using this prototype, we analyze the storage-versus-compute cost tradeoffs for different classes of StochSS simulations when deployed and executed in AWS.

**Keywords:** Cloud computing · Provenance · Cost estimation · Simulation · Replay

## 1 Introduction

Easy and inexpensive access to vast compute and storage resources, in the form of cloud computing, along with the availabili digital information (finacial, scientific, social) gathered via the Internet, have fueled the trend toward data-centric commercial application development. Data products originate from a variety of sources including mobile applications, streaming media, social networking, and large-scale analytics. Such data products in many cases require significant computational power for their generation and processing as well as substantial storage capacity for their preservation and collaborative sharing.

Scientific computing in general, and scientific simulation in particular, share many of these characteristics, but as yet, have failed to leverage the technological advantages offered by cloud computing. One reason for this lack of uptake is that the cost models associated with scientific computation are different than those associated with commercial enterprises. In a scientific context, the longevity of data (for the purposes of peer-actuated verification) is theoretically indefinite as is the need for reproducibility.

J. Altmann et al. (Eds.): GECON 2014, LNCS 8914, pp. 99–113, 2014.
DOI: 10.1007/978-3-319-14609-6_7

To aid enterprises with cost control, public cloud vendors make compute and storage resources separately available on an on-going, pay-per-use, rental basis. This "pay-as-you-go" model makes them attractive to businesses that experience transient fluctuations in computational needs, but can create infeasible long-term cost obligations for the storage of scientific results.

In this work, we investigate CLOUDTRACKER – a system for implementing the reproduction of scientific simulations in commercial cloud systems for the purposes of reproducibility and cost optimization. In many simulation contexts, the code that implements a simulation is significantly smaller than the results it produces. CLOUDTRACKER records the computational *provenance* (in a compact form) associated with a simulation so that it may be replayed exactly in a commercial cloud. Thus a scientist can choose either to store the results or to rerun the simulation when the results are needed – which ever yields the best cost-benefit relationship based on cloud storage and compute pricing. CLOUDTRACKER also facilitates data sharing (and verification) by making it possible for those, other than the progenitor, to regenerate a data set thereby aiding scientific reproducibility.

CLOUDTRACKER implements both automated provenance tracking and replay for applications that

- produce outputs deterministically from their inputs,
- use a "job manager" to automate application execution in a distributed setting, and
- can run in a cloud environment consisting of virtualized commodity and storage resources and yield the same numerical results.

Because clouds must automate the process of deploying an application (typically via a set of web services), it is possible to capture exactly the environment in which an application is executed in a cloud, including all of the operating system code, environment variables, and support library dependencies that are used. Moreover, commercial clouds operate at sufficient customer scale to make it difficult or impossible to deprecate "old" software. Operating system virtualization preserves the longevity of old releases so that they may be reconstituted years after they are first used under the same automated control. This longevity is essential for commercial adoption of clouds by enterprises as software lifecycle is a key cost control business parameter. CLOUDTRACKER leverages these properties to ensure that the results of a deterministic computation can either be stored or reproduced on demand at a later time.

In this way, CLOUDTRACKER complements previous work on data provenance for cloud systems [1, 9, 14, 18, 22]. In particular, CLOUDTRACKER records the minimal amount of meta-information necessary to re-execute an application (a.k.a a job) but it does not store the output data produced by the job itself. It captures this meta-information by observing the launch sequence of commands made by a job manager (that is responsible for running the job) and by interrogating the cloud platform for cloud configuration information associated with the job.

The work described in this paper focuses on a prototype implementation of CLOUDTRACKER for the Amazon Web Services (AWS) commercial cloud and the StochSS [20] cloud-based job manager for stochastic simulation. CLOUD-TRACKER integrates with AWS and StochSS via a well-defined API that we believe generalizes to other systems with similar application properties. It also uses the Amazon Simple Storage Service (S3) – Amazon's inexpensive and most scalable storage service – to store the meta-data associated with each job run. Finally, CLOUDTRACKER exports a graphical interface (GUI) for scientists to use to track provenance, to initiate job replay, and to extract the actionable cost analysis that CLOUDTRACKER generates.

Our results indicate that at a sufficiently large scale (jobs that take multiple hours or days to complete and generate many gigabytes or terabytes worth of data), there are significant cost differences between storage and computation. For a given job, there is a specific point in time when storage becomes more expensive than computation. CLOUDTRACKER is able to present this information to users graphically. CLOUDTRACKER's reproduction engine is also able to replay a job on a wide range of AWS virtual machine configurations (each having a different cost) to allow the user to identify the most time and cost efficient combination. This information is also reported to users through the CLOUDTRACKER Web UI to give users insight into the cost of using different cloud resources.

In the sections that follow, we overview CLOUDTRACKER and describe its prototype implementation. We next present StochSS and show how we augment its job manager to support CLOUDTRACKER. We then evaluate CLOUD-TRACKER for StochSS and present empirical results on using the system to trade off the costs of computation and storage. We follow this with a discussion of the limitations of the CLOUDTRACKER prototype, related work, and our conclusions.

## 2    CloudTracker

CLOUDTRACKER is an extensible software platform for tracking information about the execution of programs that are deployed using cloud infrastructures, such that they can be reproduced (i.e. replayed) at some later time. CLOUD-TRACKER uses this tracking information to automate replay and to help users identify the best cost trade off between re-computing their data sets and storing them using cloud resources.

CLOUDTRACKER is designed to operate alongside an arbitrary, cloud-aware job management technology (e.g. tasking systems [7,12,20], batching systems [13,21], custom scripts, and others) as depicted in Fig. 1. CLOUDTRACKER is not an interception architecture, requiring jobs to pass through before execution. Rather, it provides jobs managers with an API and library that they can use to request that CLOUDTRACKER record the execution provenance of a job. CLOUDTRACKER receives and records a unique identifier for each job to which it maps information about the execution environment of the job. Together, we refer to the map and provenance information that CLOUDTRACKER collects, stores, and manages, a *job manifest*. CLOUDTRACKER  stores the manifest with

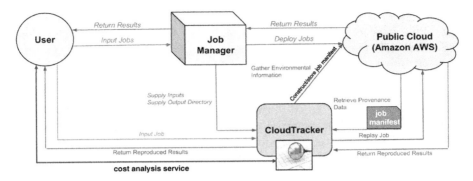

**Fig. 1.** CLOUDTRACKER System Overview. CLOUDTRACKER operates transparently alongside a job manager and with a public cloud, recording information about the execution environment of programs (jobs) into manifest files stored securely in cloud storage. At a later date, a user can use the CLOUDTRACKER web interface to specify a job to be replayed or to analyze the cost of job execution (production of the results) and result storage.

read-only access rights in a cloud datastore that is universally accessible, persistent, and immutable.

CLOUDTRACKER also provides a web service with which users can replay a previously tracked execution by selecting the appropriate job ID and specifying their cloud credentials. The service retrieves the provenance information that it has associated with the job ID and uses it to replicate the state under which the original job ran. CLOUDTRACKER sets up a virtual environment in the cloud to replay the job using the original inputs and returns the results back to the user. CLOUDTRACKER can also store the results temporarily in cloud storage or forward them directly the requester. Users can then compare the results against those reported by the progenitor of the job.

The CLOUDTRACKER service also provides users with information about the cost of a job. This cost analysis service reports the cost for storing the results of the job in the persistent object store of the cloud (e.g. the Simple Storage Service (S3) in AWS or Cloud Storage in the Google Cloud Platform). The service reports the cost of the original execution on an hourly and per-minute basis and can replay the job to determine the cost under different scenarios (e.g. using different instance sizes). Finally, the cost analysis service estimates how long the results can be stored before the cost of doing so is outweighed by that of replaying the job and reproducing the job immediately prior to the time at which the results are to be used or shared.

## 2.1   CLOUDTRACKER Implementation

CLOUDTRACKER is written in the Python programming language so that it is portable and facilitates easy integration with popular public and private cloud APIs (AWS and Eucalyptus [8]), via the publicly available boto toolkit [6].

CLOUDTRACKER exports an application programming interface (API) with which job execution systems (or individual users and scientists) can interface to provide tracking, reproduction, and cost analysis support for their cloud-based applications. We overview this API in Sect. 2.3.

The CLOUDTRACKER platform is a distributed web application that can be integrated into any cloud infrastructure or platform-as-a-service (PaaS). The CLOUDTRACKER backend provides provenance tracking (the API implementation); the frontend provides users with access to job replay and cost analysis. The backend captures and records job information provided by authenticated job managers and metadata gathered from the cloud environment. CLOUD-TRACKER manages this information in the form of a compact manifest which it stores in persistent, cloud storage using the credentials of the CLOUDTRACKER administrator. CLOUDTRACKER makes the recorded information (execution provenance) publicly readable but not modifiable to ensure trustworthy reproduction of results and datasets.

The frontend provides a web-based user interface (UI) for interacting with the CLOUDTRACKER platform. Users authenticate themselves and supply their cloud credentials (under which an application's execution is to be replayed) via the CLOUDTRACKER UI. They then select a job for which they want cost estimates or to reproduce output data. CLOUDTRACKER uses the securely stored information associated with the job ID to perform the service for the user and to return the result to the user via a web browser.

## 2.2   Leveraging Amazon Web Service Interfaces

The public cloud we use for our CLOUDTRACKER prototype is Amazon Web Services (AWS) [3] given its current position as the market leader in cloud infrastructure use [5]. We also selected it because the Eucalyptus private cloud infrastructure [15] is API-compatible with AWS and thus CLOUDTRACKER users can run CLOUDTRACKER on local cluster resources or in the public cloud without modification.

We leverage a number of recent advances in public cloud APIs from AWS to implement the CLOUDTRACKER platform. In our scenario, job managers use the Elastic Compute Cloud (EC2) service, and deploy jobs to EC2 instances. These are virtual machines, running Linux operating systems. Different machine types are available, offering different amounts of computational resources, each with their own usage price. Once configured with all of the necessary application software, libraries, and filesystem data, a snapshot of the instance can be saved as an immutable, reusable image called an Amazon Machine Image (AMI). Typically, job managers use the ID of a given AMI to launch EC2 instances to run applications in the cloud. CLOUDTRACKER records this AMI so that it can be used for the replay of a job. AMIs contain most of the relevant aspects of a job's execution environment and as such, CLOUDTRACKER need only store a small amount of information to capture this information.

CLOUDTRACKER stores job provenance information in AWS S3 using the AWS S3 manifest APIs [4]. Data in S3 are called objects and objects are grouped together into buckets. With S3, access permissions can be set at both the object and bucket level, giving users full control over who can view and edit their data.

## 2.3  Job Tracking

To perform job tracking, a job manager interoperates with the CLOUDTRACKER platform using CLOUDTRACKER API that we provide as an open source Python library. We summarize the API operations in Table 1. To initiate tracking for a new job, the job manager instantiates a new CLOUDTRACKER object. This operation sets up a communication channel with the name service and authenticates the job manager. The job manager provides CLOUDTRACKER with a unique identifier for the jobs; CLOUDTRACKER augments this with a unique identifier for the job manager (so that multiple concurrent job managers can be supported at once). CLOUDTRACKER refers to this unique identifier as the job's UUID and uses it to allocate a bucket in cloud storage and to create a manifest file in that bucket to hold the job's provenance data. CLOUDTRACKER then queries the EC2 metadata service to query details about the job's EC2 instance (given the ID passed in from the job manager) including AMI-ID and instance type. CLOUD-TRACKER writes all provenance data as key-value pairs in the manifest file.

**Table 1.** CLOUDTRACKER API

| API | Semantics |
| --- | --- |
| CloudTracker | Instantiates new CloudTracker instance |
| (uuid,instance_id) | Creates new directory in CloudTracker S3 bucket from the UUID |
| | Collects instance metadata and writes it to a manifest file |
| track_input(exec_string) | Writes executable name and input parameters to manifest |
| | Discovers input files and uploads them alongside manifest |
| track_output(output_dir) | Writes location of output directory to manifest |
| exec_state(time,size) | Computes execution time of job and size of output data |
| | Writes execution time and data set size to manifest |

To record the inputs to a job, the job manager uses the track_input() function to supply CLOUDTRACKER with the same execution string that the job manager uses to execute a job in an EC2 instance. This execution string contains the name of the executable and all of the command-line input parameters. Input files must be provided with a full file path in order to assure uniqueness and make them easier to locate. CLOUDTRACKER checks the filesystem for the existence of each input parameter, and those that do exist are assumed to be input files. Upon discovery, these files are copied and uploaded to the S3 bucket alongside the manifest. All of the other inputs are written to the manifest file itself.

Finally, the job manager uses the track_output() function to tell CLOUD-TRACKER the location of the output directory it uses for job results (other than standard output and standard error, if any). This output directory location is also written to the manifest.

CLOUDTRACKER also requires that the job manager record metadata about the execution of the job so that it can use it to estimate future costs. To do so, the job manager times the execution of jobs and computes the size of the job output. CLOUDTRACKER records this information in the manifest file of the job. This interaction relies on the job manager returning the correct values to CLOUDTRACKER; if the job manager cannot be trusted, CLOUDTRACKER can instead execute the job itself using its reproduction engine. If the job manager participates in this way, it reduces the cost of reproduction and cost analysis for future users of the job and data.

## 2.4   Job Reproduction

With all of the provenance data previously recorded, the reproduction process is straightforward. The only input CLOUDTRACKER requires from the user is the UUID of a job to be replayed and the user's public cloud credentials. CLOUD-TRACKER uses UUID to access the appropriate S3 bucket to obtain the manifest file and required input files.

CLOUDTRACKER launches an EC2 instance using the AMI ID and instance type using the user's cloud credentials. CLOUDTRACKER downloads the input files from S3 and stores them at the specified file paths. CLOUDTRACKER then reconstitutes the execution string and invokes the job. Finally, CLOUDTRACKER collects standard output, standard error, and any results in the output directory and returns them to the user via links to S3 storage on a web page. CLOUD-TRACKER also provides clean up utilities to garbage collect results no longer of interest and to reuse or terminate instances.

## 2.5   Cost Analysis

The other key component of the CLOUDTRACKER platform is the cost analysis service. The CLOUDTRACKER frontend allows users to specify or select the ID of a job for which they want to perform analyses. The platform retrieves the execution time and data set size in the job's manifest, and using pricing information provided by the cloud provider, estimates the cost of running that job and storing its data products in the cloud. The CLOUDTRACKER presents a graph that identifies the crossover point for computation and storage costs at which recomputing the result set via replay is less then continued storage. The analysis accounts for the time to produce the results themselves.

If the performance and storage data is not stored in the job manifest for the for one or more instance types, CLOUDTRACKER uses its reproduction engine to execute the jobs for the types of interest. Each instance type provides differing computational power at different costs to the user. Such runs are needed because execution time and program behavior are specific to both the application and instance type. Using this utility, CLOUDTRACKER automatically replays a job on one or more instance types in parallel. The default instance types in our EC2 prototype include seven different instance types ranging from t1.micro to c3.2xlarge. CLOUDTRACKER computes the cost of using each instance type given the execution profile of the job running within each. When the analysis is complete, CLOUDTRACKER presents the instance type that saves the most time and the most money (if different) to the user, and records this information in the job manifest for future use. CLOUDTRACKER uses reproduction if the time and size estimates for a job are not available (e.g. if not trusted, or not yet reproduced) or if requested by the user via the UI.

## 3   Prototype

To prototype CLOUDTRACKER, we target StochSS, a software platform that provides job management for simulations of discrete stochastic models [20]. Such models are useful for describing biological systems on the molecular scale (for which the number of species copies is small) and simulating their behavior accurately. StochSS "service-izes" the monte carlo based simulation engines that underly these technologies, including StochKit2 [17], ordinary differential equations, and others, by wrapping them with a web UI with which users can parameterize and customize their models, and a backend that deploys simulations on different deployment targets, including Amazon AWS.

We extend StochSS with the CLOUDTRACKER library that the job manager makes use of upon job deployment. The public StochSS VM image contains the simulation applications and their software dependencies. Upon job submission, StochSS uses the CLOUDTRACKER API to contact CLOUDTRACKER and request tracking of the job (i.e. instantiation, `track_input`, `track_output`, and `exec_state`). CLOUDTRACKER retrieves the AMI for the VM instance from the AWS metadata service and the job's ID for each unique job deployed. CLOUDTRACKER appends the ID to a unique instance ID for the StochSS instance (so that it is able to correctly handle multiple StochSS job managers concurrently). Although the simulations are stochastic, StochSS is able to extract a known seed which it includes as part of the input string for each job. Once this communication completes, users are able to use the CLOUDTRACKER UI to replay or to analyze the cost of any previously executed StochSS job.

## 4   Empirical Evaluation

We next evaluate the overheads and efficacy of CLOUDTRACKER. We overview our experimental setting and then describe our results.

## 4.1    Methodology

We empirically evaluate CLOUDTRACKER using StochSS version 1.2 and t1.micro instances in AWS for provenance tracking. The simulation engine that we use in our experiments is an ordinary differential equation with sensitivity analysis on four parameters for a dimer decay model. This job requires one input XML file and eight input parameters.

We consider two simulation job *sizes*: large and small. The large job runs for approximately 500 million steps (10 measurements per unit) and generates 1TB of output data. The small job runs for 10,000 steps which generates 22MB of output data. The instance types that we use for CLOUDTRACKER cost analysis include t1.micro, m1.small, m3.medium, m3.large, c3.large, and c3.2xlarge.

## 4.2    Empirical Evaluation

We first evaluate the overhead of CLOUDTRACKER. Figure 2 shows the manifest file for an arbitrary StochSS job in its entirety. This example is 354 bytes in size and contains all of the necessary information to reproduce the results of its representative job. The only additional information needed is the one input file, the XML model file, which can vary in size based on the model parameters. The XML file for the dimer decay model is 2.47KB.

Of course the number of inputs and total input size (files include) is program specific and varies widely. However, CLOUDTRACKER does not add any additional storage overhead to inputs and is able to compress inputs to reduce this size if needed. Since CLOUDTRACKER uses S3 to store this information, the cost of S3 storage is on $0.03 per gigabyte per month. The CLOUDTRACKER prototype currently uses fewer than ten S3 PUT operations which cost $0.005 per 1,000 requests. To retrieve provenance information, the CLOUDTRACKER prototype currently uses fewer than 10 S3 GET requests which cost $0.005 per 1,000 requests. In summary, CLOUDTRACKER is able to collect, store, and access execution provenance data at very low cost.

```
instance_type : c3.2xlarge
region : us-east-1
ami_id : ami-fcc53494
executable : /home/ubuntu/ode/stochkit_ode.py
--force :
-m : /mnt/input/9bcb7dbe-36b3-4b06-b680-b59cfc3a5658.xml
-i : 100000
--sensi :
-t : 10000.0
--parameters : c4 c2 c3 c1
--out-dir :  /mnt/output/result
exec_time : 0.999206
output_dir : /mnt/output/result
output_size : 23700332
```

**Fig. 2.** Example StochSS job manifest file - 354 bytes with a single input file.

Similarly, CLOUDTRACKER does not introduce overhead for replay beyond that required for original job execution. The process of replaying a job requires CLOUDTRACKER to launch a single EC2 instance which takes approximately the same amount of time as during the original run (on the order of a few seconds).

### 4.3  Cost Analysis

We next use CLOUDTRACKER to perform a cost analysis using the large simulation job. Using the AWS m1.small instance type, job execution (and thus replay) takes 4.49 days; for m3.medium it requires 1.18 days; and for c3.large it requires 0.53 days. Figure 3 shows three graphs that exhibit the trade-off of storage and computational costs as presented by CLOUDTRACKER. The graphs assume that the original data set is produced on Day 0.

In all three graphs, the cost of storing the 1TB output is the same and increases over time (as determined by the AWS S3 pricing model). The computation cost data shows the constant cost to produce the output data once; each graph shows the cost for each of the three instance sizes we consider. In each graph, CLOUDTRACKER also plots the Days to Recompute to show the amount of time required to recompute the data via replay (relative to Day 0) if the data sets were deleted on Day 0.

For each instance type, there is a cross-over point for computation and storage. If the data set is not used prior to this point, it is less costly to recompute

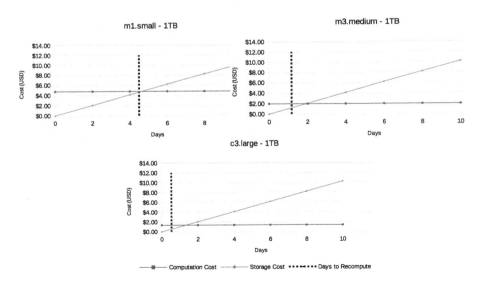

**Fig. 3.** Computation time versus storage cost for the large StochSS simulation job (1TB data set size) using m1.small, m3.medium, and c3.large instances sizes in AWS. Storage costs are the same for all three graphs because the data size is the same. The vertical dotted line represents the amount of time required to recompute the data set using CLOUDTRACKER replay on each machine.

the data. If the data is used prior to this point, it is more cost efficient to store the data. In either case, scientists and collaborators must also account for the time required to recompute the data to ensure that they have the data ready when it is needed, if they choose not to store it and instead compute it on-demand. Via its UI, CLOUDTRACKER presents these plots to the user or reports the cross-over point and replay time so that users obtain actionable insights from the tool that help them optimize the cost of cloud use.

CLOUDTRACKER also reports cost anomalies to users through its UI as part of its replay and cost analysis service. Cost anomalies are non-intuitive cost trends that may not be obvious to users. An example of a cost anomaly is when an instance price is higher than another but a computation that uses it results in a lower overall cost. Such an anomaly is depicted in the graphs in the figures. Each instance type is more expensive than the previous: m1.large costs $0.044 per hour, m3.medium costs $0.07 per hour, and c3.large costs $0.105 per hour. However, in each graph, the total cost of the computation is reduced. This is because the application is able to take advantage of the additional available resources in each case to compute in less time.

Such anomalies are application specific and hard to determine ahead of time. The CLOUDTRACKER replay mechanism executes applications using different instances sizes to establish such ground truth for users. CLOUDTRACKER can be configured to run all or part of a program and to adjust its inputs accordingly to minimize the cost of performing replay across different instances sizes. Moreover, for collaborative systems, CLOUDTRACKER can cache the results across users to employ *crowd sourcing* to estimate these costs without direct replay. Finally, CLOUDTRACKER reuses instances across job types and job managers when it is able to do so (compatible AMIs) in an attempt to consume the full instance hour being charged for.

Figure 4 shows CLOUDTRACKER analysis for the small simulation job across all of the instance sizes CLOUDTRACKER currently considers as part of its replay. We also include a more detailed description of these results in Table 2; we consider average cost on a sub-hour basis in this table. The data shows that there is a significant time savings as we increase the size of the instance types (left to right). However, once the resources are fully utilized by the application, adding more compute resources will not decrease execution time and instead will only increase cost. For this job, CLOUDTRACKER identifies the c3.large as the best instance type which is over 8 times faster and provides a 37 % reduction in cost over using t1.micro instances if the instances are used for a complete hour for this job type. CLOUDTRACKER is able to present this information to users so that they can optimize their public cloud costs when computing, replaying, and storing large data sets.

## 5    Discussion

The CLOUDTRACKER design allows provenance tracking, job reproduction, and cost analysis to happen independently of and in concert with modern job management platforms used today to deploy arbitrary programs over cloud

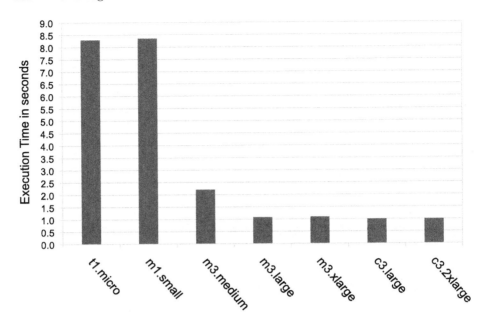

**Fig. 4.** CLOUDTRACKER execution time comparison for the small (22MB data set size) StochSS job, across the AWS instance sizes that the CLOUDTRACKERreplay service considers.

**Table 2.** EC2 Instance Comparison for the small (22MB data set size) StochSS job.

|  | t1.micro | m1.small | m3.medium | c3.large | m3.large | m3.xlarge | c3.2xlarge |
|---|---|---|---|---|---|---|---|
| Time (sec) | 8.29 | 8.35 | 2.20 | 0.99 | 1.08 | 1.09 | 1.00 |
| Rate (USD/hr) | 0.02 | 0.04 | 0.07 | 0.11 | 0.14 | 0.28 | 0.42 |
| Avg Cost (USD) | $4.6 \times 10^{-5}$ | $1.0 \times 10^{-4}$ | $4.3 \times 10^{-5}$ | $2.9 \times 10^{-5}$ | $4.2 \times 10^{-5}$ | $8.5 \times 10^{-5}$ | $1.2 \times 10^{-4}$ |
| % Time improvement vs t1.micro | None | None | 73.5 % | 88.0 % | 87.0 % | 86.9 % | 87.9 % |
| % USD savings vs t1.micro | None | None | 6.5 % | 37.0 % | 8.7 % | None | None |

infrastructures. However, there are limitations with using CLOUDTRACKER that we overview in this section and are considering as part of on-going work on this project.

First, CLOUDTRACKER supports only programs that can execute within a single virtual machine instance (i.e. distributed applications are not supported). Moreover, CLOUDTRACKER is unable to support applications for which the results generated depend on non-deterministic behavior (e.g. randomness, time-dependent inputs, external input from services not available during replay, etc.). With this work, we target scientific and data analytic programs for which the output (data product) is dependent only on program inputs (command line and files) and the VM execution environment.

Second, CLOUDTRACKER is able to interact with only those job managers capable of communicating job provenance data through the CLOUDTRACKER API. If, for example, the job manager is not capable of reporting the instance ID that is used for job execution, CLOUDTRACKER will be unable to extract the execution provenance (e.g. AMI information from the cloud metadata server) necessary to replay the job or estimate cloud costs.

Third, CLOUDTRACKER use only makes sense for programs for which the cumulative size of the inputs is significantly smaller than that of the outputs. That is, there is only an opportunity to trade off computation for storage if the computation itself does not have significant storage requirements. For some cases in which the input size is significant but they are stored (which is paid for) by a third party (e.g. public data sets [2,10,11,16,19,23] or a trusted collaborator), CLOUDTRACKER can be used to trade-off processing and storage costs.

Next, CLOUDTRACKER currently requires that users make their AMIs accessible to those with whom they wish to give reproducibility rights. That is, users can make their AMIs public for everyone to reproduce their results or to a subset of users. CLOUDTRACKER can facilitate this process through its web UI but the owner of the AMI is required to authenticate the change. Similarly, CLOUDTRACKER does not store the output data or the AMIs used for jobs under its credentials. It currently relies on the application progenitor or the job management system to do so. Such a model however requires that the AMI owners do not delete their AMIs. CLOUDTRACKER is able to make a copy of the AMI but will have to do so under the CLOUDTRACKER platform owner's credentials. As such, there is a question of who pays for and how to distribute cost across CLOUDTRACKER users. In our current prototype, we assume that AMIs are public and that they are not deleted (although CLOUDTRACKER reports any such issues to users upon reproduction/cost analysis).

# 6    Related Work

Although we are unaware of any work that employs execution provenance tracking to enable automatic and non-intrusive job replay and analysis of cloud cost trade-offs, other researchers have explored data provenance for cloud systems [1,9,14,18,22]. Muniswamy-Reddy, et al., claimed that provenance is a crucial feature currently missing from most cloud datastores, so they implemented a provenance protocol for coupling data and provenance information together in cloud storage. In addition to verification, they identify faulty data propagation as another use case for data provenance, pointing to the fact that scientists wanting to build off of one anothers work have no means to verify that she is using data processed by the correct software [14].

Abaddi and Lyle, of the University of Oxford, move beyond the idea of data provenance for applications running in the cloud to discuss the need for provenance in clouds themselves. They show how provenance can be useful in the detection of bugs and security violations, and in the identification of their origins [1].

Finally, Zhang, et al., examine the different granularities of provenance required to describe data at different levels in the cloud computing model. These levels are the application, virtual machine, physical machine, cloud, and the Internet as whole. As the focus becomes broader, so does the type of provenance that is interesting to track [22]. While our work focuses on collecting provenance information at the application and virtual machine levels, there is definitely more information to be found at those higher levels.

## 7    Conclusions and Acknowledgments

The goal of our work is to investigate and develop new tools that bring the utility and potential of cloud computing to underserved communities such as those in the scientific computing community. A key reason behind the lack of uptake in cloud use by this community in particular is the difference in the cost models that underly scientific computation versus those for commercial enterprise applications. In particular, scientists require the ability to easily reproduce datasets (scientific results) for peer review, collaboration, and extension purposes and to make these datasets available to others for long periods of time.

In this paper, we investigate a tool called CLOUDTRACKER, that provides support for cost estimation for such data life cycles. To enable this, CLOUD-TRACKER provides an easy to use cloud service (platform, client library, and UI) that extends the functionality of cloud-based job managers to facilitate automatic cost trade-off analysis between storing data and regenerating it on the fly. CLOUDTRACKER does so by tracking execution provenance so that it can reproduce the resulting data sets (for applications for which this is possible). With the ability to accurately reproduce datasets, CLOUDTRACKER is also able to estimate and report the best cost trade-off between storing data over time and reproducing it on-demand. We demonstrate the utility of CLOUDTRACKER for scientific simulations and find that it introduces negligible overhead (time and cost). We also find that for many applications there is a cross over point after which point it is more cost effective to regenerate the results rather than store them. In addition, CLOUDTRACKER is able to identify for users, opportunities for cost optimization across instance sizes offered by the cloud infrastructure.

**Acknowledgements.** We thank the reviewers for their valuable feedback on this paper. This work was funded in part by NSF (CNS-0905237 and CNS-1218808) and NIH (1R01EB014877-01).

## References

1. Abbadi, I.M., Lyle, J.: Challenges for provenance in cloud computing. In: USENIX Workshop on the Theory and Practice of Provenance (2011)

2. Amazon Public Datasets (2014). https://aws.amazon.com/datasets. Accessed 15 June 2014
3. Amazon AWS (2014). http://aws.amazon.com/. Accessed 15 Mar 2014
4. Aws manifest file options. http://docs.aws.amazon.com/AWSImportExport/latest/DG/ManifestFileParameters.html
5. Aws market share. https://www.srgresearch.com/articles/amazon-continues-to-dominate-iaaspaas-despite-strong-push-frommicrosoft-ibm
6. Boto. http://boto.readthedocs.org/en/latest/
7. Celery (2014). http://www.celeryproject.org/. Accessed 15 Mar 2014
8. Eucalyptus - Open Source, AWS-Compatible Private Cloud Infrastructure. http://www.eucalyptus.com
9. Frew, J., Metzger, D., Slaughter, P.: Automatic capture and reconstruction of computational provenance. In: Concurrency and Computation: Practice and Experience (2008)
10. Google Public Datasets (2014). https://www.google.com/publicdata/directory. Accessed 15 June 2014
11. HealthData.gov Public Datasets (2014). http://healthdata.gov/dataset/search. Accessed 15 June 2014
12. Horuk, C., Douglas, G., Gupta, A., Krintz, C., Bales, B., Bellesia, G., Drawert, B., Wolski, R., Petzold, L., Hellander, A.: Automatic and Portable Cloud Deployment for Scientific Simulations. In: IEEE Conference on High Performance Computing and Simulation (HPCS) (2014)
13. Jette, M., Yoo, A., Grondona, M.: Slurm: Simple linux utility for resource management. In: Job Scheduling Strategies for Parallel Processing (JSSPP) (2002)
14. Muniswamy-Reddy, K., Seltzer, M.: Provenance for the Cloud. In: USENIX Conference on File and Storage Technologies (2010)
15. Nurmi, D., Wolski, R., Grzegorczyk, C., Obertelli, G., Soman, S., Youseff, L., Zagorodnov, D.: The eucalyptus open-source cloud-computing system. In: 9th IEEE/ACM International Symposium on Cluster Computing and the Grid, 2009. CCGRID'09, pp. 124–131. IEEE (2009)
16. ReadWriteWeb Open Data (2014). http://readwrite.com/2008/04/09/where_to_find_data_on_the#awesm=oHspy4ZUfG9lUr. Accessed 15 June 2014
17. Sanft, K., Wu, S., Roh, M., Fu, J., Lim, R.K., Petzold, L.: StochKit2: software for discrete stochastic simulation of biochemical systems with events. Bioinformatics **27**(17), 2457–2458 (2011)
18. Simmhan, Y., Pale, B., Gannon, D.: A survey of data provenance in e-Science. SIGMOD Rec. **34**(3), 31–36 (2005)
19. Stanford Large Network Dataset Collection (SNAP) (2014). http://snap.stanford.edu/data/. Accessed 15 June 2014
20. Stoch, S.S.: http://www.stochss.org/. Accessed 20 Apr 2014
21. Thain, D., Tannenbaum, T., Livny, M.: Distributed computing in practice: the condor experience. Concurr. Pract. Experience **17**(2–4), 323–356 (2005)
22. Zhang, O., Kirchberg, M., Ko, R., Lee, B.: How to track your data: The case for cloud computing provenance. In: CloudCom (2011)
23. Zhao, B.: Social network datasets (2014). http://current.cs.ucsb.edu/socialnets/#code. Accessed 15 June 2014

# Migration to Governmental Cloud Digital Forensics Community: Economics and Methodology

Gianluigi Me$^{(\boxtimes)}$

LUISS Guido Carli University, Roma, Italy
`gme@luiss.it`

**Abstract.** The rapid growth of elastic computing services, together with a raising need to target savings, enable new IT scenarios. In particular, Law Enforcement Agencies (LEAs) can benefit of digital forensic services sharing, lowering CAPEX and OPEX especially in case of spiky utilization of forensic hardware and software resources. In fact, considering the workloads related to the size of a forensic organizational unit, the capital expenditure (CAPEX) and operational expenditures (OPEX) differently afflict the overall cost incurred to provide response to crime investigation. Hence, Government cloud community SaaS model, under strict security requirements, can represent a viable solution to dramatically lower costs of forensics units. This paper evaluates the Total Cost of Ownership (TCO) of in-house forensic farm and the TCO of a SaaS deployed as a government community cloud, providing Forensic as a Service to N forensic units. The costs assessment are part of the evaluation methodology to calculate the number of forensic crime cases needed to switch to Government cloud model from multiple independent forensic labs.

**Keywords:** SaaS · Economic evaluation · Total cost of ownership · Cost model · Digital forensics · CAPEX · OPEX

## 1 Introduction

The development of digital forensics over the last decade brought LEAs to dramatically increase case resolution effectiveness so that digital forensics, currently, represents a mandatory step in the crime investigation activity. Moreover, the huge penetration of electronic devices in daily life rapidly increased the effort in this area: e.g. FBI doubled the received cases in 2003–2012 [1] and the digital forensic area shows a 12 % growth rate in 2008–2012 compound annual [2].

In [3] Garfinkel argues that the Golden Age of Digital Forensics is quickly coming to an end of an evolution process: the pointed problems become very relevant in case of growing size of storage devices, where time to create a forensic image of a subject device and to process all of the data once it is found is

© Springer International Publishing Switzerland 2014
J. Altmann et al. (Eds.): GECON 2014, LNCS 8914, pp. 114–129, 2014.
DOI: 10.1007/978-3-319-14609-6_8

frequently insufficient. In particular, huge amounts of mobile devices with increasing memory size together with large datacenter forensics require specialized hardware equipment, huge storage capability and heterogeneous software licenses portfolio, which can be supported with high CAPEX in order to provide a prompt and complete response to crime investigation. In this expanding scenario, LEA digital forensics capacity has been strengthen in the last years, due to the huge increase of cybercrime volumes and typologies and the increasing use of Internet and digital devices to finalize common crimes [4]: however, the technological crime evolution time remains lower than the LEA organizational/technological latency due to limited budgets and finite resources.

Hence, as stated in 2006 Moore's paper [5], technological changes threaten to undermine LEA capacity for complete data analysis and the technology investments related to Digital Forensic Organizational Units (DFOUs), e.g. LEAs task forces, typically suffer of short lifetime due to rapid obsolescence of equipment versus high CAPEX needed to setup the equipment. Furthermore, the increasing digital material received by DFOUs for analysis reflects to spiky use of forensic software licenses and workload on storage and CPU cores (i.e. massive seizing for acquisition of mobile phones versus acquisition of data center storage). This scenario represents the typical fertile background for evaluating the opportunity to migrate to elastic services, providing typical cloud benefits in terms of *efficiency* (e.g. improved asset utilization, aggregated demand), *agility* (e.g. pay per use, as-a-service), *innovation* (e.g. shift focus from asset ownership to service management). In fact, when occasional or periodic load spikes happen, cloud computing is squarely tailored to provide on-demand excess resources capacity, since poor utilization rates represent a non-negligible waste factor.

In particular, IT assets in digital forensics are not used equally or continuously: as a rule of thumb, research evidences show that as computing power has indeed grown far cheaper and more plentiful, utilization rates for IT resources have rapidly decreased. All the above-mentioned considerations, in particular efficiency, agility and innovation, led many countries/regions to start the design and implementation of national strategies for Governmental Clouds (GC), e.g. in the USA in [8], in the EU in [9]), recognizing that public authorities stand to benefit from Cloud adoption both in terms of efficiency savings and in terms of services that are more flexible and turned to the needs of citizens and business. In particular, the GC, defined in [10] as an *environment running services compliant with governmental and EU legislations on security, privacy and resilience*, is going to be deployed (or in some cases, already exists) in many western countries, providing services under public body governance to state agencies, to citizens and to enterprises.

Based on the aforementioned considerations, this paper aims to provide a methodology to identify the drivers for evaluating the appropriate model and to evaluate the convenience to switch to governmental elastic services versus maintaining the independent DFOUs, considered as a community in the GC service model.

Finally, Sects. 2 and 3 will introduce the Cloud and Digital Forensics background needed to better understand economic evaluations in Sects. 6 and 7.

The Sect. 4 will identify the objectives and the limitations of the outcomes of this study, while the Sect. 8 will present the conclusions and the future works.

## 2   Government Private/Community Cloud and SaaS/PaaS Services

The National Institute of Standards and technology (NIST) defined Cloud Computing as *a model for enabling convenient, on-demand network access to a shared pool of configurable computing resources (e.g., networks, servers, storage, applications, and services) that can be rapidly provisioned and released with minimal management effort or service provider interaction. This cloud model promotes availability and is composed of five essential characteristics, three service models, and four deployment models* [16]. In particular, the deployment models defined by NIST are Public, Hybrid, Community and Private, where, in particular, the cloud infrastructure is deployed, customized, operated and maintained mainly for an organization as client supervised by cloud service provider. In the private cloud, all the resources and applications managed by the organization are strictly closed to the public. Therefore, an organization sets up a virtualization environment on its own servers, either in its own data centers or in those of a managed services provider. This structure is useful for organizations having the total control over every aspect of their infrastructure as an hard requirement. Moreover, private cloud is typically more secure than public cloud since it is customized on features that leads to more secure of their application, as consequently only selected stakeholders within organization may access and manage on a specific private cloud. Conversely, a community cloud infrastructure is procured jointly by several LEAs sharing specific needs such as security, compliance, or jurisdiction considerations. Therefore, digital forensic service for LEAs can be considered as an ICT commodity, having a common set of requirements and customers: in this case a community cloud enables the asset combination and the computing resources, data, and capabilities sharing. By eliminating the duplication of similar systems, LEAs can save money and allocate their resources more efficiently. Both private and community models fulfill the requirements of a GC forensic service provisioning: without losing generality, this paper will focus on the community cloud as the adopted model. According to [15], although a standard definition for GC services has not been widely accepted, we assume, for the purposes of this paper, that GC services fulfill the following requirements:

- Providing private (single tenancy) or community (agreed set of tenants) Cloud to host processes and store data, to run eGovernment services, controlled/ monitored locally or in a centralized way by the public body;
- Owned and managed by central government under its responsibility (private or community deployment model);
- Ensuring compliance with the infrastructure, the platform and the services with country governments and EU legislations on privacy, security and resiliency (location of the GC: on premises or off premises Cloud).

This paper will consider the GC service providing option Government to Government, where a public institution provides cloud services LEAs. Moreover, the forensic service provided by GC can be classified as critical since it handles sensitive information (related to crime investigation) and the impact of a potential failure or leakage affects the privacy of a number of citizens. The general critical service option is already in use in 29 % of EU cloud services, as well as community/private cloud are the most used deployment models [15].

**Table 1.** Cloud service models

| Service model | Delivery model |
|---|---|
| SaaS | Companies host applications in the cloud. The service being sold or offered is a complete end-user application |
| PaaS | Developers can design, build, and test applications that run on the cloud provider infrastructure |
| IaaS | System administrators obtain general processing, storage, database management and other resources |

As shown in Table 1, the SaaS and PaaS models fulfill the requirements of digital forensics applications, while IaaS provides an (typically unnecessary) increase of flexibility: in SaaS the GC offers software instances to be run in single-multi tenant mode, managing the overall system. In this model, the digital forensic operator analyses data using instances of forensic software, as it uses her/his webmail. In the PaaS, the GC delivers the necessary hardware resources where the digital forensic operators con run their own software, as Virtual Machines on a remote host. Since the forensic services provided by GC should be considered critical, in this paper the SaaS alternative will be only considered, without any loss of generality of the methodology (versus PaaS). In fact, there are substantial benefits to profit and welfare in high security-loss environments associated with introducing a SaaS alternative, according to [17].

Hence, the migration from DFOUs to GC-community introduces unseen concerns related to security, in particular data leakage: in fact, even considering the software always patched at the latest version, the magnitude of user information located in one place, together with the desirability to get the criminal investigation data, SaaS service may be more susceptible to targeted attacks (e.g. Google, Salesforce and Sony data breaches). Therefore, in order to determine the applicability of migration, as suggested in [11], after verifying the service and marketplace characteristics, the application and government readiness, the security requirements should be carefully checked. In particular, GC bodies providing forensic services have the responsibility to ensure:

- Compliance to laws, regulations, and agency requirements;
- Data characteristics to assess protections the forensic data set requires;
- Privacy and confidentiality to protect against access to information;

– Integrity to ensure data is authorized, complete, and accurate;
– Data controls (location where can be stored) and related access policies.

These aspects are discussed in Sect. 4.

## 3   The Digital Forensics

The term digital forensics refers to the scientific examination, analysis, and/or evaluation of digital evidence in legal matters [18]. Digital evidence, defined as any information of probative value that is either stored or transmitted in a digital form, once gathered, must satisfy the same legal requirements as conventional evidence, i.e. it must be:

– *Authentic*, the evidence must be original and related to the crime;
– *Reliable*, the evidence must have been collected and preserved (e.g. chain of custody) using reliable procedures that if necessary could be repeated by an independent party to achieve the same result;
– *Complete*, the evidence may be used to prove guilt as well as innocence;
– *Believable*, the evidence should be formed to convince juries and prosecutors;
– *Admissible*, the evidence was collected using procedures compliant to law.

Hence digital forensics is the collection of forensic processes applied to all (heterogeneous) digital devices, in order to transform data acquired by computers, networks, mobile devices and external memories in digital evidence. Examples of digital evidence include files stored on a computer hard drive (physically, in blocks or clusters), file fragments or data items stored in a USB memory, digital videos or audios recorded e stored in a mobile equipment, packets transmitted over a network or most recent paths in a car GPS-navigator, stored in a file. For the purpose of this paper, digital forensics is a 6-phases process:

1. *Identification:* determine items, components and data possible associated with the allegation or incident; employ triage techniques;
2. *Preservation:* ensure evidence integrity or state;
3. *Collection:* extract or harvest individual data items or groupings;
4. *Examination:* scrutinize data items and their attributes (characteristics);
5. *Analysis:* fuse and correlate material to produce reasoned conclusions;
6. *Presentation:* report facts in an organized, clear and objective manner.

This six stage process model and several other similar models [19] form the basis of the majority of digital forensic investigations. In particular, the former 3 steps are related to the acquisition (optionally performed off LEA premises), the latter to the analysis and presentation, which represent the core activities where this paper focuses for migration to GC services. In the current scenario (*as is*), the activities performed by DFOU forensic operators (basically from a LEA) are basically acquiring digital device content on a not volatile, not-rewritable memory support (optionally removable), with appropriate software/hardware tools (with data integrity as main hard requirement). The image of the seized device is, then, analyzed on premises, in a LEA forensic farm equipped with ad-hoc hardware/software: all the installed equipment has CAPEX and OPEX charged on the LEA budget. In the scenario based on FaaS (*to be*), LEA forensic operator acquires digital device content with appropriate software/hardware tools and uploads it to GC storage, to be further analyzed via digital forensic software clients through GC, typically on a VPN (Virtual Private Network) between LEA labs and GC. Consequently, all the needed equipment has CAPEX and OPEX charged on GC budget: the GC-community service dimensioning and SLA definition to set the acceptable requests loss and the allocation policy LEA are needed to appropriately share the resources. Nonetheless, this is out of the scope of this paper, which, instead, focuses on the overall costs sustained by Government to support the GC versus individual DFOUs choice. In phases 4–6, CAPEX components related to digital forensics have twofold features: the former is related to hardware and software components suffering the rapid obsolescence with continuous need of updates. In fact, e.g., the operating systems life cycle, new hardware plugs for mobile devices, new or updated data formats drive the need to have always updated equipment in order to guarantee the effectiveness of the digital investigation. The latter is related to forensic software vendors, offering a large set of common capabilities and some specialized (unique) capabilities: hence, the forensic analysis quality and completeness is strictly related to the availability of all the different tools. Therefore, the ideal forensic labs should have all the forensics equipment on the market with latest updates installed. This scenario represents a classical prerequisite for cloud adoption: in fact, as multiple software programs have to be used, many licenses can remain idle for long time (depending on how a single forensic tool is able to respond to criminal investigation requests), leading to a not-optimal utilization rate per license. For these reasons, forensic applications fall in the general classification presented in [20], where applications receiving cost benefits by running in the cloud include:

– applications with huge range of loads, occasional or periodic load spikes (crime evidences arrival process can be modeled as the sum of Poisson processes);
– capacity is hard to predict (crime evidences hardware and software resources requirements are not predictable);
– equipment purchasing is expensive and idle most of the time;
– new applications requiring additional data center space or infrastructure investment, such as new storage, cooling or power systems.

# 4 Objectives and Remarks

The main objective of this paper is to provide a methodology to evaluate the economic convenience, by central government perspective, to switch to GC community SaaS for LEAs and other governmental bodies. In particular, the enabling conditions when the transition is convenient will be highlighted together with the costs structure. The working scenario depicted in this paper foresees the invariance of forensic activities 1–3, while 4–6 are evaluated for switching to GC services. Before presenting, the following assumptions represent the baseline of the work:

*Assumption 1:* Although private cloud is the most acceptable model to store forensic images, GC community model for critical services can also fulfill the requirements at lower cost. In fact, forensic images are for restricted access only (investigators, judges, lawyers dealing with the case) and can contain confidential information. Hence it is assumed a security impact level evaluation (e.g. Impact Level, IL5, [21,22]) to establish the requirement for forensic GC services, since IL5, e.g., protects from major, long-term impairment to the ability to investigate serious crime (as defined in legislation) and protects from a number of criminal convictions to be declared unsafe or referred to appeal (e.g. through persistent and undetected compromise of an evidence-handling system);

*Assumption 2:* Laws establish evidence preserved on community cloud (with explicit rules) are admissible in court. Currently, the cloud model, due to its off-DFOU-premises feature represents a new stage in the chain of custody. If no rules (e.g. ACPO-like) apply at this stage, judge can assume the evidence as invalid;

*Assumption 3:* The network connection cost between DFOU and GC is assumed to be zero (e.g. using an already established, flat fee, available network);

*Assumption 4:* A common flawed assumption in designing distributed systems states that latency is zero, which is not true, in particular for cloud services. Using SaaS through the Internet can incur a substantial cost in terms of I/O latency. However, the presented model does not account for this latency;

*Assumption 5:* The resources are available on demand, with no loss. This assumption can be removed in presence of the queuing model and allocation policy (out of the scope of this paper, as mentioned in previous section).

## 5   Cost Evaluation

In Sect. 1 we introduced the cloud advantages related to supply-side savings. (e.g. large-scale data centers lower costs per equipment), demand-side aggregation (e.g. increasing server utilization rates), multi-tenancy efficiency (e.g. as the number of tenants increases, the application management and server cost per tenant decrease). The cost evaluation of SaaS migration of a Forensic Farm is based on the evaluation of the Net Present Value (NPV) over a time interval of the TCO of both alternatives, SaaS and N DFOUs. As a rule of thumb, organizations will adopt new technology system with the minimum NPV of the TCO over a time interval. The TCO of the GC is represented by the NPV of the sum of the OPEX and CAPEX (assumed on a seven years period). The costs related to internally based IT infrastructure are capital CAPEX, defined as *the amount of money spent for investments carried out from a long-term perspective to setup assets prior to their entering into operations.* In particular, in a forensic farm CAPEX are related to:

a. *Hardware, as Compute nodes* (split into racks), RAM (GB), Switches, connecting the racks, Controller/technology, security appliances (when the forensic lab is connected to an external network);

*b. Storage (HDs)*: in this paper it is assumed that the Organization buys storage when needed and the organization has to replace disks periodically due to failures, with an Annualized Replacement Rate (ARR), estimated at 3 %;
*c. Software Licenses* (with annual updates), computed as cost per single tenant;
*d. Security software equipment*, as firewall, anti malware, IPS/IDS etc. software, as a cost related only to GC, assuming that the DFOU labs are typically disconnected from the Internet/network, while GC is online by definition.

The Operating Costs (OPEX), defined as *recurring monthly costs of actually running the equipment*, are related to
*e. Power* (CPU + controller + Hard disks);
*f. Human resources* tasked on system/network management/administration.

Furthermore, the model does not consider invariant costs related to activities 1–3 (e.g. write blocker, forensic operator FTE, whose cost is the same on both models) as well as any costs related to new legal prescriptions (variable by countries) and CAPEX depreciation. Finally, the hardware salvage value is considered as nil, due to security prescriptions and/or legal sell-ban for hardware owned by public administrations.

# 6   CAPEX and OPEX

In equation form, the simplified standard capital budgeting format for calculating a purchased asset NPV, DFOU ($TCO^{DFOU}$) is computed as follows:

$$TCO_{(DFOU)} = \sum_{T=0}^{N-1} \frac{C_T^{DFOU}}{(1+I_R)^T} + P^{DFOU(T)} \tag{1}$$

where is the operating cost at year T, $P_{DFOU}$ represents the asset purchase (capital) cost and IR is the organizations cost of capital[1]. In particular, the DFOU TCO, in terms of hardware and software related to point (a), (b), (c), (e) and (f) is:

$$TCO_{(DFOU)} = \sum_{T=0}^{N-1} \frac{C_T^{DFOU}}{(1+I_R)^T} + \sum_{T=0}^{N-1} \frac{L_T^{DFOU}}{(1+I_R)^T} + P_{HW}^{DFOU} \tag{2}$$

where $L_T$ is the lease payment at year T for software licenses, whose updates are assumed to be billed annually. At year T, the DFOU CAPEX TCO can be further split, in particular, into 4 cost contributions:

– CPU, NAS/SAN, Storage architecture cost, $P_H$;
– $P_R$ is the cost of the hardware storage upgrades/failure repairing;
– Set of forensic software licenses, $L_S$;
– Cost of updates of forensic software licenses, $L_U$.

---

[1] The interest rate of its outstanding debt used to finance the purchase.

$$P^{DFOU(T)} = \frac{P_R^{DFOU(T)}}{(1+I_R)^T} + P_H^{DFOU(T)} + L_S^{DFOU(T)} + \frac{L_U^{DFOU(T)}}{(1+I_R)^T} \qquad (3)$$

In particular, the extra hardware needed and the repairing costs through the years, $P_H^{DFOU(T)}$ can be resumed in (4), where cost drivers are shown in Table 2.

$$P^{DFOU(T)} = ((\lceil V_T \rceil_\Omega - \lceil V_{(T-1)} \rceil_\Omega) \cdot \Omega + ARR_T) \cdot M_T \qquad (4)$$

**Table 2.** Cost drivers due to upgrades and failures

| Parameter | Description |
| --- | --- |
| $\Omega$ | Size of purchased hardware (e.g.disk drives, GBytes) |
| $ARR_T$ | Annual Replacement Ratio (typically $\in [0{,}5\,\%,13{,}5\,\%]$, assumed $3\,\%$) |
| $P_H^{DFOU}$ | Hardware cost (EUR) |
| $\lceil V_T \rceil_\Omega$ | Returns the minimum number of $\Omega$-sized hw units to manage $V_T$ |
| $K$ | Current per-hardware unit price (e.g. GByte storage, EUR/GByte) |
| $V_T$ | Expected hardware (e.g. storage) requirement in year $T$ (GBytes) |
| $M_T$ | Predicts the cost per unit (e.g. GByte of SATA disk storage at time $T$) |

I.e., for storage

- considering an overall hardware $3\,\%$ ARR (factor $0{,}03$ in formula (5)), as shown for hard disks in [23] for data centers;
- according to [24], the trend line can be approximated, using regression analysis of SATA storage prices based on Pricewatch.com, as $M_t = 1.2984 \cdot e^{0.012 \cdot T}$, where $T$ represents the time (in days) from a fixed observation data (in this case, 2003, April 23rd). Therefore, the future disk price trend conforms to the equation $K \cdot e^{C \cdot T}$, where $K$ represents the lowest storage price per GByte available to the consumer at $T = 0$; and T represents the number of years in the future. We therefore derive $M_T$ as $M_T = K \cdot e^{-0.0012 \cdot 365 \cdot T}$ and, finally, $M_T = K \cdot e^{-0.438 \cdot T}$.

In the storage case, we derive the following formulas:

$$P_{H(Storage)}^{DFOU(T)} = ((\lceil V_T \rceil_\Omega - \lceil V_{(T-1)} \rceil_\Omega) \cdot \Omega + 0.03 \cdot \Omega \cdot \lceil V_T \rceil_\Omega) \cdot K \cdot e^{-0.438 \cdot T} \qquad (5)$$

$$P_{H(Storage)}^{DFOU(T)} = (1.03 \cdot \lceil V_T \rceil_\Omega - \lceil V_{(T-1)} \rceil_\Omega) \cdot \Omega \cdot K \cdot e^{-0.438 \cdot T} \qquad (6)$$

Analogously to the abovementioned example, the formula (4) can be extended to the costs related to all the $m$ hardware components, obtaining

$$P_H^{DFOU(T)} = \sum_{j=1}^{m} ((\lceil V_T \rceil_\Omega - \lceil V_{(T-1)} \rceil_\Omega) \cdot \Omega + ARR_T^j) \cdot M_T^j \qquad (7)$$

as the overall formula taking into account the CAPEX of hardware upgrades and repairing. Hence, the formula in (3) can be upgraded to the GC case, taking into account a supplementary cost weights on all the CAPEX components related to the GC, adding the security hardware/software licenses costs needed to implement perimeter/host protection (8).

$$P^{GC(T)} = \frac{P_R^{GC(T)}}{(1 + I_R)^T} + P_H^{GC(T)} + L_S^{GC(T)} + \frac{L_U^{GC(T)}}{(1 + I_R)^T} \tag{8}$$

Finally, resuming the TCO for GC

$$TCO_{(GC)} = \sum_{T=0}^{N-1} \frac{C_T^{GC}}{(1 + I_R)^T} + P^{GC(T)} \tag{9}$$

## 6.1 OPEX

The OPEX are calculated on the basis of the electric utility cost ($\epsilon$) associated to the power consumed by hardware components (CPU cores ($W_{Cores}$), disk controllers ($W_C$), the disk units ($W_D$) and the cost of a human operator to manage the system/data, as the salary quota for data administration, $\beta$ and his salary $H_T$. These values are related to the annual increasing hardware/software need ($\lceil V_T \rceil_\Omega$) rate. Considering the parameters in Table 3, the OPEX can be modeled by the Eq. (10), as suggested in [24], resuming the costs in $C_T$:

**Table 3.** A possible set of values for calculating the OPEX

| Parameter | Description | Mock value |
|---|---|---|
| $\delta(EUR/KW)$ | Cost of electric utility | EUR 0.18 |
| $W_i(KW)$ | Hardware device power consumption | 0.5 |
| $P_D(KW)$ | Hard disk power consumption | 0.01 |
| $\lceil V_T \rceil_\Omega$ | Minimum number of hard disks | 1 |
| $\alpha$ | Workload ratio | 0,1090 |
| $H_t$ | Annual salary (data management) | EUR 35000 |

$$C_T = (365 \cdot 24) \cdot \epsilon \cdot \left( \sum_{j=1}^{n-1} W_j + W_D \cdot \lceil V_T \rceil_\Omega \right) + \beta \cdot H_T \tag{10}$$

Derived by the formula in (10), the lab accessing the GC, the OPEX of DFOU have the following upper bounded OPEX ($l$ is the number of hardware devices needed to access the GC)

$$C_T^{DFOU(GC)} = (365 \cdot 24) \cdot \epsilon \cdot \left( \sum_{j=1}^{n-1} W_j \right) \tag{11}$$

Hence, considering DFOU using some workstations to access GC SaaS (without incurring in further hw CAPEX), the formula (9) now is completed as

$$TCO_{GC} = \sum_{T=0}^{N-1} \frac{C_T^{GC}}{(1+I_R)^T} + P^{GC(T)} + \sum_N C^{DFOU(GC)} \qquad (12)$$

With assumptions in Table 3 mock values, the NPV on 7 years, the OPEX account for 33 %, while CAPEX account for 77 %, as shown in Fig. 1.

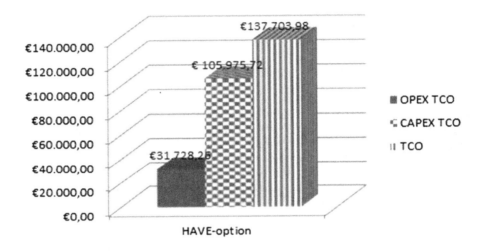

**Fig. 1.** TCO for a single DFOU, computed with mock values.

## 7    Economic Model

In 2006 Moore argued in [5] that the incentives of technology companies, LEAs and society do not always align. In particular, he cast the problem of recovering digital evidence in economic terms and how technology choices can impact the costs imposed on law enforcement, in terms of choice of proprietary and open standard formats. As a consequence of problems faced by LEAs in recovery data, the highest heterogeneous license software portfolio represents the best response. Hence, GC can represent the solution to benefit of this heterogeneity lowering the costs. In this scenario, we figure out to have N DFOUs accessing to the forensic services, namely forensic software (e.g. Encase, FTK, XRY, Cellbrite) provided by the GC. In particular, every single forensic service is bound to a maximum service capacity, represented by the related total number of software licenses available in the GC portfolio. Although the dimensioning of the GC is the target of a further paper, for the sake of methodology completeness overview, the related model can be represented as the sum of N independent Poisson processes and the related queuing model is represented by an Engset model [25], with an allocation policy following, e.g., the non cooperative resource allocation game. The well-established related literature shows that cloud services can be modeled with learning curves, in order to determine the reduction in costs per unit as experience grows while providing services with increasing maturity. The gained economies of scale are modeled by (13), where the marginal cost of producing the x-th unit, denote by c(x), is given by

$$c(x) = K \cdot x^{log_2 \alpha} \tag{13}$$

where

- $K$ is the cost to produce the first unit, As a result of the previous sections, K is represented by the TCO of the GC;
- $C(x)$, is the cost to provide the $xth$ forensic service (digital investigation case);
- $x$ is the number of digital forensic cases;
- $\alpha$ is the learning percentage (expressed as a decimal), with $\alpha \in [0, 1]$. The higher the value of $\alpha$ and $K$, the higher the production cost for the GC provider I.e., it is estimated that Amazon when running 30,000 EC2 instances, incurred in cost per instance of \$0.08/h while their original cost per EC2 instance was estimated to be \$2.20/h, representing an 80 % learning factor. As reported in [26], a typical cloud provider, as the total number of servers in house doubles, the marginal cost of deploying and maintaining each server decreases 10–25%, thus the learning factors are typically within the range (0.75, 0.9).

The Fig. 2 shows, in general, the cost comparison between the two choices, as reported in [27], for a company, where the concave line represents the in-house cost function based on the learning curve model while the straight line corresponds to the linear cost using cloud service. The sketch shows that cloud service is generally attractive for small to medium businesses. The TCO shown in the previous paragraphs applies in the learning curve costs, considering $K$ as the TCO. The total cost can be computed by integrating the above formula, obtaining

$$\frac{K \cdot x^{1+log_2 \alpha_S}}{1 + log_2 \alpha} \tag{14}$$

Conversely to well established literature [27,28] where the adoption of cloud services is related to the profits and costs of the cloud provider, it is assumed that, since the choice is between a GC and multiple governmental DFOUs, no profit should be considered for the central cloud provider. The convenience is lowering the costs less for the overall digital forensic service. Therefore, the migration to the aggregate (governmental) community cloud of the $n$ DFOUs happens when the aggregate costs of DFOUs overcome the cost of the community GC service. This is explained by the following formula:

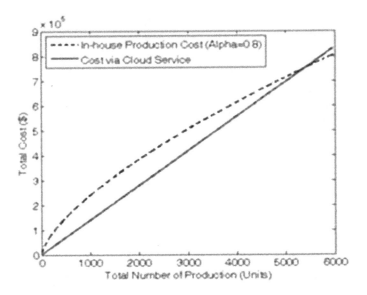

**Fig. 2.** Cost comparison: in-house vs cloud service.

$$\sum_{j=1}^{n} \frac{K_j \cdot x^{1+log_2\alpha_j}}{1 + log_2\alpha_j} > \frac{K_S \cdot x^{1+log_2\alpha_S}}{1 + log_2\alpha_S} \tag{15}$$

Assuming, for the sake of simplicity, that $\alpha_j = \alpha_F$ for all the DFOUs, the formula (15) is

$$\sum_{j=1}^{n} K_j \cdot (\frac{x^{1+log_2\alpha_F}}{1 + log_2\alpha_F}) > \frac{K_S \cdot x^{1+log_2\alpha_S}}{1 + log_2\alpha_S} \tag{16}$$

which is solved by

$$x > (\frac{(1 + log_2\alpha_F) \cdot K_S}{(1 + log_2\alpha_S) \cdot \sum_{j=1}^{n} K_j})^{log\frac{\alpha_F}{\alpha_S}2} \tag{17}$$

Posing $K_F = \sum_{j=1}^{n} K_j$ and $\alpha = \frac{\alpha_F}{\alpha_S}$

$$x > (\frac{(1 + log_2\alpha_F) \cdot K_S}{(1 + log_2\alpha_S) \cdot K_F})^{log_\alpha 2} \tag{18}$$

In the formula (18), the cost of providing the first unit of service (here, the first digital forensic investigation case) in both cases is represented by $K_S$ and $K_F$. In particular, assuming $K_F = TCO^{DFOU}$ and $K_S = TCO^{GC}$ for $T = [0, \ldots, n]$ years (which generalizes the cost of the first unit) enables the simulation of the years needed to return of the investment of migration with respect to the overall number of investigation cases. The related Fig. 3 depicts the behavior of

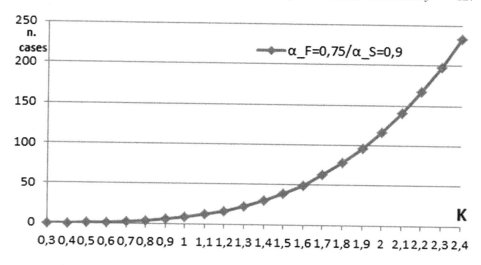

**Fig. 3.** Number of cases vs TCO ratio

convenience with respect to the ratio of TCO ($K = \frac{K_S}{K_F}$) in both cases: in fact, when the number of cases is greater than right-end member it is convenient to migrate. The Fig. 3 further shows how the formula in (18) can help the discussion: assuming $\alpha_F = 0.9$ and $\alpha_S = 0.75$ in fact, as the ratio of TCOs increases, the needed cases/per year increase exponentially in order to have convenience. Since assumed $\alpha$ values are likely for the two matching cases, the curve in Fig. 3 shows that, i.e., when the cost of the community cloud is double of the sum of all the DFOU TCO ($K = 2$), migrating to community GC is convenient for a number of cases greater than 117.

## 8    Conclusions and Future Works

The evolution of technological activities together with the increased volume of cases expected in the future make digital forensic activity squarely sitting on the G. Reese requirements for cloud convenience: if your usage patterns are relatively static, your savings in the cloud will be nominal (or potentially even nonexistent). On the other hand, if your consumption varies widely above or below planned capacity on an ongoing basis, your savings will be much higher. Hence, due to the availability of GC services and the need to rationalize the spending for LEAs, improving the quality, it is important to assess costs and evaluate alternatives. This paper has proposed a methodology to fulfill these requirements, depicting a scenario where the single DFOUs can benefit in terms of costs reduction and quality deriving from the migration to GC. The security requirement, due to the migration increased value for network attack, has been taken into account as a supplementary cost weighting on GC setup costs. Nonetheless, the results presented in this paper have to be completed, in future works, with the system dimensioning based on a queue model of the system and the allocation policy. In particular, the former describes the system behavior, following the dynamics of a continuous-time birth-death Markov process (Markov chain). This lossy system, where forensic operators enter the system if at least one of the software licenses is free, will be modeled assuming exponential inter-arrival time and service time, K servers, no queuing. The latter relies on the GC provider to supply their computing needs, requiring specific QoS to be maintained in order to meet the service requirements. The game theory approaches the problem where players want to maximize their returns which depend also on actions of other players. Vast literature (e.g. [29–31] where has been shown that Nash equilibrium always exists if the resource allocation game has feasible solutions) proposed game-theoretic method to solve the optimization problem of resource allocation from the viewpoint of the GC. Future works will complement this paper in these above-mentioned directions.

# References

1. Crane, B.: Digital Forensics: A Decade of Changes POLICE Magazine, 11 November 2013. http://www.policemag.com/blog/technology/story/2013/11/digital-forensics-a-decade-of-changes.aspx. Last access 26 February 2014
2. Forbes: 8 Hot Industries for Startups in 2013. http://www.forbes.com/pictures/fghj45fjl/4-digital-forensic-services/. Last access 26 February 2014
3. Garfinkel, S.: Digital forensics research: the next 10 years. Digital Invest. **7**, 64–73 (2010)
4. Beebe, N.: Digital forensics research: the good, the bad, and the unaddressed. In: Peterson, G., Shenoi, S. (eds.) Advances in Digital Forensics V. IFIP AICT, vol. 306, pp. 17–36. Springer, Heidelberg (2009)
5. Moore, T.: The economics of digital forensics. In: Proceedings of Workshop on Economics of Information Security (2006)
6. Cramm, S.: The truths about IT costs. Harvard Bus. Rev. **87**(2), 28 (2009)
7. Carr, N.: The end of corporate computing. Sloan Manage. Rev. **46**(3), 67–73 (2005)
8. Berstis, V.: Fundamentals of grid computing IBM Redbooks Paper, 12 November 2002. http://www.redbooks.ibm.com/redpapers/pdfs/redp3613.pdf. Last access 25 February 2014
9. Dharanibalan, G.: Want to move from CAPEX to OPEX? Think cloud. The Economic Times, 2013 2 2013. http://articles.economictimes.indiatimes.com/2013-02-27/news/37330988_1_cloud-service-providers-consumers-capital-expenditure. Last access 25 February 2014
10. Choudhary, V.: Comparison of software quality under perpetual licensing and software as a service. J. Manage. Inf. Syst. **2**(24), 141–165 (2007)
11. Kundra, V.: Federal Cloud Computing Strategy, 8 2 2011. https://www.dhs.gov/sites/default/files/publications/digital-strategy/federal-cloud-computing-strategy.pdf. Last access 25 February 2014
12. Federal Risk and Authorization Management Program (FedRAMP). www.fedramp.gov. Last access 25 February 2014
13. European Commission: Digital Agenda for Europe Available. http://ec.europa.eu/digital-agenda/. Last access 25 February 2014

14. European Commission: Unleashing the Potential of Cloud Computing in Europe, 27 September 2012. http://eur-lex.europa.eu/LexUriServ/LexUriServ.do?uri=COM:2012:0529:FIN:EN:PDF. Last access 24 February 2014
15. ENISA: Good Practice Guide for securely deploying Governmental Clouds (2013). http://www.enisa.europa.eu/activities/Resilience-and-CIIP/cloud-computing/good-practice-guide-for-securely-deploying-governmental-clouds. Last access 24 February 2014
16. Mell, P., Grance, T.: The NIST Definition of Cloud Computing. NIST-Special Publication 800–45, Gaithersburg (2011)
17. August, T., Niculescu, M.F., Shin, H.: Cloud implications on software network structure and security risks. In: Proceedings of WEIS 2013, 6 September 2013
18. Scientific Working Group on Digital Evidence (SWGDE): digital evidence standards, principles and best practices. https://www.swgde.org/documents/Current
19. Carrier, B., Spafford, E.: Getting physical with the digital investigation process. Int. J. Digital Evid. 2(2), 20 (2003)
20. Reese, G.: Cloud Application Architectures: Building Applications and Infrastructure in the Cloud. O'Reilly Media, Sebastopol (2009)
21. The National Technical Authority for Information Assurance: Extract from HMG IA Standard No.1, 10 2009. http://www.cesg.gov.uk/publications/Documents/business_impact_tables.pdf. Last access 27 February 2014
22. Gawen, E.: So what is IL3? A short guide to business impact levels HM Government-G-Cloud, 9 March 2012. http://gcloud.civilservice.gov.uk/2012/03/09/so-what-is-il3-a-short-guide-to-business-impact-levels/. Last access 27 February 2014
23. Schroeder, B., Gibson, G.: Disk failures in the real world: what does an MTTF of 1,000,000 Hours mean to you? In: Proceedings of 5th Usenix Conference File and Storage Technologies (FAST 07) (2007)
24. Walker, E., Brisken, W., Romney, J.: To lease or not to lease from storage clouds. IEEE Comput. 43(14), 44–50 (2010)
25. Brandwacht, L.: Master thesis:dimensioning the cloud, 11 January 2013. www.math.leidenuniv.nl/scripties/MasterBrandwacht.pdf. Last access 26 February 2014
26. Amit, G., Xia, C.H.: Learning curves and stochastic models for pricing and provisioning cloud computing service. Science 3, 99–109 (2011)
27. Phillips, R.L.: Pricing and Revenue Optimization. Stanford University Press, Stanford (2005)
28. Vasilakos AV, B., Lesser, V.: Evolutionary stable resource pricing strategies. In: Proceedings of ACM SIGCOMM, 17–21 August 2009, Barcelona, Spain (2009)
29. Doulamis, N., Doulamis, A., Litke, A., Panagakis, A.: Adjusted fair scheduling and non-linear workload prediction for QoS guarantees in grid computing. Comput. Commun. 30(3), 499–515 (2007)
30. Wei, G., Vasilakos, A.V., Zheng, Y., Xiong, N.: A game-theoretic method of fair resource allocation. J. Supercomput. 54, 252–269 (2010)
31. Mendel, T., Takahashi, S.: Enterprise IT budget outlook: Europe. Forrester Research, 2007. http://www.forrester.com/Research/Document/Excerpt/0,7211,41668,00.html

# Work in Progress on Pricing, Contracts, and Service Selection

# Performance Evaluation for Cost-Efficient Public Infrastructure Cloud Use

John O'Loughlin[✉] and Lee Gillam

Department of Computing, University of Surrey,
Guildford GU2 7XH, UK
{john.oloughlin, l.gillam}@surrey.ac.uk

**Abstract.** In this paper, we discuss the nature of variability in compute performance in Infrastructure Clouds and how this presents opportunities for Cloud Service Brokers (CSB) in relation to pricing. Performance variation in virtual machines of the same type and price raises specific issues for end users: (i) the time taken to complete a task varies with performance, and therefore costs also vary (ii) the number of instances required to meet a certain problem scale within a given time being variable, so costs depend on variations in scale needed to meet the requirement; (iii) different computational requirements are better satisfied by different hardware, and understanding the relationship between instance types and available resources implies further costs. We demonstrate such variability problems empirically in a Public Infrastructure Cloud, and use the data gathered to discuss performance price issues, and how a CSB may re-price instances based on their performance.

**Keywords:** Infrastructure clouds · Performance variation · Simulation · Brokers

## 1 Introduction

Infrastructure as a Service (IaaS) Clouds are multi-tenant environments where resources such as networks, storage and servers are multiplexed between large numbers of users. The main characteristics of such systems include: self-provisioning of resources, on-demand acquisition, and the illusion of infinite scalability. Clouds are a metered service, so users are charged for the (units of) resources they consume per unit of time. The ability of the provider to allow users to acquire large scale resources at speed, and then release them when no longer needed, is referred to as elasticity.

The flexibility offered by Infrastructure Clouds makes their use popular for a variety of purposes. However, a variety of concerns have been raised regarding their use including, but not limited to: data security, privacy and sovereignty; service availability and the potential for provider failure; vendor lock in; and performance. The latter concern is primarily one of variation in the performance of instances that are supposedly of the same type, and results in a number of issues for users, including:

(i) prices are the same irrespective of performance, but costs will vary with the amount of time required to undertake a task;

© Springer International Publishing Switzerland 2014
J. Altmann et al. (Eds.): GECON 2014, LNCS 8914, pp. 133–145, 2014.
DOI: 10.1007/978-3-319-14609-6_9

(ii)   as a consequence, when scaling an application the number of instances required to complete a certain amount of work in a given period of time may differ, and so the price for completing work is again variable;

(iii)  different computational requirements will be better met by certain kinds of hardware which may be more attainable in a particular geographical location and, for a given user, determining the best value to task relationship in and across instance types across all geographies for a given Infrastructure Cloud implies further costs.

There is an opportunity for a Cloud Service Broker (CSB) to address these kinds of performance and cost related issues by being able to provide instances of known performance, and re-pricing them according to such performance levels. However, accurate performance simulations would be needed in order to derive a performance distribution from which pricing schemes could, at minimum, encompass the costs of running a CSB, and beyond that to determine any profit margin. The priority for a CSB, then, is to obtain an accurate model of performance (variation).

In this paper we examine the issues that any such model of performance would need to consider. In particular, we show how performance is dependent on (1) location (2) account (3) workload and (4) VM allocation polices. The rest of the paper is structured as follows: in Sect. 2 we discuss at some length the formulation of Clouds in terms of offerings, hardware, and geographies, the intricacies of which are essential to understand for any meaningful simulation. Section 3 offers a methodology for determining performance variation in Infrastructure Clouds, with results from an example set of performance variation evaluations in Sect. 4. Based on these results, Sect. 5 discusses the opportunities and challenges for a CSB, and discusses the factors that must be taken into account when modeling performance variation. Section 6 presents our conclusions and offers suggestions for future work in respect to pricing and CSBs.

## 2  Background

Infrastructure Clouds, such as Amazon's Elastic Compute Cloud (EC2), Google's Compute Engine (GCE) and the Rackspace Open Cloud, are typically structured into Regions and Availability Zones (AZs) [1]. Regions correspond to geographical areas, and their infrastructure is isolated from each other. Amazon's EC2, for example, has 8 Regions in locations such as: North Virginia (us-east-1), Dublin (eu-west-1), and Sydney (ap-southeast-2).

Regions are physically comprised of multiple data centres, and these data centres are then structured into multiple AZs. From [2] we know that, as of 2012, the US-East-1 Region contained 10 data centres structured into 5 AZs. AZs power and network connections are independent of each other. The failure of one AZ should not, in theory, affect the operation of others in the same Region. In practice, failure cascade affecting multiple AZs has occurred on more than occasion, with one of the most serious on June 29th 2012. Rackspace is a notable exception to the AZ model, stating that they guarantee 100 % network availability [3] of the data centres which make up their Regions, and so claim there is no need to further expose the structure of the Region.

Amazon also adopts a non-exposure principle: it is entirely possible that the same AZ identifier, such as *us-east-1a*, may map to different data centres for different accounts, perhaps even different network segments. Further, larger Regions, such as US East which has 5 AZs, restrict all new customers to just 3. Therefore different accounts are quite likely to have access to quite different locations within a Region. EC2 is further complicated by the fact that there are 2 different EC2 platforms: Classic-EC2 and EC2-VPC. The primary difference between them is the more advanced network features the latter provides. In a recent change, all new accounts will only have access to EC2-VPC.

Providers use virtualisation technologies atop specific hardware and the host operating system, with Xen and KVM popular, to partition physical servers such that they can run one or more Virtual Machines (VMs). Each VM will be allocated one or more virtual CPUs (vCPUs), and the VM will be allocated CPU time via the hypervisor's scheduling. A running VM is commonly referred to as an instance, and all Cloud Infrastructure providers should support requests for on-demand instances which can be started and terminated as needed. In addition to on-demand, EC2 also supports reserved instances and spot instances [4]. Reserved instances are more akin to traditional hosting, purchased for either one year or three years, and require an up front payment that reserves the machine. In return, users are charged less per hour than for on-demand instances (depending on usage) and these can be turned on and off as required to avoid the additional usage costs - users are not charged additionally when the reserved instance is turned off. Spot instances make use of spare capacity but with unpredictability in availability. Indeed, price varies according to availability, and they can be reclaimed at any time without warning in order to support the higher value on-demand uses.

Instances are offered in a range of fixed sizes, know as instance types. Instance types typically specify some number of vCPUs, some amount of RAM, and some amount of local disk space. For example, an *m1.medium* instance on EC2 has 1 vCPU, 3.75 GB of RAM and 410 GB of local storage. Larger providers, such as EC2, GCE and HP, tend to group instance types into instance classes, also known as families. Instance types within the same instance class are typically 'multiples' of each other, for example, on EC2 the M1 class contains the *m1.large*, which has 2 vCPU, 7.5 GB of RAM and 820 GB of local storage, so has twice the resources as the *m1.medium*, whilst the *m1.xlarge* has 4 vCPU, 15 GB of RAM and 1640 GB of local storage – and so is twice the *m1.xlarge* and quadruple the *m1.medium*. The price-per-hour scales similarly. Within a given instance class, the ratio of number of vCPUs to RAM is the same for all types, and for the M1 class this ratio is 3.75, and the compute power of a vCPU is the same across the whole class. As such, larger instance types are 'more of the same' as compared to smaller types in the class. EC2 offers a range of instance classes: General Purpose, High CPU, High Memory and High Storage. Providers such as HP and GCE are following suit, albeit without any agreement on sizes.

Instance classes typically differ from each other in the following ways (1) ratio of vCPU to RAM (2) the amount of 'compute power' each vCPU in the class has (3) specialised hardware, such GPGPU cards and low latency networking. For (2), providers have devised their own ratings for specifying the amount of 'compute power' that a vCPU will have. For example, EC2 has the EC2 Compute Unit (ECU), GCE has the Google Compute Engine Unit (GCEU) and HP Cloud use the HP Cloud Compute Unit (HPCCU). Provider supplied ratings are typically defined in terms of equivalence to specified hardware. As an example, GCE define a GCEU as: '...we choose 2.75 GCEUs to represent the minimum power of one logical core (a hardware hyper-thread) on our Sandy Bridge or Ivy Bridge platform'. These measures are typically used to express the expected relative performance of instances on the same Cloud, and so, on GCE, an instance with a vCPU core rated at 5.5 GCEUs should perform twice as well as one rated at 2.75 GCEUs. How these ratings are determined is not made public.

It is generally assumed that providers use a combination of 'weights' and 'limits' [5] to provide a guaranteed amount of CPU resources per vCPU. A weight indicates an amount of CPU time that the hypervisor should schedule for one vCPU relative to other vCPUs. For example, a vCPU with weight 100 will get half the CPU time as a vCPU with weight 200. As new VMs are started on hosts, and existing ones terminate, the number of vCPUs actually running on a host will fluctuate, so the amount of CPU resource per vCPU varies. Without a limit to both the number of vCPUs that can run on a host, and a maximum weight of vCPU, a minimum amount of CPU resource per vCPU cannot be guaranteed. With such limits are in place, providers can allocate a minimum amount of resources per vCPU. However, if the physical host is not at full capacity, i.e. the number of vCPUs running is less than the specified maximum, additional CPU resources are available. Some providers let extant processes use spare cycles, and refer to 'performance bursting': a minimum CPU resource per vCPU is guaranteed but the vCPU can use any additional available capacity. Rackspace [6], in particular, allows for this, but given the difficulty in predicting when these extra resources will be available to a given VM it is hard to see how their use could be planned for in anything other than a statistical sense. Another option for managing spare CPU capacity is based on a CPU limit, which sets a maximum amount of CPU resource available per vCPU. If a limit is set above the minimum, some bursting is possible. This is a potential gain for the user but generates no income for the provider. If a limit is set at the minimum, an instance's vCPUs has an amount of guaranteed CPU time but no more. From experimental data, as presented in Sect. 4, EC2 appears to operate this way. EC2 sells spare capacity as spot instances. This strategy appears beneficial to both user and EC2 – the user gets a consistent amount of CPU each time, and so making requirements planning easier, whilst the provider generates some income from otherwise unsold cycles.

Given the different characteristics of instance classes, it would seem that different hardware platforms are required to support different instance classes. This is certainly the case for specialised hardware such as GPGPU cards. However, even for classes such as M2 High Memory and M1 General Purpose, there would appear to be 2 very good reasons for supporting these classes with their own hardware platforms: (1) VM allocation is simplified; (2) Hypervisor vCPU scheduling is simplified. For (1), the number of vCPU for a given instance type determines the RAM and local storage, so we need only find hosts that have a given vCPU capacity. By comparison, if we mix classes on hosts we need to find a host that has sufficient vCPU, RAM and local storage. For (2) we need only set the same weight and limit per vCPU for each instance type.

On EC2, it is readily possible to identify the CPU model types backing a particular instance. From this one can begin to associate platforms with instance classes - indeed, for some instance classes this is advertised: the General Purpose M3 Class runs on *Intel Xeon E5-2670 v2* (Sandy Bridge), the C3 High CPU Class runs on *Intel Xeon E5-2680 v2* (Ivy Bridge) and the R3 High Memory Class runs on *Intel Xeon E5-2670 (Ivy Bridge)*. Whilst the M3, C3 and R3, classes are currently associated with one hardware platform each, this is not the case for older instance classes. Indeed, the General Purpose M1 class is currently associated with at least 6. We have found, in addition to EC2, instance type heterogeneity exists on GoGrid, and also on Standard instance types from Rackspace. A number of papers have reported on performance variation on EC2, and some identify heterogeneity as the major cause: Armbrust et al. [15] describe EC2 performance as unpredictable; Osterman et al. [16] describe performance in the Cloud as unreliable; Yelick et al. [17] found that "applications in the Cloud...experience significant performance variations" and noted that this is in part caused by heterogeneity (of EC2); Phillips et al. [18] discovered differential performance in instances of the same type on EC2 when attempting to predict application performance. In respect to Regions, Schad et al. [19] showed that compute performance in US East N. California and EU West Dublin falls into two distinct performance bands which, upon further investigation breaks out by the two different CPU models backing their instances. Interestingly for our work, Ou et al. [20], suggest that the heterogeneous nature of Clouds can be exploited by estimating the probability of obtaining a particular CPU model backing an instance.

Understanding platform variation within an instance class, initially, is important because the compute performance of an instance is primarily determined by the platform it is running on. The time taken to complete an amount of work will depend on the hardware platform, and therefore the cost of completing the work also differs. We examine performance variation in detail in Sects. 3 and 4.

## 3   Experimental Setup

EC2 performance variations by CPU model have been widely reported on, as seen in the previous section. To produce valid simulations, we need to establish how performance varies by (1) location (2) account and (3) application. For the purpose of this paper, we explore the nature of running instances in all accessible AZs across 2 Regions (with respect to 1) using two different accounts (for 2) and a number of well known application-oriented benchmarks (3). Experiments were performed during April and May 2014, with two EC2 accounts that we refer to as account A and account B. We believe that Clouds inevitably become heterogeneous over time, and so the range of platforms backing a given instance class is also heterogeneous. We therefore choose older Regions to see if this is supported: US-East-1, which is the original EC2 Region coming online in 2006, has 5 AZs, and is the default Region for requests if no Region is selected; and EU-West-1 which is the only European based Region at the time of writing, was the second Region to come online, in 2007, and offers 3 AZs.

Being financially constrained, we decided to use instances from the spot market. This gave us access to the same resources that both reserved and on-demand instances are sold from at reduced prices. As discussed, such instances can be reclaimed by EC2 when needed, and indeed this did happen to some of the instances run by account B before they were able to finish and report back results – as such, sample numbers may not be neatly rounded: we ended up with 350 instances for A, and 161 for B. Instances ran the official EC2 Precise Ubuntu AMIs supplied by Canonical (the ami-id differs by Region).

There are numerous metrics for compute performance that include floating point operations per second (FLOPs) and millions of instructions per second (MIPS). It is generally accepted that the performance metrics that are most useful and most informative to a user are: execution time and throughput [7, 8]. Execution time is defined as the wall clock time for an application to execute, and is often referred to as application latency, and with hourly pricing for Infrastructure Clouds is a helpful measure for relating to costs. Where an application can be thought of as doing some specified unit of work, for example a file compression, an image rendering or a video transcoding, we define throughput, or application bandwidth, as the work done per unit of time. This metric allows users to relate amount of work done per unit of time to cost.

When measuring compute performance by application execution time or throughput, appropriate applications need to chosen. Applications which are CPU bound are generally good candidates, as the CPU is then the main factor in their performance. However, care must be taken in order to avoid common pitfalls. Small applications may fit into the CPU instruction cache and so their execution time will not be affected by access speeds associated with the various memory hierarchies. Difficulties in CPU comparability have led to a preference for so-called 'real world' benchmarks – CPU bound applications which are in common use, being run with realistic inputs. Such a preference is typified by the Standard Performance Evaluation Corporation (SPEC) benchmark suite [9], and we follow this approach to benchmarking.

In each of our instances, we run the following benchmarks in serial:

- Bzip2: File compression using ubuntu 10.04 ISO image for input
- POV-Ray: Photo realistic ray tracing using the standard benchmark.pov for input
- GNUGO: The Go Game with test.sgf
- NAMD: Bio molecular simulation using apoa1.namd
- STREAM: Memory bandwidth.

The first 4 benchmarks are part of the SPEC 2006 benchmark suite, with bzip2 [10] and GNUGO [11] measuring integer performance, whilst POV-Ray [12] and NAMD [13] measure floating point performance. For NAMD and POV-Ray we used the same input files as SPEC, however these were not available for bzip2 or GNUGO. The example input file for Go is freely available at the Go KGS homepage. STREAM [14] is a well known benchmark used for measuring memory bandwidth; the results reported here are for the triad kernel. The results of these experiments are described below.

## 4   Performance Variation

In this section, we present a selection of results chosen to illustrate the considerations that we believe are important, and that would need to be factored into any subsequent performance simulations.

## 4.1    Variation by CPU Model

In Fig. 1, we present a histogram of the POV-Ray execution times, with an interval width of 2.5 s. The histogram might be looked at as an emergent unimodal distribution with samples yet unseen at various intervals, but could also be seen as a multi-modal distribution. As discussed in Sect. 2, we know that performance variation if often caused by differences in the CPU model underlying the instances, and we identified 6 different CPU models backing our instances: AMD 2281, Intel Xeon E5645, Intel Xeon E5507, Intel Xeon E5-2650, Intel Xeon E5-2651 and Intel Xeon E5430.

In Fig. 2, we present a histogram broken down by CPU model, and we see that the performance of POV-Ray is primarily determined by the CPU model the instance is running on, and there is little overlap in performance of the various CPU models, with the exception of the E5-2650 and E5-2561.

It is interesting to note that the very newest hardware platform in this set, the E5-2651 is outperformed by 4 of the older platforms. The AMD 2218 is a circa 2007 CPU model and outperforms all models here apart from an isolated number of E5645. It is often assumed that as Infrastructure Clouds introduce new platforms, these will outperform older generations, and such performance improvements will accrue to users without any increases in price. This is clearly not always the case.

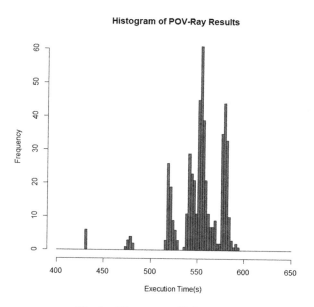

**Fig. 1.** Histogram of POV-Ray.

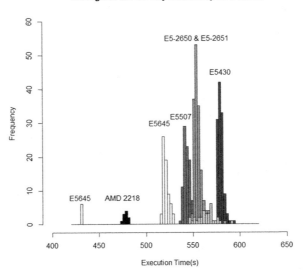

Fig. 2. Histogram of POV-Ray by CPU model.

## 4.2    Performance Variation by Application

POV-Ray results appear to depend on the CPU model, and here we have a best CPU model – the AMD 2218 (bar a few isolated E5645). It is natural to ask if we have identified a 'best' CPU model for *all* applications, and further, whether or not the ordering of CPU models by performance, is the same for different applications. Interestingly, this is not the case as the performance histograms for bzip2, GNUGO, NAMD and STREAM in Fig. 3 demonstrate, and so the relationship between CPU model and the nature of the application is important.

## 4.3    Performance Variation by Location

The physical composition of EC2 will evolve over time, for example as new Regions and AZs are added, and existing hardware is refreshed. As such, it is natural to ask if there are performance differences by location. Because identifiers such as *us-east-1a* potentially map to different locations for different accounts, we compare the mean results of the benchmarks across all these AZs for the instances for account A.

The percentage increase in mean execution time between the respective worst and best performing AZ is under 10 % for POV-Ray, 15 % for bzip2, and for STREAM the throughput difference is close to 100 %. This would seem to support an argument that, with one or two exceptions, there is a little performance difference across AZs – and so no obvious advantage in choosing one over another. However, these numbers hide a lot of detail. The histogram below shows the POV-Ray results for *us-east-1a* and *us-east-1c*, which, from Table 1, provide very similar mean performance (Fig. 4).

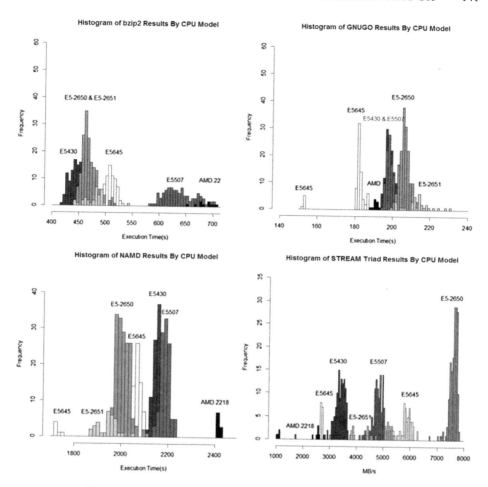

**Fig. 3.** Histograms of bzip2, GNUGO, NAMD and STREAM.

**Table 1.** Account A benchmark means across 5 AZs.

|              | us-east-1a | us-east-1c | us-east-1d | eu-west-1a | eu-west 1b |
|--------------|------------|------------|------------|------------|------------|
| POV-Ray(s)   | 559        | 551        | 569        | 519        | 558        |
| Bzip2(s)     | 520        | 473        | 481        | 511        | 544        |
| GNUGO(s)     | 196        | 203        | 198        | 184        | 198        |
| NAMD(s)      | 2154       | 2009       | 2160       | 2104       | 2183       |
| STREAM (MB/s)| 4195       | 7268       | 3669       | 4253       | 3955       |

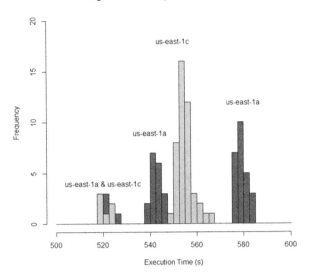

**Fig. 4.** POV-Ray us-east-1a V us-east-1c

We can see that both of these AZs have some overlap of instances which are performing around 520 s. AZ us-east-1a then has two levels of performance: one at just over 540 s and one at 580 s. Most instances in *us-east-1c* are performing around 550 s. We can best understand this by looking the percentages of CPU models found in the *us-east-1a* and *us-east-1a* respectively (Table 2).

**Table 2.** CPU model distribution

|            | E5645 | E5430 | E5507 | E-2650 |
|------------|-------|-------|-------|--------|
| us-east-1a | 12 %  | 50 %  | 38 %  | 0 %    |
| us-east-1c | 12 %  | 0 %   | 0 %   | 88 %   |

Whilst mean performance is similar for both AZs, there does appear to be a strategy a user could adopt with us-east-1a to obtain better performance: keep instances backed by E5507, and throw away the E5430 instances – a *deploy-and-ditch* strategy. Over time, most instances would then perform at 545 s or better. For *us-east-1c*, the only possibility for a similar strategy would be to keep E5645 and throw away E5-2650. With nearly 90 % of the instances in this AZ backed by the E5-2650 this would clearly be much more expensive (the cost of an E5645-only strategy in *us-east-1a* would be a similar). Where performance consistency is important to a user, it is arguable that *us-east-1c* is better than *us-east-1a*.

## 4.4 Performance Variation by Account

As different accounts appear to have access to different AZs, obtainable performance can also differ by account. The accounts used in these experiments have mappings suggesting the following AZs in US-East-1 and EU-West-1:

**Account A:** us-east-1a, us-east-1c, us-east-1d, eu-west-1a, eu-west-1b and eu-west-1c.

**Account B:** us-east-1a, us-east-1b, us-east-1d, eu-west-1a, eu-west-1b and eu-west-1c.

We compare performance for *us-east-1a* for both our accounts in Table 3:

**Table 3.** us-east-1a

| Account | POV-Ray(s) | Bzip2(s) | GNUGO(s) | NAMD(s) | STREAM MB/s |
|---------|-----------|----------|----------|---------|-------------|
| A | 559 | 520 | 196 | 2154 | 4195 |
| B | 551 | 469 | 205 | 2008 | 7342 |

For account A, there is an 11 % increase in mean bzip2 execution time and 7 % for NAMD. There is also a significant decrease in the memory bandwidth in A's instances as compared to B. Of the instances obtained by account B, 90 % were backed by the E5-2650, and the remaining was E5645. Account A obtains a mix of E5430, E5645 and E5507 – but no E5-2650. It is possible that this is simply due to chance, and is a function of resource availability at the time of request. Another possibility is that *us-east-1a* is a different location, and so a different set of resources, for both accounts. If this is the case, then for account B, performance will be consistent, but with no opportunity for obtaining better performance than is offered by an E5-2650, whilst for account A, such strategies are available.

# 5 Potential Opportunities for a CSB

Fixed prices for resources of the same type, together with a metered service, should offer users a consistent and predictable pricing for their Cloud usage. However, performance variation in instances of the same type results in variable and unpredictable costs. The absence of Service Level Agreements (SLAs) offering QoS terms with respect to compute performance presents an opportunity for a CSB who could deliver instances of known performance, at a price related to the performance. A CSB can exploit the fact that different CPU models are better, or worse, for different applications, to provide a 'match making' service between a users application specific performance needs and available Cloud resources.

Whilst a user is of course free to engage in such work themselves, there is a cost in doing so, and this cost depends upon the various factors discussed in Sect. 4. Of course, there are also costs involved for a CSB. However, by dealing with a multiplicity of application needs (from perspective clients) over a larger range of Cloud resources a CSB is likely to be able make greater use of resources obtained than an individual Cloud user. As such, the cost a CSB incurs in obtained instance of a desired performance level will, in general, be less than individual users. For example, a user wishing to run POV-Ray who obtains an instance backed by a E5430 may well look to 'ditch' this instance in favor of obtaining another CPU model. However, a CSB would view this instance as very good for bzip2 and reasonable for GNUGO.

Such a service could be advantageous to users in the following ways: (1) it offers better performance than a user may be able to obtain themselves; (2) it eliminates the variation due to differing resources (CPUs) being obtained; (3) it provides the required performance when the user requires it, so offers performance on-demand. Of course, determining appropriate pricing schemes is now crucial, for both incentivizing users and allowing the CSB to run at a profit. Consequently, developing simulations of performance pricing are needed, and in turn this requires using a realistic model of how Clouds currently works - one which takes into account that performance variation is a factor of (1) CPU model, (2) application, (3) location, (4) account.

## 6   Conclusions and Future Work

In this paper, we have discussed the nature of variability in performance in Infrastructure Clouds and how this presents opportunities for Cloud Service Brokers (CSB) in relation to pricing. We have shown that performance variation exists in various ways, for machine instances purportedly offering the same capability, across geographical regions and zones, across user accounts, and most importantly across heterogeneous hardware backing machine instances, and identified the kinds of issues that this raises for end users. Further, we have demonstrated how such variability problems present in a real Public Infrastructure Cloud and how these can be application-specific.

From the data gathered from our experiments, we have been able to suggest how performance variation could be simulated such that a CSB could consider strategies for usefully re-pricing instances based on their performance in order to ensure profitability. The next step for this work is to use such a formulation and develop and evaluate the simulation.

## References

1. Regions. http://docs.aws.amazon.com/AWSEC2/latest/UserGuide/using-regions-availability-zones.html
2. AWS Service Event. http://aws.amazon.com/message/67457/
3. Rackspace Datacenters. http://www.rackspace.com/about/datacenters/
4. EC2 Purchasing Options. http://aws.amazon.com/ec2/purchasing-options/
5. Xen Credit Scheduler. http://wiki.xen.org/wiki/Credit_Scheduler
6. Rackspace Performance Cloud Servers. http://www.rackspace.com/knowledge_center/article/what-is-new-with-performance-cloud-servers
7. Lilja, D.: Measuring Computer Performance. Cambridge University Press, New York (2000)
8. Hennessy, J., Patterson, D.: Computer Architecture a Quantitative Approach, 5th edn. Elsevier, Waltham (2012)
9. Standard Performance Evaluation Corporation. http://www.spec.org
10. Bzip2. http://www.bzip.org

11. GNU Go. http://www.gnugo.org
12. Persistence of Vision. http://www.povray.org
13. NAMD Scalable Molecular Dynamics. http://www.ks.uiuc.edu/Research/namd/
14. STREAM: Sustainable Memory Bandwidth in High Performance Computers. http://www.cs.virginia.edu/stream/
15. Armbrust, M., Fox, A., Griffith, R., Joseph, A.D., Katz, R.H., Konwinski, A., Lee, G., Patterson, D.A., Rabkin, A., Stoica, I., Zaharia, M.: Above the clouds: a Berkeley view of cloud computing, Technical Report EECS-2008-28, EECS Department, University of California, Berkeley (2009)
16. Ostermann, S., Iosup, A., Yigitbasi, N., Prodan, R., Fahringer, T., Eperna, D.: A Performance Analysis of EC2 Cloud Computing Services for Scientific Computing. In: Avresky, D.R., Diaz, M., Bode, A., Ciciani, B., Dekel, E. (eds.) Cloudcomp 2009. LNICST, vol. 34, pp. 115–131. Springer, Heidelberg (2010)
17. Yelick, K., Coghlan, S., Draney, B., Canon, R.S.: The Magellan Report on Cloud Computing for Science (2011). http://www.alcf.anl.gov/magellan
18. Phillips, S., Engen, V., Papay, J.: Snow white clouds and the seven dwarfs. In: Proceedings of the IEEE International Conference and Workshops on Cloud Computing Technology and Science, pp. 738–745 (2011)
19. Schad, J., Dittrich, J., Quiane-Ruiz, J.-A.: Runtime measurements in the cloud: Observing, analyzing, and reducing variance. Proc. VLDB Endow. 3(1–2), 460–471 (2010)
20. Ou, Z., et al.: Exploiting Hardware Heterogeneity within the same instance type of Amazon EC2. In: Presented at 4th USENIX Workshop on Hot Topics in Cloud Computing, Boston (2012)

# Balancing Leasing and Insurance Costs to Achieve Total Risk Coverage in Cloud Storage Multi-homing

Maurizio Naldi[⊠]

Department of Computer Science and Civil Engineering,
Università di Roma Tor Vergata, Via del Politecnico 1, 00133 Rome, Italy
naldi@disp.uniroma2.it
http://www.maurizionaldi.it

**Abstract.** Cloud storage multi-homing (a.k.a. as multicloud) represents a possible solution to achieve enhanced availability of one's own data and build an extremely reliable cloud environment out of relatively unreliable single cloud platforms. However, subscribing with multiple cloud providers comes at a cost. The cost of multiple subscriptions must be compared against the damage resulting from the possible temporary unavailability of the data stored on the cloud. A complementary approach is to protect against the economic damage resulting from data unavailability by subscribing an insurance policy. In this paper we investigate the complementary use of cloud multi-homing and insurance to obtain a total risk coverage against data unavailability. We provide a total cost function, which incorporates the cost of cloud subscriptions and the insurance premium, and investigate the possibility of trade-offs to achieve a total risk coverage at minimum cost.

**Keywords:** Cloud storage · Multicloud · Multi-homing · Insurance · Costs · Network Economics

## 1 Introduction

Cloud storage is a fast growing service, whereby an individual or a company stores its data on a storage facility owned and managed by a third party (the cloud provider). Resorting to cloud storage allows users to eliminate their own storage infrastructure. Migrating from an owned infrastructure to a leased one has immediate benefits but also raises several concerns, so that several issues have to be considered in the migration decision as well as a comprehensive cost model [4,9]. A major benefit in switching to the cloud consists in moving from a cost structure made of capital investments to a more flexible one based on operational expenses only [10,12,24]. However, capital investments are one-off in nature but they may lead to savings in the long run [14]. In addition, switching to the cloud may expose the cloud user to the lock-in phenomenon and price rises [13,18].

© Springer International Publishing Switzerland 2014
J. Altmann et al. (Eds.): GECON 2014, LNCS 8914, pp. 146–158, 2014.
DOI: 10.1007/978-3-319-14609-6_10

Among the several issues, an outstanding one is that related to reliability, for which very few measurement data exist and concerns have been raised [17]. Storage on multiple clouds (a.k.a. as multicloud or cloud multi-homing) has been suggested to enhance reliability [15,20].

However large the improvement in reliability due to the use of multiple clouds, we must recognize that this approach cannot zero the probability of not being able to access its own data and comes anyway at the considerable cost of multiplying the storage costs. In [11], it has been shown that an alternative strategy to protect against the risk of an unavailable platform (in [11] it was a network, but the reasoning may be applied equally well to a cloud platform) can be subscribing an insurance policy. The two solutions (multicloud and insurance) can therefore be combined to achieve total risk coverage against cloud unavailability: using multiple clouds reduces the unavailability time and the insurance policy covers the residual risk.

In this paper, we investigate this combined approach. We consider simple models for the availability of a multi-cloud configuration and the insurance premium to be paid for a given availability level and arrive at an overall cost of the multi-cloud-plus-insurance solution. The total cost model allows us to formulate the conditions under which total risk coverage can be achieved by minimizing the total cost.

The paper is organized as follows. We review reliability analyses of cloud platforms and provide a simple model for the availability of a multicloud configuration in Sect. 2. The two cost components due to storage and insurance are described respectively in Sects. 3 and 4. The optimization of costs for a combined approach (multi-homing plus insurance) is investigated in Sect. 5.

## 2    Availability of Cloud Storage Service

The visibility a user has of its data on a cloud is very limited. Despite the cost savings that appear to be a major reason to move to the cloud, the user wishes the availability of its data to be at least equal to what an in-house solution would provide. This may not be the case. In this section, we provide a very basic analysis of the reliability of a cloud solution. After reviewing some definitions of availability, we first review the current (few) works on the actual availability of commercial clouds and then report a very simple model to predict the enhanced availability resulting from a multi-homing approach to clouds. In this paper, we deal neither with specific techniques to achieve a higher availability nor with standards concerning data management interfaces or engineering guidelines (see, e.g., the work carried out within the ENSI NFV Reliability and Availability WG). We adopt a user-centric view, where the cloud storage service is either available when the user wants to retrieve its data or it is not, denying the user the possibility to access its data.

Venkatesan and Iliadis have shown that the reliability of a data center depends very little on the assumptions adopted for the time-to-failure of individual storage nodes (i.e., the assumption of independent and exponentially-distributed failure times) as long as the individual nodes are generally reliable (i.e., their mean time to failure is much longer than their mean time to repair) [23].

Baker et al. have investigated the behaviour of large-scale storage systems in the long run, assessing a wider set of failure root causes than that traditionally examined in reliability analyses [1]. They formulated strategies to improve long-term reliability, by acting primarily on the reduction of the mean time to repair.

Though addressing the related case of a data center network, Gill et al. have performed a thorough reliability analysis. They found that the data center network exhibits high reliability with more than four 9's of availability for about 80 % of the links and for about 60 % of the devices in the network [6].

Other data concerning the reliability of storage platforms tell us that the MTTR (Mean-Time-To-Repair) of individual storage nodes is in the order of tens of hours [23], while the MTTR of visible faults (those that are detected shortly after they occur) is 1.4 h for a mirrored disk and 4.4 h for a mirrored archive [1].

One of the few reliability studies concerning instead the specific case of a cloud storage platform is that performed on Google's main storage infrastructure [5]. In that study, Ford et al. investigated the availability of single components of the complex cloud environment and the impact of correlated failures, arriving at an estimate of the unavailability of data stripes (data is divided into a set of stripes, each of which comprises a set of fixed size data and code blocks called chunks), with figures in the range $10^{-7} \div 10^{-3}$ depending on the time of the day.

Since quantitative assessments of the availability of clouds based on extensive measurement campaigns are typically not reported by cloud providers, an alternative approach has been taken in [17] to try a third-party assessment based on outage as reported by customers themselves. After collecting data from a number of sources about 5 major cloud providers, it has been shown that the average duration of outages was over 8 h for 3 out of 5 providers (the actual figures ranged from 95 to 607 min).

A third party assessment of cloud storage availability has been provided in [7] for Amazon and Google, whose availability has resulted respectively equal to 99.565 % and 99.783 % (higher figures result if successive retries after the first failures are included). Some limits of that analysis have been reported in [16].

Most cloud storage providers specify the availability of their service, though they typically fail to provide guarantees or include tight performance levels in their SLA. In the survey reported in [3], 15 providers out of 17 declared at least 99.9 % availability, with 12 providers declared 100 % availability.

Whatever the availability expected from a single cloud, it has been suggested that we can achieve a higher reliability by employing multiple clouds at the same time. For example, in [15], erasure coding has been employed to create redundant data shares and spread the original data to different cloud providers. In that case, a combination of up to 7 storage providers was considered and shown to provide a lower read latency. Zhai et al. have also highlighted that the availability resulting from a multi-cloud strategy may not be as high as expected according to the independence hypothesis, since hidden interdependencies may appear due to third-party infrastructure components shared by redundant deployments [26], and have suggested the use of a recommender system to take into account those hidden interdependencies.

In this paper, we do not consider a specific strategy to disseminate data among several clouds to optimize the overall reliability. Instead we consider, for sake of simplicity, a general strategy relying on the simple replication of the same volume of data among several totally independent cloud providers. For each cloud, we assume that the service follows a simple ON-OFF process, where the data are either available for the user to retrieve or they are (temporarily) not. Unavailability of data does not mean data loss: the user will be able to retrieve again its data after the outage has ended. Under such basic assumptions, we can compute the availability in a multi-homing approach with a very simple model. For our purposes, we consider the overall availability of data over a cloud. For a single cloud, we define $A_1$ as the probability that a data retrieval operation is successful. Let's consider a customer subscribing a contract with $n$ cloud storage providers. For simplicity we assume that all cloud providers guarantee the same availability $A_1$ and that failures take place at providers independently of one another. The customer can access its data if even a single provider is operating. The probability $1 - A_n$ of not being able to retrieve the data with any of the $n$ clouds (a classical parallel configuration), where $A_n$ is the resulting availability of the data over $n$ clouds, is therefore

$$1 - A_n = (1 - A_1)^n \implies A_n = 1 - (1 - A_1)^n. \tag{1}$$

If the availability of a single cloud is expressed as the number $w_1$ of nines (e.g., if $A_1 = 0.999$ then $w_1 = 3$), the availability of a group of $n$ clouds exhibits the number $w_n$ of nines. In fact, $A_1 = 1 - 10^{-w_1}$ and

$$A_n = 1 - 10^{-nw_1} = 1 - 10^{-w_n}, \tag{2}$$

with $w_n = nw_1$. Therefore the addition of a cloud increases the number of nines by the number of nines of a single cloud. If we start with a cloud with two nines, the solution with 2 clouds will exhibit four nines, and so on.

On the other hand, Eq. (1) can be inverted to compute the number of clouds needed to achieve a desired value of availability

$$n = \frac{\ln(1 - A_n)}{\ln(1 - A_1)}, \tag{3}$$

though Eq. (3) should be modified by employing a ceiling function so as to get integer solutions.

## 3   Storage Leasing Costs

Enhancing availability through multi-homing has the obvious disadvantage of subscribing to multiple clouds and paying the pertaining costs. In this section, we review the current pricing policies of commercial clouds and provide a model to arrive at the overall cost of a multi-homing approach. We rely on the current market situation, though more advanced pricing models have been considered, especially for cloud computing [2, 22].

In [19], a survey of current cloud storage pricing practices has been presented. The survey considered 8 commercial cloud storage providers, which offer pricing plans both for consumers and business customers. It has been shown that the pricing models adopted by them can be classified into just two pricing scheme, namely Block rate pricing and Bundling pricing, with just Amazon following the former and the remaining 7 adopting the latter.

In Block rate pricing, the range of consumption is subdivided into subranges, and the unit price is held constant over each subrange. More formally, in a block rate tariff the overall price $p$ charged to the customer for a storage volume $d$ is

$$
p = \begin{cases}
v_1 d & \text{if } 0 < d \leq q_1 \\
v_1 q_1 + v_2(d - q_1) & \text{if } q_1 < d \leq q_2 \\
\cdots & \\
\displaystyle\sum_{i=1}^{m-1} v_i q_i + v_m(d - q_{m-1}) & \text{if } q_{m-1} < d \leq q_m
\end{cases}
\tag{4}
$$

where the $v_i$'s are the sequence of marginal prices, and the $q_i$'s bracket the subranges over which the marginal price is held constant. In Eq. (4), we assume that the cloud provider does not provide more than $q_m$ units of storage ($m \geq 2$). In turn, block rate pricing can be seen as a special form of multi-part tariff, where the fixed fee has been set equal to zero.

The overall charge is then a piecewise linear function of the amount of storage capacity (see Fig. 1). Diminishing prices at the margin stimulate consumption, which in turn permits the construction of large scale capacity.

The pricing model adopted by all cloud providers but one is instead bundling pricing, where several pricing schemes are proposed for a fixed fee. Each scheme allows the customer to store data up to a maximum volume. Since the pricing schemes can be sorted by the allowed maximum volume, we can derive a price-volume relationship, which is a step function. A sample price function is shown in Fig. 2.

In [19], we have also shown that a suitable approximation of such pricing models, convenient for a mathematical treatment, is the two-part tariff, In the two-part tariff scheme, where the customer pays an initial fixed fee $f$ for the first block of data (often justified as a subscription, access, or installation charge), plus a smaller constant price for each unit [25]. This model is equivalent to the block-rate scheme is just a single range is considered in Eq. (4). It is as well a linear approximation of the staircase pricing relationship applying in bundling pricing. The two-part tariff is therefore a suitable approximation of both dominant pricing plans. The overall price charged to the customer is then

$$
p_{\text{sto}} = f + v \cdot d,
\tag{5}
$$

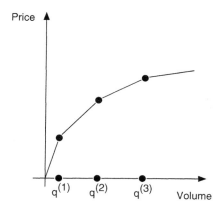

**Fig. 1.** Price-volume relationship in block rate pricing

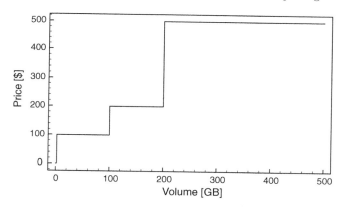

**Fig. 2.** Sample price-volume relationship in bundling pricing

where $v$ is the marginal price, and $d$ is the volume of consumption, i.e., the amount of storage volume.

If we consider a multi-homing approach, the customer is actually subscribing $n$ cloud storage contracts. If we assume, for simplicity, that all providers adopt the same two-part tariff pricing scheme, the overall expense for the customer is

$$p_{\text{sto}} = n(f + v \cdot d). \tag{6}$$

## 4   Insurance Against Unavailability

In Sect. 2, we have seen that the availability of the cloud can be improved by resorting to multiple clouds, up to the point of creating a reliable storage environment out of many relatively unreliable clouds. However, in Sect. 3 we have also seen that this involves a multiplication of storage costs. Since the ultimate negative consequence of unreliable storage is the money loss deriving from the inability to access its own data for the duration of the storage blackout, a possible remedy is the subscription of an insurance policy. In this section, we describe such a possibility and provide the formula which relates the insurance premium to the expected unavailability.

Let's assume that the customer has subscribed to $n$ different cloud storage providers, where $n$ can even be just 1. This allows the customer to expect an overall availability $A_n$ provided by Eq. (1). Though the customer can make this value arbitrarily high by increasing the number of cloud providers, this approach cannot be pushed too far. In fact, the number of providers is anyway limited and the addition of a further provider increases the cost. Though adding clouds increases quite fast the overall availability of the cloud as embodied by Eq. (2), full availability can never be reached.

A complementary approach is to accept that the availability of the cloud can never be 1, though increasingly close, and subscribe an insurance policy to cover the damage resulting from the remaining unavailability periods. The insurance solution comes of course at a cost, represented by the insurance premium, i.e., the price to be paid to subscribe the insurance policy.

In [11], the premium expression has been derived for the case where the failing system is a network and a simple ON-OFF continuous-time Markov process is assumed to model the occurrence of failures and the restoring of normal operations. The expected duration of the ON period is the MTBF (Mean Time Between Failures), while the expected duration of the OFF period is the MTTR (Mean Time To Restore). The pricing principle adopted follows the expected utility model, with the utility function exhibiting Constant Absolute Risk Aversion (CARA) property [8,21]. Since no specific features of a network are exploited, we can adopt the same model here. If we consider that the insurance policy is subscribed over the same period of time for which the cloud subscription fee applies, and we normalize all time measures to that time scale, the premium $p_{\mathrm{ins}}$ for a volume of data $d$ is

$$p_{\mathrm{ins}} = kd\frac{1 - A_n}{A_n}\left(1 + \alpha k\frac{\mathrm{MTTR}}{n}\right),\qquad(7)$$

where $\alpha$ is the risk aversion coefficient, $k$ is the money loss per data unit (e.g., per each GB) over the whole policy validity period, and the MTTR refers to a single cloud (expressed as a fraction of the overall policy validity period). The inclusion of the factor $k$ allows to account for the different value we attach to the unavailability of data, which may depend on their use: delaying the listening of an MP3 song bears probably a much lower damage than delaying the access to an X-ray image needed for a remote diagnosis.

## 5   Trade-offs in Multi-homing

In Sects. 3 and 4 we have described the two components of costs, respectively the cost of leasing storage space on several clouds and that of subscribing an insurance policy to cover against the risk of data unavailability. By combining the two operations, the user can achieve a total risk coverage strategy, where the insurance policy covers the money loss resulting from the less-than-100 % availability. In fact, the user may decide to subscribe to more clouds achieving a higher availability: the cost of storage leasing will grow, but at the same time the insurance premium will go down because of the increased availability. The overall cost of the risk coverage strategy is the sum of the cost of the two components. A trade-off can be pursued where to achieve a lower overall cost by a careful choice of the number of clouds. In this section, we examine the overall multi-homing cost and investigate the possible trade-offs.

If we recall the cost of leasing storage from $n$ cloud providers, given by Eq. (6), and the cost of subscribing an insurance policy, given by Eq. (7), we obtain the following overall cost in a multi-homing strategy

$$p_n = p_{\text{sto}} + p_{\text{ins}} = n(f + v \cdot d) + kd\frac{1 - A_n}{A_n}\left(1 + \alpha k\frac{\text{MTTR}}{n}\right) \tag{8}$$

$$= n(f + v \cdot d) + kd\frac{(1 - A_1)^n}{1 - (1 - A_1)^n}\left(1 + \alpha k\frac{\text{MTTR}}{n}\right).$$

If we consider that the availability of even a single cloud is typically very close to 1 (we can assume at least a two nine availability), we have

$$p_n \simeq n(f + v \cdot d) + kd(1 - A_1)^n\left(1 + \alpha k\frac{\text{MTTR}}{n}\right). \tag{9}$$

We see that the two components have a different behaviour when the number of clouds grows: the cost of storage grows linearly, while the cost of insurance decreases (roughly exponentially fast). Though $\lim_{N \to \infty} p_{\text{ins}} = 0$, the multi-homing approach cannot be pushed too far, because of the linear growth of storage costs which makes the overall cost grow linearly in the end. It is to be seen if we can lower the overall cost for a moderate use of multi-homing with respect to a single cloud.

Let's consider first the double-homing case, so that we have to compare $p_1$ and $p_2$. For this case, we can formulate the following theorem.

**Theorem 1.** *The double homing approach is the cheapest if the unit price of storage satisfies the following inequality*

$$\frac{f}{d} + v < k\frac{1 - A_1}{2A_1}\frac{2 + (3 - A_1)\alpha \cdot k \cdot \text{MTTR}}{2 - A_1}$$

*Proof.* Let's define the gain achieved by switching to double-homing as $\Delta_1 = p_1 - p_2$. We recall the general expression of the total cost from Eq. (8) for the cases $n = 1, 2$ we have

$$\Delta_1 = kd\left[\frac{1 - A_1}{A_1}(1 + \alpha k\text{MTTR}) - \frac{(1 - A_1)^2}{1 - (1 - A_1)^2}\left(1 + \alpha k\frac{\text{MTTR}}{2}\right)\right] - f - vd, \tag{10}$$

which after some straightforward manipulation becomes

$$\Delta_1 = kd\frac{1-A_1}{2A_1}\frac{2+(3-A_1)\alpha k \cdot \text{MTTR}}{2-A_1} - f - vd. \tag{11}$$

The double-homing strategy is economically convenient if $\Delta_1 > 0$, i.e., if

$$kd\frac{1-A_1}{2A_1}\frac{2+(3-A_1)\alpha k \cdot \text{MTTR}}{2-A_1} > f + vd, \tag{12}$$

from which follows

$$\frac{f}{d} + v < kd\frac{1-A_1}{2A_1}\frac{2+(3-A_1)\alpha k \cdot \text{MTTR}}{2-A_1} \quad\square \tag{13}$$

Some simple corollaries follow from Theorem 1, concerning the possibility of the double homing strategy being the cheapest one. We formulate the first one concerning the value of the data stored on the cloud.

**Corollary 1.** *For any amount $d$ of data stored and any couple of prices $(f, v)$, there exists a value of the data stored on the cloud for which the double homing strategy is the cheapest.*

*Proof.* Since $A_1 < 1 < 2 < 3$, the right hand side of the inequality (13) has the form $ak + bk^2$, where $a, b > 0$, and is a growing function of the unit value $k$ of the data stored. Whatever the value of $d, f, v$ appearing in the left hand side of that inequality, the right hand side can become so large as to satisfy the inequality. In fact, by solving the associated quadratic form, it can be seen that the inequality (13) is satisfied for any $k$ such that

$$k > \frac{-a + \sqrt{a^2 + 4b(f/d + v)}}{2b}. \quad\square \tag{14}$$

The second corollary concerns the amount of data stored.

**Corollary 2.** *If the marginal price $v$ satisfies the inequality $v < kd\frac{1-A_1}{A_1}\frac{2+(3-A_1)\alpha k \cdot \text{MTTR}}{2-A_1}$, there exists a number $d_1$, such that the double homing strategy is the cheapest for any amount of data stored $d > d_1$.*

*Proof.* Let $\epsilon$ be the positive quantity defined as $\epsilon = kd\frac{1-A_1}{A_1}\frac{2+(3-A_1)\alpha k \cdot \text{MTTR}}{2-A_1} - v$. Then, for $d_1 = f/\epsilon$, we have

$$\frac{f}{d_1} + v = \epsilon + v = kd\frac{1-A_1}{A_1}\frac{2+(3-A_1)\alpha k \cdot \text{MTTR}}{2-A_1}. \tag{15}$$

Hence, for any $d > d_1$ we have

$$\frac{f}{d} + v < \frac{f}{d_1} + v < kd\frac{1-A_1}{A_1}\frac{2+(3-A_1)\alpha k \cdot \text{MTTR}}{2-A_1}, \tag{16}$$

and the condition of Theorem 1 is met.

If we turn to multi-homing, we can define the quantity

$$\Delta_i = p_i - p_{i+1} \qquad i = 1, 2, \ldots, \tag{17}$$

which is the gain achieved when we add a cloud to a storage platform already consisting of $i$ clouds. For $i = 1$, we find the quantity already defined in Theorem 1. Adding a cloud leads to an overall lower cost as long as that gain is positive. We can therefore identify the optimal number $n^*$ of clouds as

$$n^* = \max i \quad : \quad \Delta_i > 0. \tag{18}$$

If we recall Eq. (8), we can write the general expression of the gain

$$\Delta_i = -(f+vd)+kd \left[ \frac{(1-A_1)^i \left(1 + \alpha k \frac{\text{MTTR}}{i}\right)}{1-(1-A_1)^i} - \frac{(1-A_1)^{i+1} \left(1 + \alpha k \frac{\text{MTTR}}{i+1}\right)}{1-(1-A_1)^{i+1}} \right], \tag{19}$$

which after some algebraic manipulation becomes

$$\Delta_i = -(f + vd) + kd(1 - A_1)^i \frac{A_1 + \frac{\alpha k \cdot \text{MTTR}}{i(i+1)}[1 + iA_1 - (1 - A_1)^{i+1}]}{[1 - (1 - A_1)^i][1 - (1 - A_1)^{i+1}]}. \tag{20}$$

Since Eq. (20) appears a bit cumbersome to obtain the optimal number of clouds, we can obtain a useful approximation by considering that $A_1 \simeq 1$, so that $iA_1 \simeq i$ and

$$\Delta_i \simeq -(f + vd) + kd(1 - A_1)^i \left[ A_1 + \alpha k \frac{\text{MTTR}}{i} \right], \tag{21}$$

so that solving the inequality $\Delta_i > 0$ is roughly equivalent to solving the simpler equation

$$n^* = \lfloor i \rfloor \quad : \quad kd(1 - A_1)^i \left[ A_1 + \alpha k \frac{\text{MTTR}}{i} \right] = f + vd. \tag{22}$$

**Table 1.** Value of parameters for the sample case

| Parameter | Value |
|---|---|
| Availability | 0.999 |
| MTTR [h] | 5 |
| Data unav. loss [€/GB] | 35 |
| Storage fixed fee [€] | 4 |
| Marginal price [€]/GB | 0.05 |
| Data volume [TB] | 10 |
| $\alpha$ | 5 |

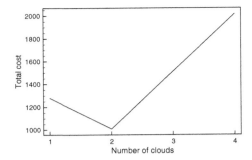

**Fig. 3.** Total cost

We can get a feeling of how adding clouds may actually help achieve a total risk coverage at a reduced cost by computing the total cost through Eq. (8) for a sample configuration. In Table 1, we report a typical set of parameter values for a month's time period. In this configuration we have considered that a single cloud delivers a three 9's availability and that not being able to access data provokes a loss of 35 € for each GB. The storage prices are those reported in [19] for the two-part tariff fitting of Amazon's prices.

In Fig. 3, we report the total cost as we increase the number of clouds. We see that: (1) the minimum cost is achieved for a double homing strategy; (2) adding a further cloud makes the insurance premium negligible with respect to the storage cost, so that for $n \geq 3$ the total cost grows linearly. The cost saving in switching from a single cloud to 2 clouds is a remarkable 21 %.

## 6   Conclusions

Storing data on multiple clouds (multicloud or cloud multi-homing) provides a higher reliability than a single cloud, but does not guarantee that data are always accessible. Complementing the use of multiple clouds with the subscription of an insurance policy against the money loss deriving from being unable to access data allows to achieve total risk coverage against cloud unavailability.

In this paper we have derived a basic cost model for this combined approach to identify the optimal configuration leading to the minimum overall cost. We have provided the conditions for double homing to be economically convenient with respect to a single cloud solution and derived the equation that leads to the optimal number of clouds. We have also shown the behaviour of the cost curve for a typical configuration, where double homing plus insurance provides total risk coverage at a cost that is 21 % less than that of a single cloud.

This study can be considered as a first step that proves the economical viability of a combined approach (multicloud + insurance) to achieve total risk coverage. Some simplistic assumptions should be removed in future works, namely assuming that data replication is complete (and therefore storage costs grow linearly), neglecting the occurrence of correlated failures (which leads to a faster growth of availability), and assuming a simple insurance pricing model (which leads to a vanishing insurance premium when the availability grows).

# References

1. Baker, M., Shah, M., Rosenthal, D.S.H., Roussopoulos, M., Maniatis, P., Giuli, T., Bungale, P.: A fresh look at the reliability of long-term digital storage. SIGOPS Oper. Syst. Rev. **40**(4), 221–234 (2006)
2. Berndt, P., Maier, A.: Towards sustainable IAAS pricing. In: Altmann, J., Vanmechelen, K., Rana, O.F. (eds.) GECON 2013. LNCS, vol. 8193, pp. 173–184. Springer, Heidelberg (2013)
3. Casalicchio, E., Silvestri, L.: Mechanisms for SLA provisioning in cloud-based service providers. Comput. Netw. **57**(3), 795–810 (2013)
4. Dutta, A.K., Hasan, R.: How much does storage really cost? Towards a full cost accounting model for data storage. In: Altmann, J., Vanmechelen, K., Rana, O.F. (eds.) GECON 2013. LNCS, vol. 8193, pp. 29–43. Springer, Heidelberg (2013)
5. Ford, D., Labelle, F., Popovici, F.I., Stokely, M., Truong, V.A., Barroso, L., Grimes, C., Quinlan, S.: Availability in globally distributed storage systems. In: 9th USENIX Symposium on Operating Systems Design and Implementation. OSDI 2010, Vancouver, BC, Canada, pp. 61–74 (2010)
6. Gill, P., Jain, N., Nagappan, N.: Understanding network failures in data centers: measurement, analysis, and implications. SIGCOMM Comput. Commun. Rev. **41**(4), 350–361 (2011)
7. Hu, Z., Zhu, L., Ardi, C., Katz-Bassett, E., Madhyastha, H.V., Heidemann, J., Yu, M.: The need for end-to-end evaluation of cloud availability. In: Faloutsos, M., Kuzmanovic, A. (eds.) PAM 2014. LNCS, vol. 8362, pp. 119–130. Springer, Heidelberg (2014)
8. Kaas, R., Goovaerts, M., Dhaene, J., Denuit, M.: Modern Actuarial Risk Theory. Springer, Heidelberg (2004)
9. Kashef, M.M., Altmann, J.: A cost model for hybrid clouds. In: Vanmechelen, K., Altmann, J., Rana, O.F. (eds.) GECON 2011. LNCS, vol. 7150, pp. 46–60. Springer, Heidelberg (2012)
10. Laatikainen, G., Mazhelis, O., Tyrväinen, P.: Role of acquisition intervals in private and public cloud storage costs. Decis. Support Syst. **57**, 320–330 (2014)
11. Mastroeni, L., Naldi, M.: Network protection through insurance: premium computation for the on-off service model. In: 8th International Workshop on the Design of Reliable Communication Networks. DRCN 2011, Krakow, pp. 46–53. IEEE (2011)
12. Mastroeni, L., Naldi, M.: Storage buy-or-lease decisions in cloud computing under price uncertainty. In: 7th EuroNF Conference on Next Generation Internet. NGI 2011, Kaiserslautern. IEEE (2011)
13. Mastroeni, L., Naldi, M.: Pricing of insurance policies against cloud storage price rises. SIGMETRICS Perform. Eval. Rev. **40**(2), 42–45 (2012)
14. Mastroeni, L., Naldi, M.: Long-range evaluation of risk in the migration to cloud storage. In: 13th IEEE Conference on Commerce and Enterprise Computing. CEC 2011, Luxembourg, pp. 260–266. IEEE (2011)
15. Mu, S., Chen, K., Gao, P., Ye, F., Wu, Y., Zheng, W.: $\mu$ LibCloud: providing high available and uniform accessing to multiple cloud storages. In: 2012 ACM/IEEE 13th International Conference on Grid Computing, Beijing, China, pp. 201–208. ACM (2012)
16. Naldi, M.: A note on "The Need for End-to-End Evaluation of Cloud Availability". ArXiv e-print 1408.0510, August 2014. http://arxiv.org/abs/1408.0510
17. Naldi, M.: The availability of cloud-based services: Is it living up to its promise? In: 9th International Conference on the Design of Reliable Communication Networks. DRCN 2013, pp. 282–289. IEEE (2013)

18. Naldi, M.: Forecast uncertainty in procurement decisions for cloud storage. In: 2014 UKSim-AMSS 16th International Conference on Computer Modelling and Simulation, Cambridge, pp. 237–242. IEEE (2014)

19. Naldi, M., Mastroeni, L.: Cloud storage pricing: a comparison of current practices. In: Proceedings of the 2013 International Workshop on Hot Topics in Cloud Services. HotTopiCS '13, Prague, pp. 27–34. ACM, New York (2013)

20. Papaioannou, T.G., Bonvin, N., Aberer, K.: Scalia: an adaptive scheme for efficient multi-cloud storage. In: Proceedings of the International Conference on High Performance Computing, Networking, Storage and Analysis. SC '12, pp. 20:1–20:10. IEEE/ACM (2012)

21. Pratt, J.W.: Risk aversion in the small and in the large. Econometrica **32**(1–2), 122–136 (1964)

22. Roovers, J., Vanmechelen, K., Broeckhove, J.: A reverse auction market for cloud resources. In: Vanmechelen, K., Altmann, J., Rana, O.F. (eds.) GECON 2011. LNCS, vol. 7150, pp. 32–45. Springer, Heidelberg (2012)

23. Venkatesan, V., Iliadis, I.: A general reliability model for data storage systems. Research report RZ3817, IBM Research, Zurich, March 2012

24. Walker, E., Brisken, W., Romney, J.: To lease or not to lease from storage clouds. IEEE Comput. **43**(4), 44–50 (2010)

25. Wilson, R.: Nonlinear Pricing. Oxford University Press, Oxford (1997)

26. Zhai, E., Chen, R., Wolinsky, D.I., Ford, B.: An untold story of redundant clouds: making your service deployment truly reliable. In: Proceedings of the 9th Workshop on Hot Topics in Dependable Systems. HotDep '13, pp. 3:1–3:6. ACM, New York (2013)

# A WS-Agreement Based SLA Implementation for the CMAC Platform

Adriano Galati[1]([✉]),[4P], Karim Djemame[1], Martyn Fletcher[2,3], Mark Jessop[2], Michael Weeks[2], and John McAvoy[3]

[1] Distributed Systems and Services Research Group, School of Computing, University of Leeds, E.C. Stoner Building, Woodhouse Lane, Leeds LS2 9JT, UK
[2] Advanced Computer Architecture Group, Department of Computer Science, University of York, York YO10 5DD, UK
[3] Cybula Ltd. R&D Team, Science Park, York YO10 5DD, UK
[4] Disney Research Zurich, Stampfenbachstrasse 48, Zurich 8006, Switzerland
adriano.galati@disneyresearch.com

**Abstract.** The emerging transformation from a product oriented economy to a service oriented economy based on Cloud environments envisions new scenarios where actual QoS (Quality of Service) mechanisms need to be redesigned. In such scenarios new models to negotiate and manage Service Level Agreements (SLAs) are necessary. An SLA is a formal contract which defines acceptable service levels to be provided by the Service Provider to its customers in measurable terms. SLAs are an essential component in building Cloud systems where commitments and assurances are specified, implemented, monitored and possibly negotiable. This is meant to guarantee that consumers' service quality expectations can be achieved. In fact, the level of customer satisfaction is crucial in Cloud environments, making SLAs one of the most important and active research topics. This paper presents an SLA implementation for negotiation, monitoring and renegotiation of agreements for Cloud services based on the CMAC (Condition Monitoring on A Cloud) platform. CMAC offers condition monitoring services in cloud computing environments to detect events on assets as well as data storage services.

**Keywords:** SLA · WS-Agreement · Requirements · Negotiation

## 1 Introduction

Cloud computing [1] is emerging as a new computing paradigm and it is gaining increasing popularity throughout the research community. One aspect of the cloud is the provision of software as a service over the internet, i.e. providing applications (services) hosted remotely. Ideally, these services do not require end-user knowledge of the physical compute resource they are accessing, nor particular expertise in the use of the service they are accessing. Whilst the cloud offers opportunities for remote monitoring of assets, there are issues regarding resource allocation and access control that must be addressed to make the approach as

© Springer International Publishing Switzerland 2014
J. Altmann et al. (Eds.): GECON 2014, LNCS 8914, pp. 159–171, 2014.
DOI: 10.1007/978-3-319-14609-6_11

efficient as possible to maximize revenues. From the service provider perspective, it is impossible to satisfy all customers' requests and a balance mechanism needs to be devised through a negotiation process. Eventually, such a process will end up with a commitment between provider and customer. Such a commitment is a commercial contract that guarantees satisfaction of the QoS requirements of customers according to specific service level agreements. SLAs define the foundation for the expected level of service agreed between the contracting parties. Therefore, they must cover aspects such as availability, performance, cost, security, legal requirements for data-placements, eco-efficiency, and even penalties in the case of violation of the SLA. An SLA is defined as an explicit statement of the expectations and obligations that exist in a business relationship between the user and the service provider. A formalised representation of commitments in the form of an SLA document is required to achieve both automated information collection and SLA evaluation. At any given point in time many SLAs may exist, and each SLA in turn may have numerous objectives to be fulfilled. Therefore, QoS attributes need to be explicitly defined with clear terms and definitions by SLAs which exhibit how service performance is being monitored, and what enforcement mechanisms are in place to ensure SLAs are met [2]. Thus, a user accessing Cloud services on demand and with defined QoS agreements which enables commitments to be fulfilled is a primary requirement. The user can specify an SLA which will guarantee resources, provide job monitoring and record violations if they are detected. The SLA document records agreement provenance allowing for auditing mechanisms after it has terminated. Although the cloud computing research community recognises SLA negotiation as a key aspect of the WS-Agreement specifications, little work has been done to provide insight on how negotiation, and especially automated negotiation, can be realised. In addition, it is difficult to reflect the quality aspects of SLA requirements. In this paper, which follows from our previous work [3], we present our SLA implementation for the management of the negotiation, the monitoring and the renegotiation phase of the agreed terms and requirements for the CMAC (Condition Monitoring on A Cloud) platform [4,5] which offers a range of analytical software tools designed to detect events on assets and complex systems as well as data storage services. For this purpose, we choose the WSAG4J framework [6,7] which is an implementation of the WS-Agreement standard [8] from the Open Grid forum (OGF). It provides comprehensive support for common SLA management tasks such as SLA template management, SLA negotiation and creation, and SLA monitoring and accounting. In the rest of this paper we present in Sect. 2 an exhaustive overview of current literature, in Sect. 3 we introduce our SLA protocol drawing attention to some aspects related to its design and integration in the CMAC platform. In Sect. 4 we present all of the requirements we consider for CMAC services, in Sect. 5 we describe our SLA implementation, and in Sect. 6 we provide the lessons we have learned throughout this experience. Finally, Sect. 7 concludes this paper.

## 2   Related Work

A Service Level Agreement (SLA) is a contract, between the service provider and the customer which specifies the function performed by the service, the agreed bounds of performance, the obligations on both contractual parties and how deviations are handled [8–10]. Unlike the provision of traditional basic services through SLAs, providing support for real-time applications over service-oriented infrastructures is a complex task that requires enhanced SLA protocols. The Grid Resource Allocation Agreement Protocol Working Group (GRAAP-WG) of the Open Grid Forum (OGF) has produced the Web Services Agreement (WS-Agreement) standard [8] to create bilateral agreements. Kubërt et al. [11] analyze different fields where SLAs are used, examine the proposed solutions, and investigate how these can be improved in order to better support the creation of real-time service-oriented architectures. The IRMOS project [12] proposes an SLA framework which introduces a chain of linked SLAs implemented on different layers in order to provide support for the provision of real-time applications. Menychtas et al. [13] present a novel cloud platform, which was developed in the frame of the EU-funded project IRMOS targeting soft real-time applications that have stringent timing and performance requirements. Their platform combines Service Oriented Infrastructures (SOIs) [14] with virtualisation technologies to manage and provision computational, storage and networking resources as well as to communicate with legacy systems such as WiFi locators. Ludwig et al. [15] describe the use of WS-Agreement for Service Level Agreements paving the way for using multiple distributed resources to satisfy a single service request. Battre et al. [16] describe the Web Services Agreement Negotiation protocol proposed by the Open Grid Forum to extend the existing specification. This proposal is the result of combining various research activities that have been conducted to define protocols for negotiating service levels or to supersede the existing "take-it-or-leave-it" protocol. The main characteristics of this proposal are the multi-round negotiation capability, renegotiation capability, and compliance with the original specification. Pichot et al. [17] propose and discuss extensions to the WS-Agreement protocol which support dynamic negotiation and creation of SLAs in an efficient and flexible manner. Some examples of WS-Agreement implementations are WSAG4J [6,7], Cremona [18] and the SORMA project [19]. WSAG4J (WS-Agreement for Java) framework is a tool developed by Fraunhofer SCAI [6,7] to create and manage service level agreements (SLAs) in distributed systems. It is an implementation of the OGF WS-Agreement specification [8]. WSAG4J helps designing and implementing SLAs and automates typical SLA management tasks like SLA offer validation, service level monitoring, persistence and accounting. It provides infrastructure components for service providers and consumers supporting the negotiation of SLAs as well as the retrieval of information about negotiated SLAs. A possible extension for WSAG4J would be the support for SLA template deployment from a tool for designing SLA templates. SLA templates can be created during the design process of a service and the deployment of an SLA template from the design tool would allow a better integration with the SLA infrastructure.

Cremona (Creation and Monitoring of Agreements) [18] was developed by IBM using an early version of WS-Agreement. It is a middleware, which supports the negotiation, monitoring, and management of WS-Agreement-based service level agreements. The provided functionality supports both parties involved in the service provisioning and consumption process, i.e. the service provider and the service consumer. SORMA (Self-Organizing ICT Resource Management) [19] implement an Open Grid Market in a comprehensive way by addressing three arguments: the economic model providing an economically sound market structure; the self-organization model, which deals with the interaction between the Grid-application and the market and provides intelligent tools; and the economic middleware model, which builds the bridge between the self-organization and the economic model on the one side and state-of-the-art Grid infrastructure on the other side.

## 3   SLA Protocol Design

In this section we draw attention to some aspects related to the design and integration of an SLA protocol for the CMAC platform to a point where it can be commercially implemented. Most research up to now provides little insight on how negotiation, and in particular automated negotiation, can be realised. In addition, it is difficult to define the quality aspects of SLA requirements. Here, we have designed an SLA protocol which is integrated in the CMAC platform. For this purpose, the main challenges that we tackle in order to provide QoS guarantees, are mainly three:

- the identification of the QoS properties, i.e. its requirements and terms, and their publication in the SLA template;
- SLA generation and negotiation control based on service requirements and assets available to satisfy customer requests, as well as the decision process to accept, reject, or renegotiate the counteroffer in the negotiation process;
- maximising providers' profit implementing an optimal service and resource allocation policy. Profits are recognised when SLA agreements are honored, generally when workload execution completes on time, otherwise penalties are incurred;

With regard to the first issue, it is not currently tackled by the WS-Agreement specification. We have decided to structure the SLA template distinguishing between *requirements* and *terms*. We assume requirements to describe sufficient conditions required by the service to be executed. More precisely, a service might have need for technical (i.e. a specific operating system, CPU capacity, amount of RAM), syntactical (i.e. defined format of the input data) and ethical requirements (i.e. majority age for the consumer to use the service). Requirements are presented exclusively by the service provider and cannot be negotiable; they are essential for the fulfillment of the service. Our SLA protocol allows negotiation based on the terms presented by the parties. In this context, the agreed terms are necessary conditions, but not sufficient, to reach an agreement; service requirements must be satisfied anyway. It is necessary to determine all the guarantee terms that will be signed by both parties. For the CMAC services we identify some terms which are QoS parameters like the delivery ability of the provider, the performance of user's workloads, the bounds of guaranteed availability and performance, the measurement and reporting mechanisms, the cost of the service, the terms for renegotiation, and the penalty terms for SLA violation. Our SLA protocol defines ad-hoc SLA template structures for each service on the base of its prerequisites. Our SLA protocol has been designed to allow negotiation only for the guarantee terms. In this respect, the WS-Agreement negotiation protocol decides whether to accept or reject the user's offer, or eventually renegotiate providing a counteroffer, if there are the prerequisites for raising one. The negotiation is quite flexible; it is based on temporal restrictions, resource constraints, previous offers and a maximum number of renegotiations is possible. Once the service requirements and the guarantee terms are met the contract has been stipulated. The negotiation constraints in the negotiation template are used to control the negotiation process. Although, virtualization of resources is a prerequisite for building a successful cloud infrastructure, we do not consider it at this stage. At this point CMAC can start monitoring the service and determining whether the service objectives are achieved or violated. Namely, if the provider has delivered the service within the guaranteed terms. At this early stage we assume only the service provider to be in charge of this process, although each party should be in charge of this task and how fairness can be assured between them is an open issue. The monitoring process helps the service provider to prevent violations of the guarantee terms by renegotiating them.

## 4   CMAC Requirements

An SLA can define different QoS for each service so as to create ad-hoc service provisions to each service consumer. In this work we target services provided by the CMAC platform [4,5]. It offers a range of analytical software tools designed to detect events on assets and complex systems as well as data storage services. In particular, in this section, we focus on the *Terms* block of the agreement template. Therefore, we identify requirements and guarantee terms of CMAC services which need to be agreed by service consumers and provider to specify ad-hoc service level agreements before creating a new binding contract. The Table 1 shows the service description terms presented in the implementation of the SLA template for CMAC. Service description terms express a functional description of the provided service. Therefore, such service description terms contain a domain specific description of the service. In particular, the Tables 1(a) and (b) list out service constraints and resources derived from the implementation of the CMAC namespace and from the OGF (Open Grid Forum) namespace respectively. CMAC users can select one service among the eeg (electroencephalogram), the ecg (electrocardiogram), and the storage of data. The eeg and ecg are both software tools designed for medical signal analysis. Such applications can

**Table 1.** Service Description Terms in the CMAC's SLA template.

(a)

| CMAC namespace | |
|---|---|
| Service | eeg |
| | ecg |
| | storage |
| Format | csv |
| | ndf |
| Time | Start, end |
| | Duration |
| | Frequency |
| Pipeline | Boolean |
| Browser | Firefox |
| | IE |
| Alerting System Failure | Critical |
| | Severe |
| Error Handling | Substantial |
| | Moderate |
| | Low |
| | Absent |
| Renegotiation | Boolean |
| Age of majority | |
| Communication of violations | email |
| | call |
| QoS communication | text |
| | post |
| Cost | Integer |

(b)

| OGF namespace | |
|---|---|
| Operating System | Linux |
| | MacOs |
| (Type, Version) | Solaris |
| | Windows |
| CPU Architecture | x86_64 |
| | x86_32 |
| (Type) | ARM |
| | sparc |
| | PowerPC |
| | mips |
| Physical Memory | Size |
| Virtual Memory | Size |
| Disk Space | Size |
| Bandwidth | Size |
| Candidate Host | Name |
| Exclusive Execution | Boolean |

read data in *cnv* (vector image files primarily associated with DB2 conversion files) and **ndf** format. CMAC allows users to request service provisioning, by allocating time-slots and frequency, between a start-time and end-time. Thus, requested services and resources are available for use during the selected time-slots. Workflows are also supported within the system. This allows users to build a pipeline of individual services and execute them as an orchestrated set of tasks via the workflow execution engine. Processes and output data can be captured via a workflow system, which can orchestrate a pipeline of processing activity. As a matter of course, CMAC archives eeg and ecg output data but they may be further processed for remote visualization on a web browser [4]. Users can decide which connection bandwidth would be suitable for the service performance and the visualization rendering of output data on the web browser. Furthermore, users can choose the alerting level for system errors and service failures. For that, CMAC can detect anomalies and system failures in signal processing and notify them to service consumers based on the selected alerting level. The error handling level is concerned with recording and communication of failures of the CMAC services. System errors and service failures are notified to CMAC users by means of the preferred communication method, that is, email, call and text. The same communication method is used to notify SLA violations and QoS auditing. CMAC also allows users to upload and make available for use any own software for processing data as long as some requirements such as the operating system and version, CPU architecture, physical memory, virtual memory and disk space can be run on an execution node. Execution nodes can be exclusively allocated or shared among CMAC users. Therefore, users can choose the terms presented in Table 1(b) both for their own and CMAC services. Service consumers can be contacted anytime to renegotiate the agreed terms if the renegotiation flag is set to true. Finally, CMAC users can define maximum cost that they are willing to pay for the service provision and must state they are over eighteen on the SLA template.

```
<?xml version="1.0" encoding="UTF-8"?>
<wsag:Template wsag:TemplateId="1"
 xmlns:wsag="http://schemas.ggf.org/graap/2007/03/ws-agreement">
  <wsag:Name>CMAC-1</wsag:Name>
  <wsag:Context>
    <wsag:ServiceProvider>AgreementResponder</wsag:ServiceProvider>
    <wsag:TemplateId>1</wsag:TemplateId>
    <wsag:TemplateName>CMAC-TEMPLATE-1</wsag:TemplateName>
  </wsag:Context>
  ...
</wsag:Template>
```

**Fig. 1.** Name and Context sections of the CMAC's SLA template described by means of the OGF XML Schema.

## 5   Implementation

The focus on service level rather than on network level enables the definition of SLA and QoS independently from the underlying network technology. Nonetheless, a service should be defined without ambiguity. Therefore, we use the WS-Agreement specification, a standard which defines a language and provides generic support to build common functionalities for advertising the capabilities of service providers, creating agreements based on templates, and for monitoring agreement compliance at runtime. In this context, WSAG4J provides support to design and create highly flexible SLAs using the WS-Agreement language and to validate dynamic agreement offers based on template creation constraints. It also supports common functionality to monitor agreements in a generic way and enables users to build and deploy WS-Agreement based services. WSAG4J allows publishing SLA templates in XML format. The Fig. 1 presents the first two sections, *name* and *context*, of an SLA template for the CMAC services which are described by means of the OGF XML schema. We name the agreement described by the SLA template as *CMAC-1*. In the *context* section we define the party that creates the agreement as "agreement responder", namely the service consumer, and assign him with a unique identifier composed of the template name and

```
...
<wsag:ServiceDescriptionTerm
 wsag:Name="TIME_CONSTRAINT_SDT" wsag:ServiceName="SAMPLE-SERVICE">
  <wsag4cmact:TimeConstraint xmlns:wsag4cmact=
"http://schemas.wsag4cmact.org/2012/10/wsag4j-scheduling-extensions">
    <wsag4cmact:StartTime>$STARTTIME</wsag4cmact:StartTime>
    <wsag4cmact:EndTime>$ENDTIME</wsag4cmact:EndTime>
    <wsag4cmact:Duration>$DURATION</wsag4cmact:Duration>
    <wsag4cmact:Frequency>$FREQUENCY</wsag4cmact:Frequency>
  </wsag4cmact:TimeConstraint>
</wsag:ServiceDescriptionTerm>
...
<wsag:ServiceDescriptionTerm
 wsag:Name="SERVICE_CONSTRAINT_SDT" wsag:ServiceName="SAMPLE-SERVICE">
  <wsag4cmact:ServiceConstraint xmlns:wsag4cmact=
  "http://www.comp.leeds.ac.uk/2012/10/CMAC-scheduling-extensions">
    $SERVICE
  </wsag4cmact:ServiceConstraint>
</wsag:ServiceDescriptionTerm>
<wsag:ServiceDescriptionTerm
 wsag:Name="RENEGOTIATION_CONSTRAINT_SDT"
 wsag:ServiceName="SAMPLE-SERVICE">
  <wsag4cmact:RenegotiationConstraint xmlns:wsag4cmact=
  "http://schemas.wsag4cmact.org/2012/10/CMAC-scheduling-extensions">
    $RENEGOTIATION
  </wsag4cmact:RenegotiationConstraint>
</wsag:ServiceDescriptionTerm>
...
</wsag:All>
</wsag:Terms>
```

**Fig. 2.** Resources described by means of the *wsag4cmact* XML Schema in the *terms* block of the CMAC's SLA template.

id, *CMAC-TEMPLATE-1* and *1* respectively for the sample presented in Fig. 1. All of the service description terms in the CMAC SLA template presented in the previous section are exposed in XML format in the *terms* section. Since the WS-Agreement is designed to be domain independent, the content of a service description term can be any valid XML document. In such a section CMAC resources and several constraints are available to users to help specifying requirements and guarantee terms of the provided services. Figure 2 presents CMAC service constraints described by means of *wsag4cmact*, Our XML schema presenting the CMAC service constraints is described by *wsag4cmact*, which is available at http://schemas.wsag4cmact.org/2012/10/wsag4j-scheduling-extensions. Both parties involved in the agreement, i.e. agreement initiator and agreement responder, must understand the domain specific service description. Our XML Schema language is shown in Fig. 4. Java interfaces and classes that can be used to access and modify XML instance data have been derived from the XML schema by means of XMLBeans which allows compiling the schema, and generating and jarring Java types. An important requirement for dynamic SLA provisioning is preventing illegal modification of agreement offers. Therefore our implementation of the CMAC's agreement template contains several sections of creation constraints which can be used by an agreement responder to define the structure and possible values of valid agreement offers. Only offers that are valid with respect to its template creation constraints are accepted by CMAC.

```
<wsag:CreationConstraints>
  ...
  <wsag:ItemConstraint>
   <xs:sequence xmlns:xs="http://www.w3.org/2001/XMLSchema">
     <xs:element name="OperatingSystem" minOccurs="1" maxOccurs="1"
                 type="jsdl:OperatingSystem_Type"/>
     <xs:element name="CPUArchitecture" minOccurs="1" maxOccurs="1"
                 type="jsdl:CPUArchitecture_Type"/>
     ...
   </xs:sequence>
  </wsag:ItemConstraint>
 </wsag:Item>
 <wsag:Item wsag:Name="ResourcesSDT_JobDefinition_JobDescription_Resources_
                       CPUArchitecture_CPUArchitectureName">
  <wsag:Location>
    ...
    $this/wsag:AgreementOffer/wsag:Terms/wsag:All/wsag:ServiceDescriptionTerm
    [@wsag:Name='RESOURCE_SDT']/jsdl:JobDefinition/jsdl:JobDescription/
    jsdl:Resources/jsdl:CPUArchitecture/jsdl:CPUArchitectureName
  </wsag:Location>
  <wsag:ItemConstraint>
  <xs:simpleType xmlns:xs="http://www.w3.org/2001/XMLSchema">
    <xs:restriction base="xs:string">
  <xs:enumeration value="sparc"/>
     <xs:enumeration value="powerpc"/>
     <xs:enumeration value="x86_32"/>
     <xs:enumeration value="x86_64"/>
     ...
  </xs:restriction>
  </xs:simpleType>
  </wsag:ItemConstraint>
  ...
</wsag:CreationConstraints>
```

**Fig. 3.** Snippets of creation constraints in the CMAC's SLA template.

Our creation constraints support CMAC in finding out acceptable values for service descriptions. Besides, they protect the agreement responder from accepting offers that are created in an illegal way. The CMAC agreement template we have designed helps both the agreement initiator and the responder to come to a common understanding of the provided service in the context of an SLA. The agreement offer is valid only if all of the offer items are valid according to the specified item constraints. Figure 3 shows snippets of value and structural constraints described in jsdl of the CMAC SLA templates. The first item refers to the resources defined in the *terms* section of the CMAC SLA template. Here, they must occur once. The second item refers to the CPU architecture name. The location tag points to the **CPUArchitectureName** field which is also defined in the *terms* section. A string type can be assigned to such a variable and CMAC users can choose a CPU architecture out of the ones provided in the list. The third snippet of Fig. 3 defines the structural constraints of the agreement offer. They specify which child elements can be part of a certain offer, the order with which such child elements must occur, their cardinality and how they are clustered. This part implies that the *context* and the *terms* sections must be specified in the CMAC SLA template, whereas its *name* section is optional.

```
<?xml version="1.0" encoding="UTF-8"?>
  ...
  <xs:complexType name="FrequencyConstraintType">
    <xs:sequence>
      <xs:element name="StartTime" type="xs:dateTime" minOccurs="0" maxOccurs="1" />
      <xs:element name="EndTime" type="xs:dateTime" minOccurs="0" maxOccurs="1" />
      <xs:element name="Duration" type="xs:int" minOccurs="0" maxOccurs="1" />
      <xs:element name="Frequency" type="xs:int" minOccurs="0" maxOccurs="1" />
    </xs:sequence>
  </xs:complexType>
  <xs:simpleType name="FormatConstraintType">
      <xs:restriction base="xs:string">
              <xs:enumeration value="csv"/>
              <xs:enumeration value="ndf"/>
<xs:enumeration value="plain"/>
      </xs:restriction>
  </xs:simpleType>
  <!-- ecg: electrocardiogram, eeg: elettroencephalogram -->
  <xs:simpleType name="ServiceConstraintType">
<xs:restriction base="xs:string">
<xs:enumeration value="ecg"/>
<xs:enumeration value="eeg"/>
<xs:enumeration value="storage"/>
</xs:restriction>
  </xs:simpleType>
  <xs:simpleType name="AlertingSystemFailureConstraintType">
      <xs:restriction base="xs:string">
              <xs:enumeration value="Critical"/>
              <xs:enumeration value="Severe"/>
          <xs:enumeration value="Substantial"/>
           <xs:enumeration value="Moderate"/>
          <xs:enumeration value="Low"/>
          <xs:enumeration value="Absent"/>
      </xs:restriction>
  </xs:simpleType>
  ...
</xs:schema>
```

**Fig. 4.** CMAC's XML Schema.

## 6    Lessons Learned

Several questions and problems surfaced during the development of the Service
Level Agreement for the CMAC platform. Being CMAC a software platform
which offers condition monitoring services to detect events on assets and data
storage services in cloud environments, these questions mainly focused on the
"how" to implement and "what" requirements need to be taken into account
to design an SLA protocol to provide CMAC services. The answers that were
found are described here as the lessons learned. Several lessons were learned
between the initial analysis phase and the actual implementation of the SLA.
During the first phase we identified and analyzed terms and requirements for
each of the CMAC services. Therefore, the first lesson is to decide at an early
stage what the provided services are so as to identify all of their requirements
and determine how they will be defined in the document structure of the SLA.
Besides, the identification of QoS properties, namely, service requirements, guarantee terms and their publication in the SLA template strongly help designing the process to accept, reject or renegotiate an offer and to monitor SLA

violations accordingly. For the purpose, we have chosen the WSAG4J framework which helps designing and implementing SLAs and automates typical SLA management tasks like SLA offer validation, service level monitoring, persistence and accounting. In this work we provide a practical lesson on using WSAG4J to define and provide specific services of the CMAC platform. From the best of our knowledge, this is the first employment of WSAG4J for a real-world cloud platform. Therefore, we provide evidence that WSAG4J is a suitable tool for designing SLA agreements. It provides support to design and create highly flexible SLAs using the WS-Agreement language and to validate dynamic agreement offers based on template creation constraints. One more lesson is about the possibility to differentiate between the different SLA components. After investigating service requirements it became clear that some aspects of the service needed more attention than others. Therefore, it would help untangling the components of the provided services and focus on such parts individually, rather than on the services as a whole. Furthermore, the work presented in this paper is part of a common project where researchers and software engineers from both academia and industry are involved. However, some members were not involved in this SLA implementation and would have to work with it as being part of the entire project. This emphasised the need for a specific and readable document based on the WS-Agreement specification and service requirements. An SLA document that can be understood and easily adapted, even by people who have not been involved in the earlier SLA implementation, including descriptions of taken decisions on both document structure and services. A final lesson we learned is that in cloud environments an agreement should not been seen as a rigid contract that cannot be renegotiated and meant to be used only in case of conflicts or agreement violations. It is a document that tries to bring two or more parties into conformity for a common agreement. Therefor commitments on QoS results might not always be enough. A balance between commitments on final results and service performance should be defined by flexible agreements from both service provider and service consumer in order to achieve a fair cooperation. The lessons we have learned provide us with basis references for the development of WS-Agreement based SLAs. Our recommendations provide practitioners with a set of operational SLA concepts. In particular, the identification and definition of requirements of cloud services play a key role in the design of suitable SLA agreements and efficient SLA protocols. By focusing on the gathered requirements and by modelling the SLA process step by step all of the researchers and software engineers involved in this project were able to discuss and contribute to the SLA definition process and the final implementation. Both aspects lead to a well-structured and understandable SLA document, which is the basis for successful service delivery in cloud environments.

## 7   Conclusions

Currently, WS-Agreement provides little insight on how negotiation, and in particular automated negotiation, can be realized. In addition, it is difficult to define the quality aspects of SLA requirements. This paper presents an SLA protocol designed to guide the negotiation, the monitoring and the renegotiation phase of the agreed terms to maximize revenues in the CMAC platform. Besides, we also provide a clear distinction between quality aspects of SLA requirements. In this work we integrate our SLA protocol into the CMAC platform which offers a range of analytical software tools designed to detect events on assets and complex systems as well as data storage services. For this purpose, we choose the WSAG4J framework which is a tool to create and manage service level agreements in distributed systems. In this work, we have developed the first SLA protocol for the CMAC platform with the intention to maximize revenues by designing an appropriate resource allocation process based on time restrictions and related service parameters agreed during the negotiation phase and possibly modified by means of renegotiations. The lessons learned provide us with basis references for the development of WS-Agreement based SLAs. Our recommendations provide practitioners with a set of operational SLA concepts. In particular, we draw attention to the identification and definition of requirements of cloud services as fundamental for the design of suitable SLA agreements and efficient SLA protocols. In future work we would like to implement and evaluate the renegotiation protocol we have designed in this work. We would also like to consider varying expiration times based on historical records to handle the duration of the negotiation phase so as to enhance its flexibility. Besides, we would also like to provide service consumers with estimates on previous service executions along with service performance measurement methods, measurement periods and data analysis reports, which will help choosing suitable service requirements. Moreover, we are examining the possibility of integrating the SLA protocol with service pricing and discounting policies to apply when SLA commitments are not satisfied.

**Acknowledgments.** We would like to thank Wolfgang Ziegler, Oliver Wäldrich and Hassan Rasheed from the Fraunhofer Institute SCAI for their valuable advices. This research is partly funded by the University of Leeds through a Knowledge Transfer Secondement grant, and the European Union within the 7th Framework Programme under contract ICT-257115 - OPTIMIS.

# References

1. Buyya, R., Yeo, C.S., Venugopal, S., Broberg, J., Brandic, I.: Cloud computing and emerging IT platforms: vision, hype, and reality for delivering computing as the 5th utility. Future Gener. Comput. Syst. **25**(6), 599–616 (2009)
2. Keller, E., Ludwig, H.: The WSLA framework: specifying and monitoring service level agreements for web services. J. Netw. Syst. Manage. **11**, 57–81 (2003)
3. Galati, A., Djemame, K., Fletcher, M., Jessop, M., Weeks, M., Hickinbotham, S., McAvoy, J.: Designing an SLA Protocol with Renegotiation to Maximize Revenues for the CMAC Platform. In: Cloud-enabled Business Process Management (CeBPM 2012), Paphos, Cyprus (2012)

4. Hickinbotham, S., Austin, J., McAvoy, J.: Interactive graphics on large datasets drives remote condition monitoring on a cloud. In: The Proceedings of the Open Access Journal of Physics: Conference Series, Part of CMAC project, for Cybula Ltd. and the University of York, COMADEM2012, pp. 18–20 (2012)
5. Liang, B., Hickinbotham, S., Mcavoy, J., Austin, J.: Condition monitoring under the cloud. In: The Proceedings of the Digital Research 2012, Oxford (UK) (2012)
6. Battré, D., Hovestadt, M., Wäldrich, O.: Grids and Service-Oriented Architectures for Service Level Agreements, pp. 23–34. Springer, Berlin (2010)
7. Wäldrich, O., Ziegler, W.: WSAG4J - Web Services Agreement for Java. https://packcs-e0.scai.fraunhofer.de/wsag4j
8. Andrieux, A., Czajkowski, K., Dan, A., Keahey, K., Ludwig, H., Kakata, T., Pruyne, J., Rofrano, J., Tuecke, S., Xu, M.: Web Services Agreement Specification (WS-Agreement), GRAAP-WG, OGF recommendation. http://www.ogf.org/documents/GFD.192.pdf
9. OGF GFD.120: Open Grid Services Architecture - Glossary of Terms, J. Treadwell (2007)
10. SLA Management Handbook: Volume 2 Concepts and Principles, Release 2.5, TeleManagement Forum, GB 917–2 (2005)
11. Kubërt, R., Gallizo, G., Polychniatis, T., Varvarigou, T., Oliveros, E., Phillips, S.C., Oberle, K.: Service level agreements for real-time service-oriented infrastructures. In: Achieving Real-Time in Distributed Computing book: From Grids to Clouds, Chap. 8. IGI Global Books, Information Science Pub (2011)
12. IRMOS Project. http://www.irmosproject.eu
13. Menychtas, A., Kyriazis, D., Gogouvitis, S., Oberle, K., Voith, T., Gallizo, G., Berger, S., Oliveros, E., Boniface, M.: A Cloud platform for real-time interactive applications. In: 1st International Conference on Cloud Computing and Service Science (CLOSER 2011), Noordwijkerhout, The Netherlands (2011)
14. Erl, T.: Service-oriented Architecture: Concepts, Technology, and Design. Prentice Hall PTR, Upper Saddle River (2005). ISBN: 0-13-185858-0
15. Ludwig, H., Nakata, T., Wäldrich, O., Wieder, P., Ziegler, W.: Reliable orchestration of resources using WS-agreement. In: Gerndt, M., Kranzlmüller, D. (eds.) HPCC 2006. LNCS, vol. 4208, pp. 753–762. Springer, Heidelberg (2006)
16. Battré, D., Brazier, F.M.T., Clark, K.P., Oey, M.A., Papaspyrou, A., Wäldrich, O., Wieder, P., Ziegler, W.: A proposal for WS-agreement negotiation. In: Proceedings of the 11th IEEE/ACM International Conference on Grid Computing, pp. 233–241 (2010)
17. Pichot, A., Wieder, P., Wäldrich, O., Ziegler, W.: Dynamic SLA-negotiation based on WS-Agreement, CoreGRID TR-0082, Technical report (2007)
18. Ludwig, H., Dan, A., Kearney, R.: Cremona: an architecture and library for creation and monitoring of WSAgreements. In: Proceedings of the International Conference on Service Oriented Computing (ICSOC172004), pp. 65–74. ACM, New York (2004)
19. Neumann, D., Stoesser, J., Anandasivam, A., Borissov, N.: SORMA – building an open grid market for grid resource allocation. In: Veit, D.J., Altmann, J. (eds.) GECON 2007. LNCS, vol. 4685, pp. 194–200. Springer, Heidelberg (2007)

# A Domain Specific Language and a Pertinent Business Vocabulary for Cloud Service Selection

Mathias Slawik[(⊠)] and Axel Küpper

Telekom Innovation Laboratories, Service-centric Networking,
Technische Universität Berlin, Berlin, Germany
{mathias.slawik,axel.kuepper}@tu-berlin.de

**Abstract.** As more cloud computing offerings become available globally, cloud consumers' efforts of gathering relevant information to support their service selection are raised considerably. On the one hand, high-volume marketplaces, such as Salesforce AppExchange, feature non-formalized offering descriptions. This abstinence of a service formalization impedes cloud consumers' capabilities to both rapidly assess the fulfillment of their selection criteria and to compare different services uniformly. On the other hand, contemporary research on formalized service marketplaces faces significant challenges in its practical application, especially its ease of use and pertinence. In this article we present a novel textual domain specific language for describing services, a pertinent business vocabulary of selection criteria, and a brokering component. These artifacts raise cloud consumers' capabilities while being practically applicable, pertinent to businesses, and easy to use.

**Keywords:** Cloud service brokering · Domain-specific language · Service description language · Cloud computing

## 1 Introduction and Motivation

According to the NIST Definition of Cloud Computing [23] one of the cloud characteristics is *on-demand self-service*: consumers and providers are exempt from having human interaction in order to provision computing capabilities. Therefore, the description of cloud offerings becomes a crucial basis for service selection by cloud consumers.

The service descriptions found within high-volume SaaS marketplaces, such as Salesforce AppExchange [32] and the Google Apps Marketplace [13], rely on nonformalized information, e.g., free text, images, and some structured fields, e.g., author and category. While such content is appropriate for marketing purposes, other uses are impeded as unstructured text is insufficient for comprehensive search and uniform service comparison. Therefore, advanced use cases within service marketplaces require the formalization of service descriptions.

There are state-of-the-art research platforms for marketplaces and service descriptions, e.g., the Unified Service Description Language (USDL) marketplace [33], SPACEflight [37], and the FI-Ware Repository and Marketplace [34].

© Springer International Publishing Switzerland 2014
J. Altmann et al. (Eds.): GECON 2014, LNCS 8914, pp. 172–185, 2014.
DOI: 10.1007/978-3-319-14609-6_12

They use advanced service models, such as USDL [25], as well as expressive ontologies, such as Linked-USDL [26], and the Web Service Modeling Ontology for the Internet of Services (WSMO4IoS) [39] to describe services.

Applying such research within a small and medium enterprises (SME) application domain is one concept of the TRESOR project, whose architecture we present in [42]. This publication presents the contributions of the TRESOR service broker which matches customer requirements to cloud service capabilities in order to support the service selection decisions by SME cloud consumers. The broker provides a service description mechanism, a matchmaking component, as well as means to support cloud consumers in their service selection.

While realizing the TRESOR service broker we observed four challenge areas in the application of contemporary research within an SME domain. These motivate our contribution and are described in the following paragraphs:

1. **Business pertinence.** Advanced models and ontologies can expressively and extensively describe services as well as support their global publication and interlinking using Linked Data principles. However, we did not find any model or ontology which specifically represents the selection criteria of SME cloud consumers. To ensure the pertinence of the TRESOR broker to businesses we contribute a derivation of such a vocabulary based on current empiric research.

2. **Tooling complexity.** We observed an absence of specialized knowledge and skills for effective application of semantic technologies and tools in the SME application domain. To be able to successfully establish the cloud broker in this domain, it has to utilize common technologies and feature a simple design. Consequently, we created the Service Description Language - Next Generation (SDL-NG) framework which features a *Ruby-based internal textual domain specific language (DSL)*. This framework presents simplified semantics and a clean syntax, while allowing the vocabulary and service descriptions to be processed by text-, XML-, as well as RDF-based technologies.

3. **Documentation reuse.** Due to the self-service nature of cloud computing, cloud services have to be extensively documented. Without changing this documentation (e.g., by introducing annotations), contemporary models and ontologies cannot easily reuse those descriptions, creating *information redundancy* in service descriptions. A common reuse mechanism is parsing cloud vendors websites. We observed that it is a challenging task to integrate website parsers with language frameworks without raising complexity. As our DSL is executed as Ruby-code it can integrate arbitrary operations into service descriptions, creating self-sufficient entities wherein static elements and possibly highly dynamic external content, such as cloud spot market prices, are easily blended.

4. **Modeling defiances.** There are some traits of cloud services, which cannot be represented effectively with contemporary models and ontologies, such as *modeling service variants, price calculation*, as well as *dynamic properties*. While we do not address these in our current work, we outline and delineate impending contributions in this area at the end of this publication.

**Publication structure.** We apply the Information Systems Research Framework by Hevner et al. [15] which also structures this publication: Sect. 2 formulates the application environment and its requirements to ensure research *relevance*. To maintain research *rigor*, the related work is contrasted with the requirements in Sect. 3. The *design* of the approach is presented in Sect. 4. Section 5 contains its *assessment* and further development, while Sect. 6 concludes this publication.

## 2    Application Environment and Requirements Analysis

This section outlines the characteristics of the SME application domain, presents our requirements analysis methodology, and enumerates the resulting requirements. These are contrasted with the related work in Sect. 3 and provide the basis for the design evaluation in Sect. 5.

**Application environment.** The application environment are service ecosystems consisting of SMEs participating in public SaaS marketplaces as cloud consumers and providers. One example is the TRESOR ecosystem which brings together SMEs from the health sector to offer and consume secure and trusted cloud services.

Three fundamental reasons underly having SMEs as the application domain: First, SMEs play an important economic role. In Europe, for example, 99.8 % of all enterprises are SMEs and 66.5 % of the EU workforce is employed by an SME [44]. Second, SMEs receive significant benefits from cloud services as investigated by Lacity et al. in [20]. This provides a compelling reason for SMEs to participate in SaaS ecosystems as targeted by our approach. Third, the health sector aimed by TRESOR is dominated by SMEs. This allows us to incorporate first-hand experience and provides an appropriate evaluation environment.

**Requirement analysis: methodology and results.** To identify the requirements for our contribution we applied a multi-stage approach combining different methodologies. These are explicated in the following paragraphs:

**First stage (Months 1–6).** We first studied cloud-related literature to become familiar with the state-of-the-art. Concurrently, we joined multiple stakeholder group discussions to identify mutual and preliminary use cases, requirements and concepts. We published the results of this preliminary phase in [42].

**Second stage (Months 7–18).** We adjusted the Volere Requirements Specification Template [3] to capture stakeholder requirements iteratively: conducting topic-focused stakeholder workshops, analyzing and modelling the requirements using UML, and presenting, discussing, and adjusting the results. We identified 186 requirements which motivate previous publications [5,6,41] and [47]. We also joined a panel of experts from the accompanying research and other projects from the SME-focused "Trusted Cloud" intiative [12]. There, we compared all approaches to cloud description, matchmaking, and brokering. These group discussions let us assume that our requirements are not TRESOR specific, but are shared requirements for a range of cloud marketplaces. We assume that they can therefore also benefit from our contribution.

**Current stage (Months 16–36).** We derived implementation tasks from the requirements and evaluated the related work regarding its suitability to provide the foundation for the cloud broker implementation. We identified six requirements, which allow pinpointing the deficiencies of the current state-of-the-art and the advancements presented by our approach. They consist of *functional* and *non-functional* requirements, as defined by ISO/IEC/IEEE 24765 [18]. The following requirements have been identified:

**R1 (Functional): Capture service aspects pertinent to businesses.** The cloud service formalization has to contain selection criteria which are pertinent to potential service consumers, as they use it for service selection on a marketplace.

**R2 (Functional): Prevent redundant information.** A new formalization has to prevent the introduction of redundant information by allowing to reuse existing description sources.

**R3 (Functional): Support the service selection by cloud consumers.** There are many SME service procurement agents which do not have extensive expertise in cloud computing. The formalization should therefore not only list selection criteria, but also support consumers in assessing the criteria fulfillment.

**R4 (Non-functional): Low description effort.** Any provider's description effort presents an entry barrier for cloud marketplace participation. Therefore, a new cloud formalization has to present measures to lower the efforts for describing services.

**R5 (Non-functional): Low language definition effort.** SaaS ecosystems have to adapt the service formalization to their audience, as only some selection criteria are universal. The cloud formalization has to provide a mechanism for easy adaptation to different scenarios.

**R6 (Non-functional): Simple and usable tooling.** Any software which is needed to interact with the formalization has to be usable with reasonable efforts by the respective target group, e.g., SME cloud service providers.

# 3   Related Work

This section presents the state-of-the-art in the area of our contribution and contrasts it to the previously stated requirements. Fulfillment or dissatisfaction of specific requirements are designated by + and − as a requirement number suffix. For partly fulfilled requirements, a ○ is used. The end of this section summarizes the analysis of the related work.

## 3.1   Pertinent Selection Criteria for Businesses

Repschläger et al. have conducted two studies regarding the selection criteria of cloud consumers: In [28] they present "selection criteria for Software as a Service" based on literature review, an extensive market analysis, and an evaluation guided by expert interviews. The "Cloud Requirement Framework" (CRF) is outlined in [29]. It was devised using the same methodology and provides a well-grounded conceptual basis for structuring SaaS, PaaS, and IaaS selection criteria.

The "Cloud Service Check" [9] is a German catalog of cloud selection criteria with an extensive rationale providing guidance to assess different cloud service offerings. It is one of the results of the German research project Value4Cloud [10], whose application area are also SME cloud ecosystems.

The "Service Measurement Index" (SMI) is provided by the Cloud Service Measurement Initiative Consortium, led by Carnegie Mellon University [4]. It is far more extensive than related works. The SMI uses relative measures for assessing cloud offerings, i.e., "points" awarded for a service KPI are relative to the customer requirements and therefore differ for each respective service evaluation.

**Analysis.** The preceding works offer empiric knowledge whose incorporation into a solution design is the prerequisite for fulfilling Requirements 1 and 3.

### 3.2   Domain Specific Languages (DSLs)

Domain specific languages (DSLs) are tools to realize parts of computer systems. A comprehensive overview of DSLs is given by Fowler in [11] who defines DSLs as "a computer programming language of limited expressiveness focused on a particular domain". Fowler differentiates between *external* and *internal* DSLs: An external DSL is "external" to an implementation language, e.g., regular expressions, SQL, and XML. An internal DSL is "a particular way of using a general-purpose language", for example, a "fluid API" [7] and C++ template metaprogramming. Fowler recognizes a strong DSL culture in the programming language Ruby, which we chose for implementing our approach.

**Analysis.** According to Fowler, one of the main benefits of using a DSL is the domain specificity which fundamentally supports the communication with domain experts. DSLs can therefore help to fulfill Requirements 4 and 5.

### 3.3   High-Volume SaaS Marketplaces

Their revenue and the number of users make Salesforce AppExchange [32] and the Google Apps Marketplace [13] prototypical high-volume SaaS marketplaces. Instead of an elaborate cloud service formalization, they utilize data models with a small number of service attributes, such as free-text, images, provider info, and a categorization.

**Analysis.** Capturing information pertinent to businesses is solely dependent on the capability of the service provider to describe their services using unstructured information [R1○]. If providers participate in multiple marketplaces, the lack of a formalization introduces redundant information [R2−]. There is no support for consumers to assess criteria, as the information about selection criteria fulfillment has to be collected manually [R3−]. A guidance by a formalization is absent. Therefore, authoring service descriptions and enforcing a common structure between different descriptions is a non-trivial endeavor [R4−] [R5−]. The majority of contemporary software interacting with the simple data models of such marketplaces can be regarded as very mature, simple and usable [R6+].

### 3.4  Future Cloud Marketplaces and Service Description Languages

The features of future cloud marketplaces are postulated by Akolkar et al. in [2], who emphasizes on "intelligence" achieved by a solution repository and a deep question answering ability (DeepQA [17], such as the IBM Watson technology [16]). Akolkar refers to the work of Legner [21], who asserts the need for "more sophisticated classification schemes which reflect the vocabulary of the target customers". Our contribution contains such a vocabulary. To realize "intelligence" Akolkar proposes to use semantic technologies (e.g. OWL [45]) in a "vast knowledge base" using "recent advances in NLP, Information Retrieval, and Machine Learning to interpret and reason over huge volumes" [2]. There are recent research approaches sharing the mindset of Akolkar, such as FlexCloud (WSMO4IoS) and Linked-USDL:

**FlexCloud (WSMO4IoS).** The goal of the FlexCloud project is "developing methods and mechanisms for supporting a secure cloud lifecycle" [8]. It proposes a service description language, a registry, and a discovery system, which are presented by Spillner and Schill in [40]. The authors base their propositions on the analysis of twelve existing languages and their lack of meeting the authors' requirements of being "easily usable, freely available, versatile, extensible and scalable". Our requirement analysis yielded similar requirements. The authors created WSMO4IoS [39] which is based on one of the analyzed languages, the Web Service Modelling Language (WSML) [46]. Any work on WSML has ceased in 2008 having implications on the applicability of the work to current use cases. The usability of WSML tools is also impeded due to the outdated technological base of the WSMO IDE "WSMO Studio" [35].

**Linked-USDL.** Another recent proposal is the Linked-USDL, which is presented by Pedrinaci, Cardoso, and Leidig in [26]. It extends USDL proposed by Oberle et al. in [25]. According to Pedrinaci et al., USDL failed to gain adoption due to "complexity, difficulties for sharing and extending the model" [27]. USDL is based on the Eclipse Modeling Framework [43], Linked-USDL utilizes OWL [45] and reuses existing ontologies.

**Analysis.** Linked-USDL, WSMO4IoS, and our approach are motivated by the shortcomings of contemporary service description languages. Yet, we focus on supporting manual service selection by SME cloud consumers, while Linked-USDL and WSMO4IOS have a very broad scope: Linked-USDL aims "to maximise to the extent possible the level of automation that can be achieved during the life-cycle of services" [26]. WSMO4IoS has the goal of "covering as many XaaS domains as possible" and "unify these services as much as possible while restricting the domain specific service characteristics as little as possible" [40].

This broad scope and the lacking enterprise evaluation environment are the supposed reasons behind the failure of Linked-USDL and WSMO4IoS to capture most of the selection criteria identified in Sect. 3.1 [R1−]. Linked-USDL and

WSMO4IoS cannot capture HTML descriptions [R2−] or support SME users in their cloud service selection [R3−]. Due to the expressive power of the utilized ontologies and the broad scope of both approaches, the description and language definition effort can be regarded as high in comparison to DSLs and JSON/XML-based models, especially for SME users [R4−][R5−]. There are basic editors for Linked-USDL [22] and WSMO4IoS [38] which could be both reasonably used by SME users. Yet, the extension of both languages is only supported by ontology design software which targets expert users [R6○].

We have discussed both USDL and Linked-USDL with Leidig and Oberle to get design recommendations for our contribution.

### 3.5   Summary

The analysis of the related work clearly shows the lack of a solution fulfilling all of the enumerated requirements of SME cloud ecosystems. While there has been extensive research about pertinent selection criteria, almost none of them are reflected within service description languages, as well as contemporary and future cloud marketplaces. Furthermore, the benefits of using DSLs to capture service-domain specific information is not used in any of the analyzed contributions.

## 4   Formalizing Cloud Service Descriptions

Our contribution is divided into three main elements, which also structure this chapter: *The SDL-NG framework*[1] provides the metamodel and DSL framework for vocabulary definition and service description. A *pertinent business vocabulary*[2] uses the SDL-NG framework to formalize empiric knowledge about selection criteria. The *service broker*[3] builds upon the SDL-NG framework and the business vocabulary to provide a user interface to interact with the system.

### 4.1   SDL-NG Framework

The Service Description Language - Next Generation (SDL-NG) framework is built using the Ruby programming language to enable the specification of a service vocabulary as well as the description of services using this vocabulary in the form of domain specific languages.

The design of the SDL-NG framework is motivated by the requirements and the analysis of the related work: A DSL lowers description and language definition efforts (R4 & R5), especially in relation to service description languages using semantic technologies. From our past experience using Ruby as well as other programming languages we presume that a Ruby-based DSL can provide a simpler and more usable tooling (R6) than the language tools of WSMO4IoS

---

[1] https://github.com/TU-Berlin-SNET/sdl-ng.
[2] Contained as `/examples/vocabulary` in the SDL-NG source.
[3] https://github.com/TU-Berlin-SNET/tresor-broker.

**Listing 1.1.** Example vocabulary definition

```
1  type  :cloud_service_model
2  cloud_service_model  :saas
3  cloud_service_model  :paas
4  cloud_service_model  :iaas
5  service_properties  do
6      string  :service_name
7      cloud_service_model
8  end
```

**Listing 1.2.** Example service description

```
1  service_name  "Google␣Drive␣for␣Business"
2  cloud_service_model  saas
```

and Linked-USDL. As the service description is in fact program code, it can be augmented by libraries to implement the integration of existing sources (R2), e.g., scraping HTML documents for feature descriptions. Another benefit of using Ruby is the low "syntactic noise", i.e., the overhead characters not conveying semantic meaning (semicolons, brackets, etc.) are considerably lower in Ruby than in other programming languages, such as Java and C++.

The remainder of this subsection presents the SDL-NG *description life-cycle*, its *metamodel and type system*, as well as its *HTML parsing* and *export capabilities*.

**Description life-cycle.** The general life-cycle of service descriptions consists of the *vocabulary definition* and its *instantiation* in service descriptions. The main task of the vocabulary is to define the properties a service can have, their types, and their documentation. Vocabulary descriptions can be distributed over multiple files. An example SDL vocabulary description is shown in Listing 1.1. Line 1 defines a new **Type: CloudServiceModel**. Afterwards, some **CloudServiceModel** instances are defined. Starting from Line 5, new properties are added to the **Service** class: A string property named **service_name** and a property of the type **CloudServiceModel** with an auto-generated name **cloud_service_model**. Additional files contain the multi-lingual documentation of the vocabulary.

Listing 1.2 shows a service description, based on pairs of **Service** property names and their values. Setting the value of a property is in fact an invocation of a Ruby method on a **Service** instance. The predefined instances are referred by their identifier, e.g., the **saas** instance of **CloudServiceModel**.

**Metamodel and type system.** The SDL-NG metamodel and type system are based on Ruby classes forming a simple data model: **Types** containing **Property** instances. Properties of **Type** instances are set to either one or many values, e.g., a **String** containing a service name, or other **Type** instances, e.g., the **Firefox** instance of the **Browser Type**. Any property value can be annotated to capture the "fine print" of service descriptions which cannot be modeled effectively using the vocabulary. Retrieving and setting properties is internally delegated to reflective methods, allowing custom persistence options, such as the default in-memory

**Listing 1.3.** HTML parsing with SDL-NG

```
1  fetch_from_url(<URL>⁴, <CSS>⁵).each do |header|
2     feature header.content.strip, header.search('~p')[0]
3  end
```

persistence and the MongoDB-based persistence used by the cloud broker. An SDL user does not need to know how to instantiate a specific Ruby class in order to set a property, as all classes are wrapped. These wrappers allow simple class instantiation with strings and numbers, e.g., using the string `"1 $"` to create a money value instead of having the user know to write `Monetize.parse("1 $")`. Wrapped strings and numbers are retained in the wrappers to ease the serialization of property values.

**HTML parsing.** Preventing redundant information (R2) requires a simple mechanism to retrieve HTML SaaS descriptions. To ensure low efforts (R4) and simple tooling (R6), static service information and parsing commands should be defined in a self-sufficient service description. As SDL-NG descriptions are Ruby code, static information (e.g. `service_name "My service"`) as well as HTML parsing commands (e.g. `fetch_from_url(...)`) can be easily blended (e.g. `service_name fetch_from_url(...)`). Listing 1.3 illustrates the combination of HTML parsing and service description by showing the retrieval of **Feature** properties from the Google Drive for Business documentation. This example highlights the brevity, conciseness, and accessibility which can be achieved using language-internal DSLs. Besides statically reusing parts of websites for service description, the integration of external information can be highly dynamic in nature, e.g., when integrating spot market prices for cloud resources.

**Export capabilities.** To further prevent redundancies (R2), the vocabulary and descriptions should be consumable by other information systems. SDL-NG allows exporting descriptions as XML and the vocabulary as a corresponding XML Schema Definition (XSD) [36]. To support semantic processing, exporting descriptions to RDF is also possible. Generating a Web Ontology Language (OWL) [45] from the vocabulary is planned for one of the next releases.

### 4.2 A Pertinent Business Vocabulary

We have defined a vocabulary of selection criteria using the SDL-NG framework on the basis of empiric results from Repschläger et al. and the Cloud Service Check. It consists of 37 **Type** classes, 31 **Service** properties and 52 **Type** instances, covering a broad range of criteria, structured according to the Cloud Requirement Framework: **Characteristics**, e.g., cloud service model, service categories, **Charging**, e.g., charge unit (user account, floating license), **Compliance**, e.g., data location, audit options (e.g. audit logging), **Delivery**, e.g., billing and payment options, **Dynamics**, e.g., the duration for provisioning an

---

⁴ http://www.google.com/enterprise/apps/business/products.html.
⁵ div.apps-content-set:nth-child(3) div.product-section-features h3.

end user, **Interop**, e.g., features, interfaces, and compatible browsers, **Optimizing**, e.g., maintenance windows and future roadmaps, **Portability**, e.g., exportable and importable data formats, **Protection**, e.g., the communication protection (HTTPS, VPN, TCTP), **Provider management**, e.g., support availability, **Reliability**, e.g., offline capabilities, **Reputation**, e.g., year of service establishment, and **Trust**, e.g., providers' financial statement, reference customers. To achieve low description efforts (R4), `Service` properties are designed for high readability, e.g., "`employs 49829`", or "`is_protected_by https`".

### 4.3   The Service Broker

The service broker is part of the TRESOR ecosystem and offers an authoring interface for service descriptions, a repository query interface, cloud consumer search profiles, management of description versions, a description update workflow, and a module for booking and provisioning third party cloud services. The broker is built on the basis of the Ruby on Rails web framework [14] and uses MongoDB [24] for description persistence. To meet Requirements R4 and R6 (low description effort and simple tooling) the service broker includes a customized version of the Ace JavaScript editor [1] to allow comfortable authoring of service descriptions. To guide description authors, the broker can present a comprehensive listing of all properties and predefined instances of the business vocabulary in the form of a "cheat sheet". It is covered by 102 test cases, which cover 93,5 % of source lines of code.

## 5   Assessment and Outlook

We carried out an *analytical evaluation*, contrasting our contribution to its requirements, an *experimental evaluation*, where we applied the SDL-NG framework in an SME setting, and a preliminary *empirical evaluation*.

**Analytical Evaluation.** To ensure *capturing service aspects pertinent to businesses(R1)* we extensively and thoroughly compiled requirements from SME stakeholders, included empiric studies in our work, discussed it with the authors of the Cloud Requirement Framework and the Cloud Service Check, and participated in expert panels to assure its relevance for different use cases. To *prevent redundant information (R2)* the SDL-NG framework can integrate HTML descriptions as well as export them to XML/XSD and RDF. We *support the service selection by cloud consumers (R3)* by including rationale and extensive property documentation. By relying on text files containing property-value pairs SDL-NG presents *low description effort (R4)*. The language definition also relies on a simple textual syntax, leading to *low language definition effort (R5)*. Our *tooling is simple (R6)*, having a simple meta- and data model and consisting of only 1.200 source lines of code.

**Experimental evaluation.** The SDL-NG source repository contains descriptions of two widely used SaaS services, Google Apps for Business and

Salesforce Sales Cloud. These descriptions test the vocabulary pertinence and simplicity and also present a trial of the integration of external HTML content, as well as the XML/XSD and RDF export functionality. So far, we did not encounter challenges in the application of the SDL-NG framework.

**Empirical evaluation.** While designing our contribution we regularly presented preliminary stages to different project and external partners to carry out short explorative expert interviews to gain their first impressions on the respective state of our contribution. To test the usability of our approach in the SME domain we will carry out user studies at the end of the project.

**Outlook.** The outlook of our contribution is the "Open Service Compendium": by refining the vocabulary, creating an easy to use web interface, and opening up the service broker, we want to create a crowd-sourced "Wikipedia for Services", where any user can describe any service and use the broker to support their service selection. Four additional challenges have been identified which need to be addressed to create such a system:

**Modeling service variants.** Modeling the large amount of possible combinations of SaaS offering's variants and optional features is not feasible. The Open Service Compendium will use a *feature model* [19] based variant modeling. The features would contain `Service` property values, so that any offering description can be created through selecting features and combining properties.

**Price modeling and calculation.** Contemporary price models and ontologies are either lacking in sophistication, are too complicated, or cannot capture existing SaaS services. The Open Service Compendium should capture the price models of common SaaS offerings to the degree that potential service consumers can easily estimate their consumption charges. By combining the price and feature model, complex charging rules can also be supported.

**Property brokering information.** The Service Compendium should be able to assess the tendency of property values, i.e., if a value is better or worse than another value. This provides the basis for implementing analytic processes, such as the analytic hierarchy process [30] and the analytic network process [31] to support users with their service selection. We also want to include the findings of the CSMIC [4] to automate the measurement of service selection criteria fulfillment.

**Dynamic vocabulary.** To keep usage efforts of large vocabularies low, the vocabulary should be dynamically adaptable. For example, it should be possible to define category-specific properties. Furthermore, the definition of derived properties, e.g., "Cloud Storage per Euro" could help service comparison considerably.

## 6    Conclusion

Finding suitable cloud services is a laborious task, especially for SMEs. To support SMEs with their service selection better than current approaches we have created a novel DSL, a pertinent business vocabulary, and a brokering component. As we apply and evaluate the components in an appropriate SME environment we ensure their *relevance*. We have designed them *rigorously*, building upon empirical studies and established state-of-the-art. By publishing our work as open source software and by continuously engaging with the service community we want to further advance our work towards an "Open Service Compendium", which can support a broad range of cloud consumers in their service selection.

# References

1. Ajax.org B.V.: Ace (2014). http://ace.c9.io
2. Akolkar, R., Chefalas, T., Laredo, J., Peng, C.S., Sailer, A., Schaffa, F., Silva-Lepe, I., Tao, T.: The future of service marketplaces in the cloud. In: 2012 IEEE 8th World Congress on Services, pp. 262–269 (2012)
3. Atlantic Systems Guild Ltd.: Volere Requirements Specification Template (2014)
4. Carnegie Mellon University: CSMIC: Cloud service measurement initiative consortium (2012). http://csmic.org/
5. Ermakova, T., Fabian, B., Zarnekow, R.: Security and privacy system requirements for adopting cloud computing in healthcare data sharing scenarios. In: Proceedings of the AMCIS (2013)
6. Ermakova, T., Huenges, J., Erek, K., Zarnekow, R.: Cloud computing in healthcare - a literature review on current state of research. In: Proceedings of the AMCIS (2013)
7. Evans, E.: Domain-Driven Design: Tackling Complexity in the Heart of Software. Addison-Wesley, Reading (2003)
8. FlexCloud: FlexCloud (2014). http://flexcloud.eu/
9. fortiss GmbH: CloudServiceCheck (2014). http://www.value4cloud.de/de/cloudservicecheck
10. fortiss GmbH: Value4Cloud (2014). http://www.value4cloud.de
11. Fowler, M.: Domain-Specific Languages. Addison-Wesley, Reading (2011)
12. German Federal Ministry for Economic Affairs and Energy: Trusted Cloud (2014). http://www.trusted-cloud.de/
13. Google: Google Apps Marketplace (2014). https://www.google.com/enterprise/marketplace/home/apps/?pli=1
14. Heinemeier Hansson, D.: Ruby on rails (2014). http://rubyonrails.org
15. Hevner, A.R., March, S.T., Park, J., Ram, S.: Design science in information systems research. In: Gupta, A. (ed.) MIS Quaterly, pp. 75–105. SciTePress, Lisbon (2004)
16. IBM: Watson (2014). http://www.ibm.com/smarterplanet/us/en/ibmwatson
17. IBM Research: The DeepQA Research Team (2013). http://www.research.ibm.com/deepqa
18. ISO/IEC/IEEE: Systems and software engineering - Vocabulary (2010)
19. Kang, K.C., Cohen, S.G., Hess, J.A., Novak, W.E., Peterson, A.S.: Feature-oriented domain analysis. Technical report, FODA) (1990)
20. Lacity, M., Reynolds, P.: Cloud services practices for small and medium-sized enterprises. MIS Q. Executive **13**(1), 31–44 (2014). Management Information Systems Research Center, Minneapolis
21. Legner, C.: Is there a market for web services? In: Di Nitto, E., Ripeanu, M. (eds.) ICSOC 2007. LNCS, vol. 4907, pp. 29–42. Springer, Heidelberg (2009)

22. Leidig, T.: Simple editor for linked USDL descriptions (2013). https://github.com/linked-usdl/usdl-editor
23. Mell, P., Grance, T.: The NIST Definition of Cloud Computing. National Institute of Standards and Technology, Gaithersburg (2011)
24. MongoDB Inc: mongoDB: Agile and Scalable (2014). http://www.mongodb.org
25. Oberle, D., Barros, A., Kylau, U., Heinzl, S.: A unified description language for human to automated services. Inf. Syst. **38**(1), 155–181 (2013)
26. Pedrinaci, C., Cardoso, J., Leidig, T.: Linked USDL: a vocabulary for web-scale service trading. In: Presutti, V., d'Amato, C., Gandon, F., d'Aquin, M., Staab, S., Tordai, A. (eds.) ESWC 2014. LNCS, vol. 8465, pp. 68–82. Springer, Heidelberg (2014)
27. Pedrinaci, C., Cardoso, J., Leidig, T.: Presentation: linked USDL: a vocabulary for web-scale service trading (2014). http://slideshare.net/cpedrinaci/linked-usdl-a-vocabulary-for-webscale-service-trading
28. Repschläger, J., Wind, S., Zarnekow, R., Turowski, K.: Selection criteria for software as a service: an explorative analysis of provider requirements. In: Proceedings of the AMCIS (2012)
29. Repschläger, J., Zarnekow, R., Wind, S., Klaus, T.: Cloud requirement framework: requirements and evaluation criteria to adopt cloud solutions. In: Pries-Heje, J., Chiasson, M., Wareham, J., Busquets, X., Valor, J., Seiber, S. (eds.) Proceedings of the 20th European Conference on Information Systems (2012)
30. Saaty, T.L.: What is the analytic hierarchy process? In: Mitra, G., Greenberg, H.J., Lootsma, F.A., Rijkaert, M.J. (eds.) Mathematical Models for Decision Support. NATO ASI Series, pp. 109–121. Springer, Berlin (1988)
31. Saaty, T.L.: Analytic Network Process: Encyclopedia of Operations Research and Management Science, pp. 28–35. Springer, New York (2001)
32. Salesforce: AppExchange (2014). https://appexchange.salesforce.com
33. Sap, AG: USDL marketplace (2012). http://sourceforge.net/projects/usdlmarketplace
34. Sap, AG: FI-Ware marketplace and repository reference implementation (2013). https://github.com/service-business-framework
35. Simov, A., Dimitrov, M.: WSMO studio (2008). http://sourceforge.net/projects/wsmostudio/files
36. Sperberg-McQueen, C.M., Thompson, H.: XML schema (2014). http://www.w3.org/XML/Schema
37. Spillner, J.: SPACEflight - A versatile live demonstrator and teaching system for advanced service-oriented technologies. In: IEEE (ed.) Proceedings of the 21st CriMiCo, pp. 455–456. IEEE (2011)
38. Spillner, J.: wsmo4ios-editor (2012). http://serviceplatform.org:8000/trac/browser/packaging/scripts/develtools/wsmo4ios-editor
39. Spillner, J.: WSMO4IoS (2013). http://serviceplatform.org/spec/wsmo4ios/
40. Spillner, J., Schill, A.: A versatile and scalable everything-as-a-service registry and discovery. In: Desprez, F., Ferguson, D., Hadar, E., Leymann, F., Jarke, M., Helfert, M. (eds.) CLOSER 2013 Proceedings, pp. 175–183. SciTePress, Lisbon (2013)
41. Thatmann, D., Slawik, M., Zickau, S., Küpper, A.: Deriving a distributed cloud proxy architecture for managed cloud service consumption. In: CLOUD 2013 Proceedings, pp. 614–620. IEEE, California (2013)
42. Thatmann, Dirk, Slawik, Mathias, Zickau, Sebastian, Küpper, Axel: Towards a Federated Cloud Ecosystem: Enabling Managed Cloud Service Consumption. In: Vanmechelen, Kurt, Altmann, Jörn, Rana, Omer F. (eds.) GECON 2012. LNCS, vol. 7714, pp. 223–233. Springer, Heidelberg (2012)

43. The Eclipse Foundation: Eclipse Modeling Framework Project (EMF) (2014). http://www.eclipse.org/modeling/emf
44. The European Commission: A Recovery On The Horizon: Annual Report on European SMEs 2012/2013 (2013)
45. W3C OWL Working Group: OWL 2 Web Ontology Language Document Overview: W3C Recommendation 11/12/2012 (2012). http://www.w3.org/TR/owl2-overview
46. WSML Working Group: Web Service Modeling Language (2008). http://www.wsmo.org/wsml
47. Zickau, S., Küpper, A.: Towards location-based services in a cloud computing ecosystem. In: Ortsbezogene Anwendungen und Dienste, pp. 187–190 (2012)

# Economic Aspects of Quality of Service

# Towards Petri Net-Based Economical Analysis for Streaming Applications Executed Over Cloud Infrastructures

Rafael Tolosana-Calasanz[✉], José Ángel Bañares, and José-Manuel Colom

Dpto. de Informática e Ingeniería de Sistemas, Universidad de Zaragoza,
Zaragoza, Spain
{rafaelt,banares,jm}@unizar.es

**Abstract.** Streaming Applications are complex systems where the existence of concurrency, transmission of data and sharing of resources are essential characteristics. When these applications are run over Cloud infrastructures, the execution may incur an economical cost, and it can be therefore important to conduct an analysis prior to any execution. Such an analysis can explore how economic cost is interrelated to performance and functionality. In this paper, a methodology for the construction of this kind of applications is proposed based on the intensive use of formal models. Petri Nets are the formalism considered here for capturing the active entities of the system (processes), the flow of data between the processes and the shared resources for which they are competing. For the construction of a model aimed at studying different aspects of the system and for decision-taking design, an abstraction process of the system at different levels of detail is needed. This leads to several system models representing facets from the functional level to the operational level. Petri Net models are used to obtain qualitative information of the streaming application, but their enrichment with time and cost information provides with analysis on performance and economic behaviours under different scenarios.

**Keywords:** Economical cost of clouds · Petri Nets · Streaming application

## 1 Introduction

Over the last years, with the advances and development in sensor networks & technologies, there has been a growing number of sensors that are monitoring physical or environmental conditions, such as temperature, humidity, wind, etc. These sensors transmit their measurements continuously, forming a sequence of data elements known as a *data stream*. A number of applications exploit these data streams with different purposes–ranging from military applications monitoring battlefield to industrial and consumer applications, such as applications that help create Smart Cities and Smart Buildings, or applications for health

© Springer International Publishing Switzerland 2014
J. Altmann et al. (Eds.): GECON 2014, LNCS 8914, pp. 189–205, 2014.
DOI: 10.1007/978-3-319-14609-6_13

care monitoring, and natural disaster prevention. Moreover, these applications often have to deal with significants amounts of data that need to be processed *continuously* in (near) real-time, leading to the need for distributed computational infrastructures.

Hence, in such a context, the complexity of streaming applications arises from the confluence of concurrency, transmission of data and the use of distributed resources. From a conceptual design perspective, a streaming application can be seen a set of *Computational Processes (CPs)* that receive data continuously, and the data dependencies among them. Besides, a CP may require the synchronization of several input streams to conduct the computation. In order to execute such applications, CPs and their data transmissions involved require resources, including computational machines, network and storage. In the activity of mapping, resource management is involved, and its effectiveness can be measured from various system properties [15], namely economical cost, performance, and functionality. Nevertheless, depending on the target infrastructure the policies and the mechanisms involved for such an activity may be different. For instance, unlike in traditional distributed systems, load balancing in a Cloud infrastructure is not about evenly distributed the load among servers, but in minimizing the cost of providing the service. Hence, the goal is to adapt the computational power to the actual workload. It would be therefore important to conduct an analysis prior to any execution of a given workflow, analysis that must explore minimal and maximal boundaries of the economical cost of the execution of a streaming specification, in relationship with its performance and its workload.

In this paper, we propose a Petri net-based, model-driven and stepwise refinement methodology for streaming applications over Clouds. The central role in this methodology is assigned to a set of Petri Net models describing the behavior of the system including timing and cost information. The goal is to use these models in an intensive way before the deployment of the application in order to understand the system, and to obtain properties of the different solutions adopted. In some cases, the observations may induce or recommend changes into the application with the purpose of modifying parts of the design and assure agreed specifications. The consideration of Petri Nets is based on the natural descriptive power for the concurrency, but also for the availability of analytic tools coming from the domain of Mathematical Programming and Graph Theory. These tools are based on a structural analysis that support the reasoning on properties without the construction of the state space –which for such a class of systems is prohibitive.

Additionally, Petri Nets support the use of formal verification techniques such as standard Model Checking Techniques for the verification of qualitative properties. These techniques can be based on the construction of the state space of a streaming application (the complete set of reachable markings of the net by the occurrence of transitions). Then, any property to be verified can be expressed in logic terms. In case the property is satisfied, the answer of the Model Checker is just a confirmation of this, but if the property is false, then the model checker gives counterexamples that proof that the property does not hold. The main advantage is that usual properties like deadlock-freeness, liveness, home space, maximal sets of concurrently fireable transitions, mutual exclusions, etc. can be decided. In practice, the applicability of the approach is limited to *bounded* systems with a finite state space and with a moderate size. Conclusions hold *only for the initial marking* being considered. Our models for streaming application can be exploited to understand the most appropriate approach for solving the problem: strategy(ies) for decomposing the problem into processes, communication needs and resources required for satisfying functional and non-functional requirements. Taking into account that the model is a Petri Net, we can consider it as an executable specification. Therefore, it can be simulated in order to reach this understanding or simply to obtain performance or economic boundaries, which can be obtained by enriching it with time and cost information. In other words, simulation is an analysis technique. It may be useful to discover some (un)desirable behaviors, but in general it does not allow to proof the (in)existence of some properties.

The other way to exploit the models is through the extraction of structural information from the net. Structural information allows to obtain properties that are guaranteed mainly for the net structure, i.e. the places, the transitions and the token flow relation represented by means of the arcs. On this regard, a classical example is the information obtained from the marking invariants guaranteed by the structure of net (weighted sums of the contents of tokens of some places of the net that remain constant for any reachable state and, in particular, for the initial marking of the net). Invariants or other structural objects of the net give valuable information on the net behavior that can be used to detect, for example, a sequential execution of activities that reduces the net concurrency –i.e. because there are not enough tokens to fire transitions simultaneously. Let us suppose, for example, that we have a marking invariant that says that the sum of the contents of tokens of a set of places is equal to 1 for all reachable states. This means that in the set of places contained in the invariant one and only one of the places can contain exactly one token. Therefore, all the places are in mutual exclusion, moreover, all output transitions of these places are in mutual exclusion (they cannot be never concurrently fired). With this information a designer can decide to increase the contents of tokens of these invariants to increase the degree of concurrency, or he/she can modify the structure of the net in order to remove all these limiting invariants for the concurrency. From the above comments, we can say that a first phase for exploiting the models is to determine *the correction of the adopted solution*, verifying all the good properties expected are satisfied. As a second step, when a property is not satisfied, the model can be used for *detecting the causes of the problems* or anomalies in it that prevent it to behave as expected. Then, the understanding of the causes can lead to a *modification of the model*.

In the case of this paper, Petri Nets must capture the active entities of the system CPs, the flow of data between the processes (Data Transmission Processes) and the shared resources. The final Petri Net models can be exploited as a universal specification to be used with multiple platforms and languages. Taking into account the complexity of the involved elements in the system, the proposed approach decomposes the construction of the model in several stages. This leads to several system models representing facets from the functional level to the operational level. Petri Net models are used to obtain qualitative information of the streaming application, but their enrichment with time and cost information provides with analysis on performance and economic behaviours under different scenarios.

We validate our methodology through the wavefront algorithm, a Matrix-Vector multiplication in streaming fashion [12,13]. First, we create a Functional model describing the behavior of computations and data transmissions. After that we apply structural analysis techniques to verify that the functional behavior of our model was the expected: the wavefronts are propagated through the array in an orderly way. In order to verify some quantitative properties (the throughput of transitions) we add a timing interpretation to some transitions of the net, from which we can derive the economic cost. The reminding of this paper is structured as follows. In Sect. 2, related work is briefly discussed. In Sect. 3, our methodology is proposed. The Matrix-Vector multiplication example is studied in Sect. 4, and finally the conclusions are given in Sect. 5.

## 2    Related Work

Due to importance of processing data generated in a stream fashion, well-known workflow systems such as Kepler [10,19], Triana [9], or JOpera [5] have already incorporated data streaming workflow patterns to be used by users in their workflow specifications. The idea is that a sequence of more than one task is applied sequentially to a data stream [20]. In general terms in pipelined workflows, performance is typically measured in terms of throughput, and therefore the throughput is conditioned by the slowest task. For such a reason, it is important that all the tasks execute in the same time, which is challenging due to the variability and heterogeneity of computational resources as well as the programs that execute the tasks. Thus, task merging and workflow transformation is essential prior to mapping the tasks onto distributed resources in order to achieve the minimal variation in execution time of tasks. We believe that our proposal in this paper can help analyze the influence of the different design decisions in the task-mapping process on workflow throughput and other properties such as economical cost. Other proposals like [23] utilised Petri Nets for predicting the execution time (makespan) of Taverna workflows at a functional level.

Regarding the problem of workflow mapping of tasks and task clustering has been studied deeply in the Pegasus workflow system [14] for workflow DAGs. In particular, in [8], the authors highlight the problems that arise with current task clustering techniques as they are based on over simplified workflow models. They investigate the causes and propose a number of task balancing methods to address these imbalance problems. To the best of our knowledge, there is no analogous work for streaming workflows. Our model can be useful for system analysis, but at this stage is intended for human assistance rather than for autonomic system.

On the other hand, stream processing frameworks such as Yahoo's S4 [18], or IBM InfoSphere Streams [4] provide streaming programming abstractions to build and deploy tasks as distributed applications at scale for commodity clusters and clouds. Nevertheless, even that these systems support high input data rates, they do not consider variable input rates, which is our focus in this paper.

Additionally, the work in [1, 21, 22] is focused on designing a system architecture that processes data streams and exploits autonomic computing principles for resource management in an elastic infrastructure. It consists of a sequence of nodes, where each node has multiple data buffers and computational resources – whose numbers can be adjusted in an elastic way. They utilize the token bucket model for regulating, on a per stream basis.

In the Performance Engineering community, traditionally, three methods have been proposed, sometimes in complementary ways, to reveal how a system performs: direct measurement, simulation and analytical techniques. Although all of them allow system engineers to undertake testing before development, and at a lower cost, both simulation and analytical methods share the goal of creating a performance model of the system/device that accurately describes its load and duration of the activities involved. Performance models are often described in some formalisms including queuing network models [16], stochastic process algebra [3] or Petri nets [17] that provide the required analysis and simulation capabilities. A great number of these studies try to derive Petri net performance models from UML diagrams [2] and to compute performance metrics such as response time. Our emphasis in here is to exploit the inherent nature of Petri Nets for modelling concurrency, which serves.

# 3   Model Construction for the Economical Analysis

In the next subsections, we introduce the basic principles for the modular construction of the Petri Net models for our proposal. After that, we introduce different interpretations in the models in order to analyze properties related to the qualitative behavior of the system, the performance of the application or the economical costs of the deployment and execution.

## 3.1   Modular Construction of the Functional Petri Net Model of the Streaming Application

The construction of the functional model is based on the identification of the basic modules that compose an application of this class. These modules are the Computational Processes (CPs) and the Data Transmission Processes (DTPs). CPs accomplish functional operations and transformations on data, and DTPs allow data dependencies to be conducted among CPs. Both of CPs and DTPs need resources to accomplish the corresponding operation, and these resources also appear in the model, but at a conceptual, and generic way. Later in subsequent model refinements, specific resource constraints of different computational infrastructures will be added, such as limitations in parallelism, capacity, economic cost, etc.

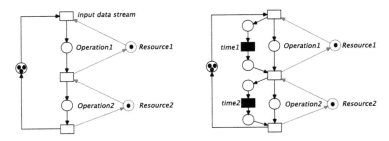

**Fig. 1.** A Computational Process with Resources composed by 2 sequential states each one requiring a different type of resource. (a) Untimed model; (b) Timed model assigning $time_i$ units of time to the execution of the $operation_i$.

- **Characterization of a CP.** A CP can be viewed as a sequence of operations to be applied to a set of data elements coming from different input data streams, a type of elementary computational task of the application. We assume a CP consists of multiple instances, Computational Threads (CT), that are executed concurrently. A CP is modeled as a Petri Net, $\mathcal{N}$, and a CT as a token that moves through $\mathcal{N}$. The places (partial states) of $\mathcal{N}$ are related to the different operations (either transformations, handling or assembly/disassembly operations) to be carried out by the thread. There exists a special place named *Idle* representing the inactive state of the threads and its initial marking is the maximum number of supported threads executing simultaneously this CP. The transitions of $\mathcal{N}$ allow a CT to progress towards its final state representing the end of the computation for the input data elements, the production of the output data elements and the restarting the thread for the processing of the next data elements on the stream. A CP has distinguished input points (output transitions of the Idle place) of data elements from the input streams and output points (input transitions of the Idle place) of data elements of the output streams. The execution of a CP is achieved by the execution of a computation path, and several of them can exist in the same CP. A computation path is a sequence of transitions fireable in $\mathcal{N}$, whose occurrence represents the obtention of a computed data record.

   In Fig. 1.a, a CP with two sequential states is represented. A token in the place *Operation1* or *Operation2* represents a thread executing the code corresponding to the operation 1 or 2, respectively, required by the computational task modeled by means of this CP. A thread executes these operations sequentially following the firing sequence: (1) *Input Data Stream* representing the acquisition of the data records from the input stream to realize the computational task; (2) *Change* representing the end of the operation 1 and the beginning of the operation 2; (3) *Output Data Stream* representing the delivery of the data records obtained after the computation to the output stream. The model presented in Fig. 1.a is untimed. The addition of timed information to a CP is introduced by the addition of a sequence place-transition-place in parallel with a process place representing an operation of the computational

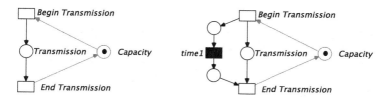

**Fig. 2.** A Data Transmission Process with capacity for a single data record. (a) Untimed model; (b) Timed model

task that consumes time. The transition added is labeled with time information representing the duration of the computational operation. In Fig. 1.b, the CP from Fig. 1.a is represented by assigning *time1* and *time2* units of time to the execution of the operations 1 and 2, respectively, according to the previously announced construction for the introduction of timing in the model. Observe that all transitions of Fig. 1.a are immediate that is, do not consume time.

– *Characterization of the Data Transmission Processes.* CP can transmit data elements to other CP in the form of a stream sent by means of a physical/virtual device such as a FIFO queue implemented in memory or a communication channel in a communication network. That transmission behavior is captured by a *Data Transmission Process* DTP. A data element to be transmitted is modeled as token that moves through a Petri Net, $\mathcal{N}$, representing an Elementary DTP with capacity for a single data record. The places of $\mathcal{N}$ are related to the states in which a data element can be in the transmission device. The transitions of $\mathcal{N}$ allow a data record to progress from the source to the destination. The construction of a transmission device for a stream with a capacity for $k$ data elements sequentially ordered requires of the concatenation of $k$ of these elementary DTPs. The model in Fig. 2.a is untimed and firing sequence of transitions *Begin Transmission* and *End Transmission* represents the movement of a single data element of a stream from the source (the final transition of any kind of Process) to a destination (the initial transition of any kind of Process). In Fig. 2.b, the DTP of Fig. 2.a is represented by assigning $time_1$ units of time to the transmission of a data element (according to the previously announced construction for the introduction of timing in the model).

– *Incorporation of Resources to each Computational and Data Transmission Process.* We consider any hardware/software element part of the execution environment (i.e. a processor, a buffer, a server, a communication channel, etc.) as a resource with a given capacity. In the case of a buffer, its capacity can be the number of positions to allocate elements, a processor may have a number of cores that can be considered as its capacity, etc. Moreover, in the execution environment, there exist several resource types and for each of them, a number of identical instances can be available, representing either the number of available copies of the resource to be used (or its capacity). In all cases, the considered resources are conservative, i.e. there is no resource leakage. On the other hand, each state of a CP, for its corresponding processing step, requires a (multi-)set of resources (including the buffering capacity to hold the thread itself). In our model, a resource type is represented by means of a place whose initial marking represents either the number of available copies of the resource or its capacity. A resource place has input (output) arcs to (from) those transitions of a CP that moves a Thread to (from) a state that requires (was using) a number of copies of this resource type. In the case of DTPs, resource places represent the capacity of the storage device for transmission. The CP of Fig. 1.a requires two different types of resources that are modeled by means of the places *Resource1* and *Resource2*. Observe that the CP requires a copy of *Resource1* to realize the operation 1 and a copy of *Resource2* to realize the operation 2. in the DTP of the Fig. 2.a the resource place is the place named *Capacity* that represents the size of the storage in the transmission device measured in number of data records, in the figure is equal to one (the initial marking of the place *Capacity*).

– *Construction of the global model by composition of the Modules with resources.* In order to obtain the global model of the Streaming application, a number of CPs with their corresponding DTPs (accomplishing the data dependencies among them) must be composed. Besides, the resources needed must also be considered at this step. The composition is based on the fusion of the resource places representing the same resource type in the different Modules. The initial marking of the resources, after the fusion, normally is computed as the maximum of the initial markings of the instances that have been merged. The other composition operation is the fusion of a transition representing the production of data records of an output stream in a module with the transition representing the consumption of data records of an input stream belonging to a different module. Observe that it is possible to connect directly two CP without intermediate DTPs, one of the processes acts as producer of data records and the other as consumer of data records but without any intermediate buffer.

## 3.2   Modular Construction of the Operational Petri Net Model of the Streaming Application

The functional Petri Net model is derived from a specific algorithm that actually processes a number of given data streams. As already seen, it consists of a composition of computational tasks and the data dependencies among them. In consequence, a *minimal* number of constraints coming from the final execution environment can be taken into account and, in many cases, the functional model is constructed under a number of hypothesis that may not hold when targeting a specific infrastructure – i.e. the resources required in order to reach the maximum degree of parallelism inherent in the model will not be available, or in case there are resources available, but the economic cost of its usage exceeds the budget, etc. Therefore, refining the functional model with the operational submodel aims at introducing specific resource constraints that may alter either economic cost, performance or even functionality. The alteration of the expected

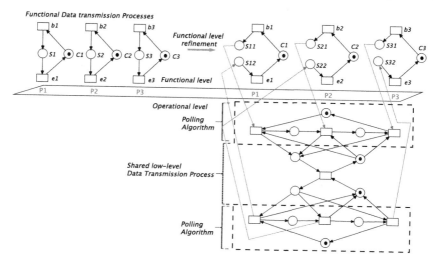

**Fig. 3.** Refinement of the Functional Petri Net model to take into account the operational data transmission process that must be shared for three functional data transmission processes

and observed behavior at the functional model may even induce changes into the functional model in order to better target a particular execution environment. In other words, the reason for the operational submodel is to consider explicitly those actual characteristics of a final execution environment, or to compare the response of the application under different deployment scenarios. In this section, we refine the Functional Petri Net model according to the characteristics of the execution environment. Nevertheless, the list of possible constraints imposed by the operational level is very large for the space in this paper. Hence, the following is an illustration on how the operational Petri Net model can be constructed from the Functional Petri Net model in two cases of relevance.

The first one corresponds to the case in which the functional Petri Net model has several DTPs that they were initially independent, but finally in the operational model they must be merged together within the same low-level DTP. The actual refinement procedure is depicted in Fig. 3. There, three independent DTPs, $P_1$, $P_2$ and $P_3$, are displayed that were already present in the Functional Petri Net Model. Nevertheless, the design decision to be taken is that the three Processes must share the same Low-Level Data Transmission Process of capacity 2. The refinement of the model requires the splitting of each place $s_i$ of a DTP $P_i$ in 2 places: (1) $s_{i1}$ represents the request of transmission to the low level; (2) $s_{i2}$ represents the end of the transmission. These two places are connected with a low-level DTP of capacity two, as depicted in the figure. Observe that in order to recognize the process requesting the transmission, in the low-level DTP a Polling Algorithm to serve the requests has been implemented that is equal to the Polling Algorithm to send the acknowledgements to High-Level DTPs. The other aspect to take into account in the refinement activity is that in case of having timing information for the processes $P_1$, $P_2$ or $P_3$, this information must be removed before the actual refinement; since, after the refinement the original information, it has no significance. The reason for this is that in the refined model the consumption of time is in the Low-Level DTP.

Another case arises when several CPs of the Functional Petri Net Model, which use resources types in isolation, must share the resources between all CPs. This provokes the rise of competitive relationships. A typical scenario for this transformation appears when the number of CPs is higher than the number of processors and the actual parallelism is limited.

### 3.3   Exploiting Petri Net Models for the Economical Analysis

A first phase for exploiting the models is to determine *the correction of the adopted solution*, verifying all the good properties expected are satisfied. As a second step, when a property is not satisfied, the model can be used for *detecting the causes of the problems* or anomalies in it that prevent it to behave as expected. Then, the understanding of the causes can lead to a *modification of the model*.

Finally, the addition of *performance*-oriented interpretations to the model allows us to compute measurements such as throughput, utilization rates, queue lengths, etc., from which it is possible to determine the time consumed in a particular computation or the resources that have been involved. Both the time consumed and the number of resources involved can be utilised to evaluate the economic cost. The kind of performance measurements that are required to be computed and how they must be exploited for an economic analysis depends on the semantics of the elements in the model and its connection to the real system (streaming application). In the next section we discuss an example of this.

## 4   Case Study: Wavefront Algorithm for Matrix-Vector Multiplication in Streaming

In order to illustrate our methodology, we are making use of the Matrix-Vector Multiplication problem in streaming fashion, in particular, the Wavefront Algorithm [12], which represents a simple solution for large arrays. Due to space limitations, we are focused on Functional analysis, and no particular target infrastructure for the operational analysis is considered here. Let us examine how an algorithm from Linear Algebra can be executed on a square, orthogonal $3 \times 3$ wavefront array (Fig. 4).

Let $A = (a_{ij})$ be a $3 \times 3$ matrix, and let $X^{(k)} = (x_i^{(k)})$, $Y^{(k)} = (y_i^{(k)})$ and $Z^{(k)} = Y^{(k)} + A \cdot X^{(k)} = (z_i^{(k)})$ be $3 \times 1$ matrices for $k = 1, 2, 3$. Initially, the elements of $A$ are stored in the array of processors ($a_{ij}$ in processor $P_{ij}$). The elements $x_i^{(k)}$, for $k = 1, 2, 3$ are stored from data streams on the top of the i-th column of processors. The elements $y_i^{(k)}$, for $k = 1, 2, 3$ are stored from data streams to the left of the i-th row of processors. The computational process

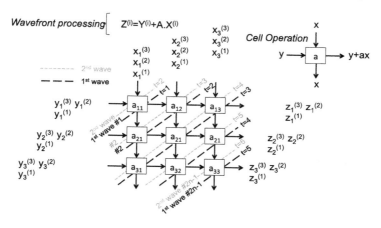

**Fig. 4.** Wavefront processing of $Z^{(k)} = Y^{(k)} + A \cdot X^{(k)}$, $k = 1, 2, \dots$.

starts with processor $P_{11}$, where $y_1^{(k)} + a_{11}x_1^{(k)}$ is computed. The appropriate data is then propagated to the neighbour processors $P_{12}$ (the result of $P_{11}$) and $P_{21}$ (the input data on the top of $P_{11}$, $x_1^{(k)}$), which execute their respective (similar) operations. The next front of activity will be at processors $P_{31}$, $P_{22}$ and $P_{13}$. At the end of this step, $P_{13}$ outputs $z_1^{(1)}$. A computation wavefront that travels down the processor array appears. Once the wavefront sweeps through all the cells, the first computation for $k = 1$ is finished. Similar computations can be executed concurrently with the first one by pipelining more wavefronts in succession immediately after the first one. The wavefronts of two successive computations never intersect, since once a processor performs its share of operations for a given computation, the next set of data that it will receive can only be from the next computation.

## 4.1  A Functional Petri Net Model of the Wavefront Algorithm for $Z^{(k)} = Y^{(k)} + A \cdot X^{(k)}$, $k = 1, 2, \dots$

The functional Petri Net model of the wavefront algorithm sketched in Fig. 4 is constructed in a modular fashion. The basic models we need in this case are: (1) A module to describe the Computational Process carried out in a node of the wavefront array; (2) A module to describe de Data Transmission Processes of the input and output data streams to/from the wavefront array. These modules are depicted in Fig. 5. To construct the global model nine instances of the CP of Fig. 5.a are needed. The modules of this type belonging to the same row are composed via the fusion of the transition $End\_i1$ with the transition $Sync\_i2$; and the transition $End\_i2$ with the transition $Sync\_i3$. These transitions fusions represent the transmission of the result elaborated by the column 1 or 2, as input to the columns 2 or 3, respectively, without intermediate buffering. Each one of the CPs of the first column is composed with a DTP representing the input stream of the corresponding i-th component of the vector $Y^{(k)}$ via the fusion of the transitions $Sync\_i1$ and $end$. Each one of the CPs of the last column is composed with a DTP representing the output stream of the corresponding i-th component of the vector $Z^{(k)}$ via the fusion of the transitions $End\_i3$ and $begin$. Each one of the CPs of the first row is composed with a DTP representing the input stream of the corresponding i-th component of the vector $X^{(k)}$ via the fusion of the transitions $Sync\_1i$ and $end$. Finally, we connect two CPs belonging to the same column but located in rows 1 and 2, or in rows 2 and 3, by means of a Internal DTP describing the flow of the corresponding component of the vector $X^{(k)}$ through the rows of the array. This connection is done by the fusion of the transitions $Sync\_1j$ and one transition $begin$ and the corresponding transition $end$ with the transition $Sync\_2j$ (similarly for the case of rows 2 and 3).

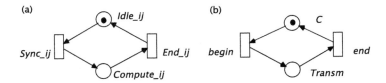

**Fig. 5.** Basic modules for the construction of the functional Petri Net model of the wavefront algorithm for $Z^{(k)} = Y^{(k)} + A \cdot X^{(k)}$, $k = 1, 2, ....$ (a) Computational Process associated to a node; (b) Data Transmission Process for the external/internal data streams.

Figure 6 depicts an untimed functional Petri Net model of the wavefront algorithm for $Z^{(k)} = Y^{(k)} + A \cdot X^{(k)}$, $k = 1, 2, ....$ This net model is isomorphous to the flow model in Fig. 4.

The addition of time to the model of Fig. 6 will be done in the way described in the previous section: adding a sequence place-transition-place in parallel with the place representing the activity that consumes time. The new added transition will be labeled with the time information. In the example, a timed sequence will be added in parallel with each place $Compute\_ij$ representing the duration of the computation realized by the CP located at row i-th, column j-th. Moreover, a timed sequence will be added in parallel to each place $Transm$ representing the consumption of time in the transmission of a data element in the corresponding DTP.

## 4.2    Analysis of the Model

According to the proposed methodology in this paper, we proceed now to exploit the model we have obtained in Fig. 6.

## 4.3    Structural Analysis

First, we try to determine the correction of design obtained. This is realized exploiting the structural properties of the net. This net is a *strongly connected*

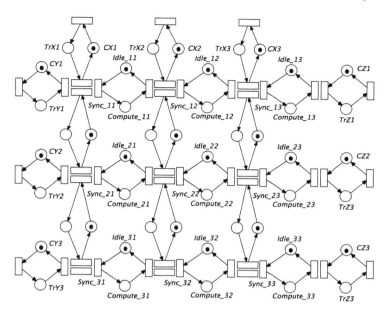

**Fig. 6.** Untimed functional Petri Net model of the wavefront algorithm for $Z^{(k)} = Y^{(k)} + A \cdot X^{(k)}$, $k = 1, 2, \ldots$.

*marked graph* (a subclass of Petri nets in which each place has only one input and one output transition, being strongly connected in the sense of graph theory). Moreover, in this net all circuits contain at least one token. From these characteristics, we obtain the following functional properties of the model:

(1) Any transition of the net is fireable from any reachable state of the net (the net is *live*, thus deadlock-free). The minimal repetitive sequence of transition firings contains all transitions of the net exactly once (it is guaranteed from the existence of only one T-invariant: right annuller of the incidence matrix of the net). This is a necessary condition for the execution of a wavefront in the array.

(2) The wavefronts propagate in an orderly manner without colliding one into another. This can be concluded when taking into account the maximal difference between firings (in any firing sequence) of a transition $Sync\_ij$ with respect to its: (1) right neighbor transition $Sync\_i(j + 1)$ is equal to 1. To see this, observe that both transitions are covered by a circuit containing only one token. This circuit enforces a strict alternation in the firing of both transitions starting with the firing of $Sync\_ij$; (2) left neighbor transition $Sync\_i(j - 1)$ is equal to 0. The reason is the same that in the previous case: the existence of a circuit with a token that enforces the alternation of both transitions starting with the transition $Sync\_i(j - 1)$; (3) bottom neighbor transition $Sync\_(i + 1)j$ is equal to 1. Once again, this can be proven by means of the vertical circuit covering both transitions and containing only

one token; and (4) top neighbor transition $Sync\_(i-1)j$ is equal to 0. All these values can be obtained from the so called marking invariants of the net (that in the case of marked graphs are the elementary circuits of the net) and can be computed in a structural way.

(3) CP in a right to left diagonal can operate concurrently, but two right to left adjacent diagonals cannot fully operate concurrently. This can be easily proven observing that the 4 transitions $Sync\_ij$, $Sync\_i(j+1)$, $Sync\_(i+1)j$ and $Sync\_(i+1)(j+1)$ are covered by an elementary circuit containing only two tokens. This means that only two transitions of these 4 transitions can be concurrently fired. But taking into account the firing relations enumerated in the previous point, only two scenarios are possible: (1) concurrent firing of the transitions $Sync\_ij$ and $Sync\_(i+1)(j+1)$; (2) concurrent firing of the transitions $Sync\_i(j+1)$ and $Sync\_(i+1)j$. This points out the initial statement about the mutual exclusion in the execution of right to left neighbor diagonals.

(4) The maximal concurrency can be obtained putting to work concurrently all CPs in odd right to left diagonals or all CPs in even right to left diagonals. This property can be obtained from the previous property extended to the full array.

The previous analysis, without the need for an exhaustive simulation or construction of the state space, points out that it is not possible to have the nine CPs working/executing concurrently. This anomaly or bottleneck limiting concurrency is due to the existence of the circuits covering four transitions, but containing only two tokens as those described in the previous point 3. in order to reach a fully concurrent operation of the nine CPs, we can modify the initial design to enforce circuits with four tokens, covering the four transitions as in the previous point 3. Thus, we can introduce a DTP between two consecutive CPs in a row, decoupling the two CPs by the introduction of a buffer of capacity 1. An alternative solution to enforce the circuits with four tokens to avoid the property of point 3, is to introduce and additional DTP of capacity 1 connected to the already existing between two rows in the same column. This additional buffering enables a design with the maximal possible concurrency in the steady state of the processing of the streams: nine simultaneous computational processes.

**Economical Analysis.** For an economic analysis, the pricing models in [11] could be considered, including pricing cost associated to different data transfers, CPU time or storage usage. For the sake of simplicity in here, we are just considering an economic cost per CPU usage through time, information that can be added into the model in the following way:

(1) Let us assume, under a deterministic timing interpretation, a time $\alpha$ for the timed transitions added to represent the duration of the input of data elements from the streams corresponding to the vectors $Y^{(k)}$ and $X^{(k)}$ (timed transitions in parallel with the places $TrYi$ and $TrXi$, a time $\beta$ for transitions corresponding to the execution of the code of the CPs (timed transitions added in parallel with the places $Comp\_ij$), and a time $\gamma$ for transitions corresponding to the internal transmissions in the wavefront array. A reachable

(exact) bound of the throughput of the system can be computed through structural techniques as in [6], obtaining a value equal to the inverse of $max\{\alpha, \beta, \gamma\}$. In general, under a stochastic timing interpretation, the computed bounds following [6] can be eventually improved (in [7] a search for embedded queueing networks was considered).

(2) A bound of the mean cycle time for this net (the elapsed time between two consecutive firings of a transition) is the inverse of the throughput, from this value, we can compute the economic cost for the processing of streams of length $k = n$, assuming the cost of the time unit per CPU, $p$: $Cost = max\{\alpha, \beta, \gamma\} * n * p * 9$. It allows the designer to have an accurate estimation of the cost taking into account the pricing applied to CPU time consumed. Note that this analysis corresponds to the functional level and no information on the operational level has been considered. In this case, the model is designed with nine CPs having each nine computational resources in isolation.

(3) Taking into account that the model in Fig. 6 is a marked graph an optimal scheduling policy is just the earliest-firing-time policy (i.e. fire the transitions as soon as possible).

The previous analysis has be done on the functional Petri Net model. In case we wanted to introduce a particular operational level, we would have to proceed to the refinement of the previous functional Petri Net model and proceed to a similar analysis to the previously carried out: the timing and pricing information that are currently in the Functional level would be removed, and then they would be appearing in the new refined submodel. Besides, in such a refined model, the relationship between economic cost and performance can be studied: i.e. how the performance behaves when the economic cost is reduced.

## 5   Conclusions and Future Work

In this paper, we have shown that Petri Nets (eventually with an associated interpretation) are useful formal models to describe and analyze functional, performance and economical properties (of interest for the designer) of streaming applications. The separation between the graph-based structure of the model and dynamic properties such as the marking, enables the use of many structure-based analysis techniques. Through a simple Matrix-Vector multiplication in streaming fashion, the wavefront algorithm, we have shown the underlying methodology in the use of Petri Nets. First, the modeling task has been realized in a modular fashion using the subnet describing the behavior of computations and data transmissions. After that, we have applied some structural analysis techniques (due to their good tradeoff between decision power and computational complexity) to verify that the functional behavior of our model was the expected: the wavefronts are propagated through the array in an orderly way. In order to verify some quantitative properties, namely throughput and economic cost, have added a timing interpretation to some transitions of the net, and have assumed an associated CPU pay-per-use cost.

**Acknowledgements.** This work was supported by the Spanish Ministry of Economy under the program "Programa de I+D+i Estatal de Investigación, Desarrollo e innovación Orientada a los Retos de la Sociedad", project id TIN2013-40809-R.

# References

1. Bañares, J.Á., Rana, O.F., Tolosana-Calasanz, R., Pham, C.: Revenue creation for rate adaptive stream management in multi-tenancy environments. In: Altmann, J., Vanmechelen, K., Rana, O.F. (eds.) GECON 2013. LNCS, vol. 8193, pp. 122–137. Springer, Heidelberg (2013)
2. Bernardi, S., Merseguer, J.: Performance evaluation of UML design with stochastic well-formed nets. J. Syst. Softw. **80**(11), 1843–1865 (2007)
3. Bernardo, M., Ciancarini, P., Donatiello, L.: Aempa: a process algebraic description language for the performance analysis of software architectures. In: Workshop on Software and Performance, pp. 1–11 (2000)
4. Biem, A., Bouillet, E., Feng, H., Ranganathan, A., Riabov, A., Verscheure, O., Koutsopoulos, H., Moran, C.: Ibm infosphere streams for scalable, real-time, intelligent transportation services. In: Proceedings of the 2010 ACM SIGMOD International Conference on Management of Data, SIGMOD '10, pp. 1093–1104. ACM, New York (2010). http://doi.acm.org/10.1145/1807167.1807291
5. Bioernstad, B.: A Workflow Approach to Stream Processing. Phd thesis, ETH Zurich, Computer Science Department (2008). http://e-collection.ethbib.ethz.ch/view/eth:30739
6. Campos, J., Chiola, G., Colom, J.M., Silva, M.: Properties and performance bounds for timed marked graphs. IEEE Trans. Circ. Syst. I: Fundam. Theor. Appl. **39**(5), 386–401 (1992)
7. Campos, J., Silva, M.: Embedded product-form queueing networks and the improvement of performance bounds for petri net systems. Perform. Eval. **18**(1), 3–19 (1993)
8. Chen, W., Ferreira da Silva, R., Deelman, E., Sakellariou, R.: Balanced task clustering in scientific workflows. In: 2013 IEEE 9th International Conference on eScience (eScience), pp. 188–195 (2013)
9. Churches, D., Gombas, G., Harrison, A., Maassen, J., Robinson, C., Shields, M., Taylor, I., Wang, I.: Programming scientific and distributed workflow with Triana services: Research articles. Concurr. Comput. Pract. Exper. **18**(10), 1021–1037 (2006)
10. Dou, L., Zinn, D., McPhillips, T., Kohler, S., Riddle, S., Bowers, S., Ludascher, B.: Scientific workflow design 2.0: demonstrating streaming data collections in kepler. In: 2011 IEEE 27th International Conference on Data Engineering (ICDE), pp. 1296–1299, April 2011
11. Gohad, A., Narendra, N.C., Ramachandran, P.: Cloud pricing models: a survey and position paper. In: 2013 IEEE International Conference on Cloud Computing in Emerging Markets (CCEM), pp. 1–8. IEEE (2013)
12. Kung, S.Y., Arun, K.S., Gal-Ezer, R.J., Rao, D.V.B.: Wavefront array processor: Language, architecture, and applications. IEEE Trans. Comput. **31**(11), 1054–1066 (1982). http://dblp.uni-trier.de/db/journals/tc/tc31.html#KungAGR82
13. Kungt, H., Leisersont, C.E.: Systolic arrays (for vlsi), p. 256. Social Industry Application, Philadelphia (1979)

14. Lee, K., Paton, N., Sakellariou, R., Deelman, E., Fernandes, A., Mehta, G.: Adaptive workflow processing and execution in Pegasus. In: Third International Workshop on Workflow Management and Applications in Grid Environments (WaGe08), Kunming, China, pp. 99–106, 25–28 May 2008
15. Marinescu, D.C.: Cloud Computing: Theory and Practice. Morgan Kaufmann, Boston (2013)
16. Menascé, D.A., Gomaa, H.: A method for design and performance modeling of client/server systems. IEEE Trans. Software Eng. **26**, 1066–1085 (2000)
17. Murata, T.: Petri nets: Properties, analysis and applications. Proc. IEEE **77**, 541–580 (1989)
18. Neumeyer, L., Robbins, B., Nair, A., Kesari, A.: S4: distributed stream computing platform. In: Proceedings of the 2010 IEEE International Conference on Data Mining Workshops, ICDMW '10, pp. 170–177. IEEE Computer Society, Washington, DC (2010). http://dx.doi.org/10.1109/ICDMW.2010.172
19. Ngu, A.H.H., Bowers, S., Haasch, N., McPhillips, T., Critchlow, T.: Flexible scientific workflow modeling using frames, templates, and dynamic embedding. In: Ludäscher, B., Mamoulis, N. (eds.) SSDBM 2008. LNCS, vol. 5069, pp. 566–572. Springer, Heidelberg (2008)
20. Pautasso, C., Alonso, G.: Parallel computing patterns for Grid workflows. In: Proceedings of the HPDC2006 Workshop on Workflows in Support of Large-Scale Science (WORKS06), Paris, France, 19–23 June 2006
21. Tolosana-Calasanz, R., Bañares, J.A., Rana, O.F.: Autonomic streaming pipeline for scientific workflows. Concurr. Comput. Pract. Exper. **23**(16), 1868–1892 (2011)
22. Tolosana-Calasanz, R., Bañares, J.Á., Pham, C., Rana, O.F.: Enforcing qos in scientific workflow systems enacted over cloud infrastructures. J. Comput. Syst. Sci. **78**(5), 1300–1315 (2012)
23. Tolosana-Calasanz, R., Rana, O.F., Bañares, J.A.: Automating performance analysis from Taverna workflows. In: Chaudron, M.R.V., Ren, X.-M., Reussner, R. (eds.) CBSE 2008. LNCS, vol. 5282, pp. 1–15. Springer, Heidelberg (2008)

# Autonomous Management of Virtual Machine Failures in IaaS Using Fault Tree Analysis

Alexandru Butoi[✉], Alexandru Stan, and Gheorghe Cosmin Silaghi

Business Information Systems Department, Babeş-Bolyai University,
Cluj-Napoca, Romania
{alex.butoi,alexandru.stan,gheorghe.silaghi}@econ.ubbcluj.ro

**Abstract.** Cloud IaaS services bring the novelty of elastic delivery of computational resources in a virtualized form and resource management through easy replication of virtual nodes and live migration. In such dynamic and volatile environments where resources are virtualized, availability and reliability are mandatory for assuring an accepted quality of service for end users. In this context specific fault tolerance strategies are needed. Using concepts from fault tree analysis, we propose a distributed and autonomous approach where each virtualized node can assess and predict its own health state. In our setup each node can proactively take a decision about accepting future jobs, delegate jobs to own replicated instances or start a live migration process. We practically evaluate our model using real Xen log traces.

**Keywords:** VM fault tolerance · Fault trees · Fault agent · Xen log traces

## 1 Introduction

Cloud computing is continuously changing the way we do computation in any domain: business or science. It comprises the idea of delivering computation as a service in a pay-per-use manner through virtualization technology. In the Infrastructure-as-a-Service (IaaS) model, resources are virtualized and delivered as "a service" using Service Level Agreements (SLA) which guarantee certain levels of quality of service (QoS) for end users. Within IaaS, service reliability and availability are of a great importance for a successful service delivery and these objectives can be achieved through complex distributed fault tolerant design. Virtualization brings elasticity in resource provisioning of the cloud, with the meaning that if end users request additional computing resources, they can be provisioned on-demand, transparent to the user.

In general, cloud providers pay a cost for supplying the above mentioned service characteristics: reliability, availability and elasticity. Thus, fault tolerant models that can mitigate provider costs with high levels of QoS are of great interest.

In this paper we develop and evaluate a fault tolerance model for achieving the above-mentioned characteristics within the IaaS cloud model. We use

© Springer International Publishing Switzerland 2014
J. Altmann et al. (Eds.): GECON 2014, LNCS 8914, pp. 206–221, 2014.
DOI: 10.1007/978-3-319-14609-6_14

machine replication and live migration as basic tools and present a fault tolerant design to pro-actively decide when replication and live migration processes should be initiated. With the help of fault tree analysis, we are able to predict the health state of a virtual machine and based on this, to keep high levels of reliability and availability.

The paper is organized as follows. Section 2 describes the problem under study and presents some basic concepts from Fault Tree Analysis. Section 3 details our fault tolerance model, Sect. 4 disseminates the experimental results of a primary implementation of the model. Section 5 reviews several important results in the field, and conclusion ends the paper.

## 2    Background

In this section we describe and formally present the problem under study and some insights about the modeling tool used in this respect.

### 2.1    Problem Specification

We approach a data center where computing power is delivered under the paradigm of "Infrastructure as a Service". IaaS is achieved with the help of a virtualization technique like Xen. Each deployed virtual machine (VM) requires a certain amount of resources, like CPU, RAM, bandwidth and storage, taken from the global pool of the data center. When a VM is instantiated, a service level agreement (SLA) is created for that VM, indicating the amount of resources allocated for the VM. Total available resources of the data center diminishes with every instantiated VM. For this paper, we will work only with the four types of resources enumerated above, without restricting the generality of our approach to other types of resources.

For a successful IaaS service delivery, two characteristics are mandatory to be accomplished: availability and reliability. Service availability is measured with the help of the accepted failure rate of the VM, denoted by $natural_Q$, expressed as the time the machine is not available for usage out of the total time the machine is allocated on the data center. Required service availability is included in the SLA created for a new VM.

A common practice for assuring availability and fault tolerance of the services is replication, where a VM is accompanied by a synchronized VM in a kept similar state. Replication in virtual environments is approached by a large number of authors using techniques like asynchronous checkpoint-recovery replication [4,5] or other more sophisticated techniques based on memory content similarity [7]. In our approach we will assume that each instantiated VM is accompanied by a replica, kept synchronous with the parent using one of the techniques enumerated above. The replica runs in parallel the same processes as the cloned VM. When the VM becomes unavailable, the replica should assure the continuity of the service. Of course that replication imposes extra resource usage generating extra costs for the data center owner.

When the replica fails too, there is a high probability to have a service outage, diminishing the availability figure of the IaaS service. In this case, we can use the elasticity characteristic of the cloud, migrating the machine to a healthy one, using the live migration process [1,12,17]. Live migration incurs allocating a new VM only on-demand basis, and transferring all processed from the unhealthy VM to this new VM; all the migration process being transparent to the cloud user. Live migration consumes the available resources in the data center and incurs additional costs for the IaaS provider. Live migration concurs with other VM creation requests on the data center, and we will model this to obtain the failure probability of the live migration process.

We assume that each VM, during its lifetime, generates events that can be used for VM failure prediction.

To keep service availability at high rates and make the data center resource management operations transparent to the cloud user, including replication and live migration, in this paper we develop a fault tolerance model able to monitor the health state of the running machines and to predict the failure of a VM. Based on this model, we can construct a decision strategy about when to pro-actively transfer the control from a VM to its replica or when to apply the live migration. For our modeling, we will use the fault trees analysis, presented in the next subsection. Having in mind not to overload the virtualization hypervisor or to require other centralized mechanism for running the fault tolerance model, we apply fault tree analysis in decentralized way, such us that each machine to be able to autonomously run the fault tolerance mechanisms.

## 2.2    Fault Tree Analysis

Fault tree analysis was introduced by the U.S. Nuclear Regulatory Commission as the main instrument used in their reactor safety studies. Fault-tree models are part of an analytical technique studying specified undesired states of systems and their systems [9].

Basic fault tree analysis uses graphical tree representation of failure nodes of the system connected together by AND/OR gates. Each node is the equivalent of a subsystem and is characterized by the estimated probability of failure of the represented system or subsystem. Each node of the system can be further decomposed using a fault tree.

In our study we will use the analysis procedure of parallel subsystems - the AND gate, depicted in Fig. 1.

In our case of a parallel system, the whole system is considered crashed when all subsystems that work in parallel are crashed. Having the fault probability for each subsystem $P(S_1)$ and $P(S_2)$, we can compute the failure probability of general fault of the parallel system: $P(S) = P(S_1 \cdot S_2) = P(S_1) \cdot P(S_2)$.

In terms of reliability $(Q)$ and unreliability $(R)$ at a time $t$ we have [9]: $Q(t) = \prod_{i=1}^{n} Q_i(t)$ and $R(t) = 1 - Q(t) \Rightarrow R(t) = 1 - \prod_{i=1}^{n} Q_i(t)$, where $Q_i$ represents the reliability of the $i$th subsystem.

In the context of virtualized environments, we will evaluate the health state of a virtual machine based on the events triggered in the environment using fault

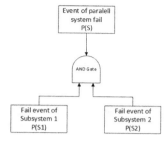

**Fig. 1.** Fault tree representations for parallel two-component systems [9]

trees. Crash imminence will be assessed based on the health state of a VM and its replicas.

## 3 Approach

In this section we present our approach for fault tolerance analysis, based on the above-mentioned fault trees, using concept of fault agents, described below.

### 3.1 Fault Agents

As presented in Sect. 2.1, a VM can have two types of relations with other VMs running in the datacenter, defined as follows: *replication* - between a virtual machine and its clone and *migration* - between a virtual machine and its clone obtained by live migration.

We equip each VM with a fault agent, capable of building the fault tree for the VM according to the relations between that VM and others (replicas or migrated ones). In order to have a bottom-up approach of the problem, the fault agent conceptually resides in the virtual machine and take as input events raised by the hypervisor in the relation with that VM.

The fault agent implements fault tree analysis principles to process the events delivered by the hypervisor and to predict the reliability of the associated virtual machine. The fault agent acts proactively on the behalf of the VM, taking the decision of transferring the control to its replica or to start the live migration process. Having a virtual machine $v_k$ and its replica $r_k$, the fault agent computes the fault tree described in Fig. 2.

The fault tree presented in Fig. 2 has two types of fault nodes:

(1) the computation nodes are fault nodes which correspond to a running or possible running (live migrated) virtual machines. $N_{v_k}$ represents the fault node of the virtual machine $v_k$, $N_{r_k}$ represents the fault node of its replica $r_k$, and $M_{r_k}$ is the fault node of the on-demand future migrated virtual machine.

(2) the aggregation nodes or the decision nodes do not have real corresponding virtual machines, but they aggregate the fault probabilities of the subsystems

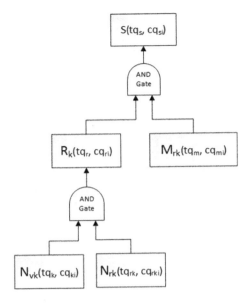

**Fig. 2.** Fault tree model of one replicated virtual machine

and are important for the fault agent to take decisions. $R_k$ represents the fault node of the subsystem resulted from the replication relation of $v_k$ with $r_k$ and it is computed from $N_{v_k}$ and $N_{r_k}$. $S$ represents the fail node of the whole system obtained out of the replication and live migration relations; it is computed from $R_k$ and $M_{r_k}$.

$R_k$ nodes are of great importance, as the fault agent residing on replicas will decide when a live migration has to start, assessing when the replication process is unreliable.

Each node in the fault tree stores two failure probabilities at time $t$: $tq_i$ is the theoretical fault probability of the node and $cq_i$ is the computed fault probability of a node at time instance $t_i$. For each VM, the theoretical fault probability $tq$ is initialized with the value of the maximum accepted fault rate, according to user-accepted QoS of that VM. Computed $cq$ indicators of the computation nodes are initialized with 0 and computed from the events raised by the hypervisor in relation with the VM. Composite $tq$ and $cq$ indicators of aggregation nodes are calculated in the fault tree according to AND gate rules. Below, we fully specify the life cycle of each fault agent.

The fault agent life cycle has two phases:

1. *The fault tree initialization phase* takes place once, when the VM is started and the fault agent is deployed. The fault tree is constructed using the model presented above. In this phase the $tq$ indicators are computed as follows:
   1. $tq_k$ of $N_{v_k}$, $tq_{r_k}$ of $N_{r_k}$ and $tq_m$ of $M_{r_k}$ are initialized with the values of the natural fault probabilities of the virtual machines ($natural_Q$); these values can be found in SLA service availability specification.

2. $tq_r$ of $R_k$ is computed as following: $tq_r = tq_k \cdot tq_{r_k}$ (AND gate output)
3. $tq_s$ of $S$ is computed as following: $tq_s = tq_r \cdot tq_m$ (AND gate output)

2. *The reasoning phase*: the fault agent captures events raised by the VMs or by the hypervisor and updates the $cq$ indicators with the fault probability induced by each event. Each event indicates either the well-being of the system - describing the successful completion of a VM process or it is an undesired event and brings in a fault probability.

The computed probability of failure $cq$ of each node of the tree is updated and recalculated every time an event is raised by the VM. In this phase the $cq$ indicators are computed as presented in the next two subsections.

## Computation of $cq$ for the VM Nodes and Replicas

1. If at time $t_i$ an error event $E_i(p)$ is raised by $v_k$, inducing a probability $p$ for the machine to crash:
   (a) update the $cq$ indicator of the computation node $N_{v_k}$: $cq_{k_i} = cq_{k_{i-1}} + p$
   (b) recompute the $cq_{r_i}$ of the replication decision node $R_k$: $cq_{r_i} = cq_{k_i} \cdot cq_{r_{k_i}}$
   (c) recompute the $cq_s$ of the aggregation system node $S$: $cq_{s_i} = cq_{r_i} \cdot cq_{m_i}$
   (d) announce all the agents of other VMs which are in direct relation with $v_k$ to update their fault tree with the new values
2. If at time $t_i$ a non-error event $NE_i(p)$ is raised by $v_k$, where $p$ is the probability that this event not to take place - thus leaving space for an error event:
   (a) update $cq$ indicator of the corresponding fault node: $cq_{k_i} = max(0, cq_{k_{i-1}} - p)$
   (b) recompute $cq_{r_i}$ and $cq_s$ as explained at 1.
   (c) announce all the agents of other VMs which are in direct relation with $v_k$ to update their fault tree with the new values

Strictly positive $cq$ indicates the unhealthy state of a VM. When a non-error event is produced, the $cq$ is decreased, and after several non-error events, we consider that the virtual machine heals from an unreliable state to healthy one.

When a virtual machine raises an event and the corresponding fault node is updated, the agent announces other agents deployed in other machines which are in direct relation with the current one: for example if $v_k$ updates its corresponding node, the replica agent will be announced to update the corresponding node too in her internal fault tree.

## Computation of $cq$ indicator for the migration fault node $M_{r_k}$. While the $N_{v_k}$, $N_{r_k}$ and $R_k$ nodes are handled based on fault probabilities associated with each raised event originating in the corresponding VMs, the fault probability $cq_{m_i}$ of the live migration node $M_{r_k}$ is computed according to the chance of the VM to migrate at a time $t_i$, being aware that the available resources to be provisioned during the live migration process are limited and there can be other agents simultaneous claiming those resources at time $t_i$. Thus, $cq_{m_i}$ represents the probability of the VM not to be able to migrate at time $t_i$ and is computed as described bellow.

Virtual machine $v_k$ can migrate only if it has enough resources for all four types required. Given that $p_{storagefail}(t_i)$, $p_{cpufail}(t_i)$, $p_{ramfail}(t_i)$, $p_{bandfail}(t_i)$ represent the failure probabilities due to lack of a given type of resources, the probability of $v_k$ not being able to migrate due to insufficient resources (migration fault probability) at time $t_i$ is:

$$p_{v_k}(t_i) = p_{storagefail}(t_i) \cdot p_{cpufail}(t_i) \cdot p_{ramfail}(t_i) \cdot p_{bandfail}(t_i). \qquad (1)$$

Now, we need to compute the values $p(r)_{fail}$ for each of the above mentioned resources: storage, cpu, ram, bandwidth, where $r$ is the requested stock of each resource needed in the live migration process.

For each resource type required by $v_k$, we compute the probability of not having enough resources at time $t_i$. We assume that at time $t_i$ there are $TC$ concurrent requests for the total $RS(t_i)$ stock of resource available at the data center at time $t_i$.

If $NCMALR$ represents the number of claims requesting at least the stock $r$ of the resource and $NCMLR$ represents the number of claims requesting less than the stock $r$ of resources, it gives that the probability of a successful migration requesting $r$ resources $p(r)_{func}$ is

$$p(r)_{func} = \frac{NCMLR}{TC} \qquad (2)$$

and the probability of not being able to complete live migration because of the lack of resources $p(r)_{fail}$ is

$$p(r)_{fail} = 1 - p(r)_{func} = \frac{NCMALR}{TC} \qquad (3)$$

A resource claim is a $j$-subset of $RS(t_i)$. Total possible concurrent requests $TC$ is equal with the number of $j$-subsets on $| RS(t_i) |$ elements and is therefore given by the binomial coefficient $\mathbf{C}^j_{|RS(t_i)|}$. Thus, the total number of possible resource claims is equal to:

$$TC = \sum_{j=1}^{|RS(t_i)|} \mathbf{C}^j_{|RS(t_i)|} = \sum_{j=0}^{|RS(t_i)|} \mathbf{C}^k_{|RS(t_i)|} - \mathbf{C}^0_{|RS(t_i)|} \qquad (4)$$
$$= (1+1)^{|RS(t)|} - \mathbf{C}^0_{|RS(t_i)|} = 2^{|RS(t_i)|} - 1$$

The total number of claims $NCMLR$ requesting less than $r$ resources can be found using dynamic programming, solving the subset sum problem for a maximum $r$ resources, using the recurrence below:

$$NCMLR(RS(t_i), | RS(t_i) |, r) = \qquad (5)$$
$$NCMLR(RS(t_i) \setminus \{x_{|RS(t_i)|}\}, | RS(t_i) | -1, r)+$$
$$NCMLR(RS(t_i) \setminus \{x_{|RS(t_i)|}\}, | RS(t_i) | -1, r - x_{|RS(t_i)|})$$

With this approach, we can compute the four failure probabilities $p_{storagefail}(t_i)$, $p_{cpufail}(t_i)$, $p_{ramfail}(t_i)$, $p_{bandfail}(t_i)$.

The above heuristic computes only the probability of a VM not being able to migrate due to insufficient amount of required resources at time $t$. There can be situations when there are enough available resources to migrate but the live migration fails due to specific migration error or crashes. For the completeness of the approach we need to add another probability component $p_{residual}$ representing the probability of live migration process fault due to causes other than lack of resources. The probability of $v_k$ not being able to migrate is the probability of not being able to migrate because of not enough resources at time t and the live migration residual probability:

$$cq_{m_i}(t_i) = p_{storagefail}(t_i) \cdot p_{cpufail}(t_i) \cdot_{ramfail}(t_i) \cdot p_{bandfail}(t_i) \cdot p_{residual}(t_i) \quad (6)$$

## 3.2  Quantifying the Error Impact on Each Node

In our modeling, the pernicious effect of errors decays over time. Thus, a non-error event or events occurring after an error event indicates that the VM recovered somehow from the crash and the probability of failure decreases.

We considered three types of temporal error impact on the system: (1) punctual impact; (2) stochastic linear decay impact; (3) stochastic exponential decay impact. Below, we present the mathematical modeling for these sorts of decays.

**Punctual Impact.** Punctual impact means that a non-error event following after an error event totally heals the machine. Mathematically, decay intervenes as a Heaviside step function $E(t_{err}) \cdot (1 - H[t_{err} + 1])$ and full decay instantaneously occurs at time $t_{err} + 1$. The differential equation of the process is $\frac{dE}{dt} = E(t_{err}) \cdot (1 - \delta(t_{err} + 1))$. Figure 3 shows this sort of decay function.

**Fig. 3.** Punctual error impact on the system

**Stochastic Linear Decay Impact.** The linear model uses a constant rate of decay, and is the most simple decay function. It has the specific meaning of error impact decreasing in arithmetical progression. The differential equation of the process is $\frac{dE}{dt} = -\lambda_d$ paired with the initial condition $E(t_{err}) = E_{t_{err}}$, where $\lambda_d$ is the linear decay rate. Full decay intervenes after time $t_{err} + \frac{E_{t_{err}}}{\lambda_d}$. Figure 4 shows this type of decaying impact.

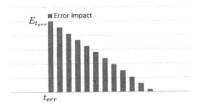

**Fig. 4.** Linearly decaying error impact on the system

We used a stochastic alternative of this equation of the following form: $\frac{dE}{dt} = -\lambda_d + \sigma \cdot dw(t)$, where $\sigma$ is the volatility around the linear decaying trend and $w(t)$ is a Wiener noise. The stochastic decaying process encounters an absorbing barrier at $E = 0$.

**Stochastic Exponential Decay Impact.** The error impact is subject to exponential decay which decreases at a rate proportional to the initial impact. The process can be expressed by the differential equation $\frac{dE}{dt} = -\lambda_d E$, where $E(t)$ is the error impact at time $t$ and $\lambda_d$ is the exponential decay constant.

The solution to this equation is an exponential rate of change $E(t) = E_{t_{err}} e^{-\lambda_d t}$ $t \geq t_{err}$ where $E_{t_{err}} = E(t_{err})$ is the initial error impact on the system at time $t = t_{err}$.

In this case, the error occurrence in the system will induce an infinite impulse response with an impact decreasing exponentially, but never reaching zero and having half-live original impact at time $t_{1/2} = t_{err} + \frac{\ln(2)}{\lambda_d}$. Figure 5 illustrates an example of this type of decaying impact.

We used a stochastic derivation of the exponential decay of the following form: $\frac{dE}{dt} = -\lambda_d \cdot E(t) + \sigma \cdot dw(t)$. The stochastic decaying process encounters an absorbing barrier at $E = 0$.

We used one of the three types of decay functions presented above for computing the update healing probability for each error event occurring at one computation node followed by non-error events (see computation of $cq$ for VM and replica nodes in Subsect. 3.1).

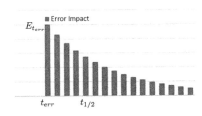

**Fig. 5.** Exponentially decaying error impact on the system

### 3.3    Proactive Decision Making Algorithm

The agent takes a decision to relocate the running processes from the VM to the replica or to start live migration by comparing $cq$ with $tq$ using a threshold.

Given a threshold $0 < f < 1$, the decision process at time $t_i$ for transferring the control to replica or to migrate takes place as follows:

1. for node $N_{v_k}$, if $\frac{cq_{k_i}}{tq_k} \geq f$ then the corresponding virtual machine $v_k$ is unreliable: transfer the control to its replica, $r_k$, only if the replica is reliable: at node $N_{r_k}$, $\frac{cq_{r_{k_i}}}{tq_{r_k}} < f$
2. for the replication composite node $R_k$, if $\frac{cq_{r_i}}{tq_r} >= f$, then both $v_k$ and $r_k$ became unreliable: try to migrate the healthiest machine only if the migration process is reliable: node $M_{r_k} : \frac{cq_{m_i}}{tq_m} < f$
3. for the root node $S$, if $\frac{cq_{k_i}}{tq_k} \geq f$ then the system is in an unreliable state

The possible decisions taken by the fault agent are:

1. REPLICATED - the control has to be transferred to replica- taken upon node $R_k$.
2. MIGRATED - the VM and its replica are unreliable and the migration is needed - taken upon node $R_k$.
3. OK-when a computation node is in a reliable state
4. REPLICATED to OK/MIGRATED to OK - when a VM is becoming reliable again and can be reversed from its previous state (replicated/migrated) to its normal state.
5. REPLICATION FAIL/MIGRATION FAIL - when the replication or migration process is unreliable too.
6. UNRELIABLE - a computation node is declared unreliable

## 4    Experimental Results

Our aim was to evaluate the strategy of migration as a secondary plan for QoS assurance, when the VM and it's replica are in a fault state. We study the evolution of computed fault probability of $R_k$ node which is used to take the decision of migration.

We simulated a virtual machine together with its replica requiring 2 CPUs, 2 GB of RAM, 100 MB/S of bandwidth and 10 GB of storage, and a maximum accepted failure rate of 0.1 % with a threshold $f = \frac{cq_{ki}}{tq_k} = 0.8(80\%)$, varying the number of errors raised by the VM. Using traces generated from real Xen virtualization logs, we studied the behavior of the fault agent for the cases when the migration is needed in the above mentioned error impact scenarios: punctual error impact, linear decay impact and exponential decay impact. The XEN hypervisor was hosting similar VM configurations, having a medium load/hour. It produces three types of log records labeled as: ERROR, DEBUG and INFO. For our experimental setup, we used only the ERROR and INFO labeled log records while the DEBUG records targets the development process of XEN engine.

## 4.1   Error Samples Generated from Traces

The event samples for simulation runs were obtained by parsing each record of the XEN log file obtaining a specific event in the initial sample of VM events. If the log record was labeled as an ERROR, an event error was generated, while another was labeled as INFO a non-error event was generated. For each new created event a simple probability was computed:

1. if the log trace was labeled as ERROR the probability is calculated as
   $\frac{1+\text{number of ERRORS raised before current error}}{\text{total number of events}}$;
2. if the log trace was labeled as INFO the associated probability is calculated as
   $\frac{1+\text{number of INFO raised before current error}}{\text{total number of events}}$;

After parsing all records we obtained a small sample of error and non-error events on which we applied three bootstrapping procedures: bootstrap with no decay effect - producing event queues in which each error has punctual impact, bootstrap with linear decay effect-producing an event queue in which every error has a linear decay impact and bootstrap with exponential decay effect - having as output an event queue in which error events have the effect of exponential decay. Every bootstrap procedure generates a number of event queues from the initial sample using the bootstrap procedures. In our simulations, a linear decay rate of 0.5 and an exponential decay rate of 0.8 where used, specifying the decreasing effect of the decay process.

For a more representative sample of error events, we performed bootstrapping on the event traces pool in order to evaluate our model near the limits and obtaining a larger event sample while preserving the structural characteristics of the initial sample. After each sample was generated using the bootstrap method we computed some descriptive indicators and histograms of the error events contained in the sample (Fig. 6).

On the x-asis we plot the number of error events generated in each event queue by bootstrap routine. On y-axis we plot the frequencies of error occurrences in event queue obtaining the histograms of the error events in the samples. The error distributions are close to the normal distribution indicating that the bootstrap procedures generates robust and representative event samples.

## 4.2   The Different Error Impact Models in Assuring QoS

Previous simulations using randomly generated events from a homogeneous Poisson process showed that for an error rate below 13.41 % per VM the replication cq indicator of fault node $R_k$(the replication node) is below the tq and migration is not needed. When the error rate is higher than 13.41 % per Vm, migration is needed as we can see in Fig. 7, when $cq$ value peeks very close to $tq$ value. Next, in every case of error decays, we analyzed the evolution of $cq$ indicator of the replication node $R_k$ in relation with the maximum accepted failure rate of 0.001 (99.9 % of availability of the service). Moreover these observations where

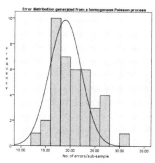

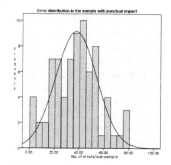

**(a)** Homogeneous Poisson process sample (Mean:19.88; Std.Dev:4.02; Skewness:0.37)

**(b)** Punctual error impact sample (Mean:37.60; StdDev:18.19; Skewness:0.79)

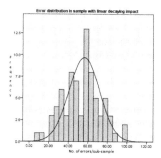

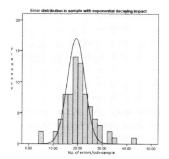

**(c)** Linear decay error impact sample (Mean:53.89; Std-Dev:19.25; Skewness:0.002)

**(d)** Exponential decay error impact sample(Mean:19.95; Std-Dev:6.17; Skewness:0.69)

**Fig. 6.** Error distribution in the different scenario event samples

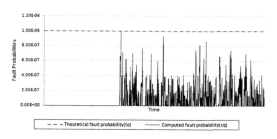

**Fig. 7.** Computed probability (cq) evolution on replication node for 13.41 % errors from Poisson homogeneous process

made after 3000 VM events when migration was needed. Bellow this value no migration was needed.

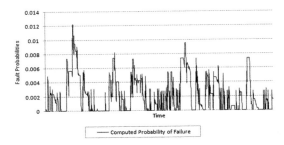

**Fig. 8.** Computed probability (cq) evolution on replication node in punctual error impact scenario [Average: MIGRATED-7 %; MIGRATED-OK-0.2 %]

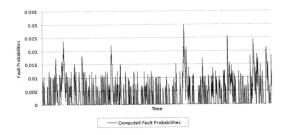

**Fig. 9.** Computed probability (cq) evolution on replication node in linear decay error impact [Average: MIGRATED-6.36 %; MIGRATED-OK-0.23 %]

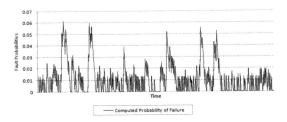

**Fig. 10.** Computed probability (cq) evolution on replication node in exponential decay error impact [Average: MIGRATED-10.3 %; MIGRATED-OK-0.13 %]

Figures 8, 9 and 10 present a comparative view of the evolution of cq indicator calculated for the replication node in each 3 event samples scenarios. The data used for these representations was considered from the moment when the fault agent is starting to take the decision for live migration due to VM and replica unreliability.

When the level of 0.001 $natural_Q$ is passed by the cq indicators live migration is required. Observing the frequency and amplitude of peeks correlated with the average percentage of live migration in each case, we can state that in the linear decay error impact scenario we have the smallest number of migrations, followed by the punctual decay error scenario and exponential decay error impact when live migration rate is the highest. Moreover the cq values have the natural tendency to return back to the imposed threshold of 0.001. This can be explained due to the compensation power of the non-error events.

## 5    Related Work

Reliable cloud computing infrastructures require specially selected and optimized conditions for which the hardware equipment are not primarily conceived [6,20]. The complexity and the heterogeneity of hardware infrastructures can make cloud-based systems prone to significant amounts of failures and functioning incidents [11]. In failure-prone environments, fault tolerance is playing an essential part when assuring high levels of reliability and availability of the services [15]. To tolerate failures, these environments are characterized by systematic resource replication. By replicating individual virtual machines, fault tolerance and resource costs of applications can be improved [19].

There are many symbolic representations used to describe the ability of a distributed system to cope with failures. In this paper, we describe the failure behaviour of a fault tolerant system through fault tree models [2,10], which are well fitted to present the different levels of errors specific to cloud computing infrastructures [8,18].

System virtualization technology is at the foundation of the cloud computing. Through virtualization, extra hosts can be easily added or removed at any time after the computing infrastructure has been set up. Thus, cloud infrastructure can start at initial modest scales, and then scale up progressively, rendering system services in a flexible and scalable way [16]. Virtualization [13] is highly beneficial since virtual machine instances level up computing resources stemming from potentially hundreds of thousands of commodity servers with heterogeneous CPU, memory and storage characteristics. When the replicas are located at physical hosts with different geographical location, the failures incidence on different replicas can become increasingly independent and the system much more reliable [3,21].

Application deployment on virtual machines instances within clouds bring new risks as failures in data centres are normally outside the clouds clients' control. Traditional approaches in assuring fault tolerance require the users to have very good knowledge of the base mechanisms. Cloud computing, on the other hand, through the abstraction layers, make transparent the architectural details for their clients. This changes the paradigm in approaching fault tolerance, as the cloud computing platforms need to address clients' reliability and availability concerns. Our approach is employing Xen [14] as a virtualization system but it is not constrained to it.

## 6    Conclusions

The paper presents a novel approach to autonomous management of virtual machine faults in Infrastructure as a Service cloud model, by deploying fault agents which conceptually reside in each virtual machine. Having the objective of avoiding QoS breaches, using fault tree analysis, fault agents can decide whether the virtual machine is reliable. To preserve the availability rate of the VMs, we use a strategy which combines active machine replication and live migration. When replication strategy fails, the migration process of virtual machine is used in order to assure continuity of the service.

We evaluated our fault tolerance model using a practical approach by generating virtual machine events traces from production Xen engine logs. We tested our model for robustness in a stress evaluation setup by using bootstrapping. Considering three sorts of error impact behaviors: punctual impact, linear decay and exponential decay, we showed that after an error event is raised, several consecutive non-error events can have the power to establish the reliable status of a virtual machine. Further work will focus on autonomous establishing when to apply each impact behavior and which one suits best for the IaaS setups.

**Acknowledgements.** This work was co-financed from the European Social Fund through Sectoral Operational Programme Human Resources Development 2007-2013, project number POSDRU/159/1.5/S/134197 "Performance and excellence in doctoral and postdoctoral research in Romanian economics science domain". G.C. Silaghi acknowledges support from UEFISCDI under project JustASR - PN-II-PT-PCCA-2013-4-1644.

# References

1. Atif, M., Strazdins, P.: Adaptive parallel application resource remapping through the live migration of virtual machines. Future Gener. Comput. Syst. **37**, 148–161 (2014)
2. Bobbio, A., Portinale, L., Minichino, M., Ciancamerla, E.: Improving the analysis of dependable systems by mapping fault trees into bayesian networks. Reliab. Eng. Syst. Saf. **71**(3), 249–260 (2001)
3. Clark, C., Fraser, K., Hand, S., Hansen, J.G., Jul, E., Limpach, C., Pratt, I., Warfield, A.: Live migration of virtual machines. In: Proceedings of the 2nd Conference on Symposium on Networked Systems Design & Implementation, NSDI'05, vol. 2, pp. 273–286. USENIX Association (2005)
4. Colesa, A., Mihai, B.: An adaptive virtual machine replication algorithm for highly-available services. In: 2011 Federated Conference on Computer Science and Information Systems (FedCSIS), pp. 941–948. IEEE (2011)
5. Cully, B., Lefebvre, G., Meyer, D., Feeley, M., Hutchinson, N., Warfield, A.: Remus: high availability via asynchronous virtual machine replication. In: Proceedings of the 5th USENIX Symposium on Networked Systems Design and Implementation, San Francisco, pp. 161–174 (2008)
6. Feller, E., Rilling, L., Morin, C.: Snooze: a scalable and autonomic virtual machine management framework for private clouds. In: 12th IEEE/ACM International Symposium on Cluster, Cloud and Grid Computing (CCGrid), pp. 482–489. IEEE Press, May 2012
7. Gerofi, B., Vass, Z., Ishikawa, Y.: Utilizing memory content similarity for improving the performance of replicated virtual machines. In: 2011 Fourth IEEE International Conference on Utility and Cloud Computing (UCC), pp. 73–80. IEEE (2011)

8. Guerraoui, R., Yabandeh, M.: Independent faults in the cloud. In: Proceedings of the 4th International Workshop on Large Scale Distributed Systems and Middleware, LADIS '10, pp. 12–17. ACM Press (2010)

9. Haimes, Y.: Risk Modeling, Assessment, and Management. Wiley, New York (2005)

10. Jhawar, R., Piuri, V.: Fault tolerance management in iaas clouds. In: IEEE First AESS European Conference on Satellite Telecommunications (ESTEL), pp. 1–6. IEEE Press (2012)

11. Jhawar, R., Piuri, V.: Fault tolerance and resilience in cloud computing environments. In: Vacca, J.R. (ed.) Cyber Security and IT Infrastructure Protection, pp. 1–28. Syngress (2014)

12. Jin, H., Deng, L., Wu, S., Shi, X., Chen, H., Pan, X.: Mecom: live migration of virtual machines by adaptively compressing memory pages. Future Gener. Comput. Syst. **38**, 23–35 (2014)

13. Kim, D.S., Machida, F., Trivedi, K.S.: Availability modeling and analysis of a virtualized system. In: Proceedings of the 2009 15th IEEE Pacific Rim International Symposium on Dependable Computing, PRDC '09, pp. 365–371. IEEE Computer Society (2009)

14. Nagarajan, A.B., Mueller, F., Engelmann, C., Scott, S.L.: Proactive fault tolerance for hpc with xen virtualization. In: Proceedings of the 21st Annual International Conference on Supercomputing, ICS '07, pp. 23–32. ACM Press (2007)

15. Nicolae, B., Cappello, F.: BlobCR: Virtual disk based checkpoint-restart for HPC applications on IaaS clouds. J. Parallel Distrib. Comput. **73**(5), 698–711 (2013)

16. Sampaio, A.M., Barbosa, J.G.: Towards high-available and energy-efficient virtual computing environments in the cloud. Future Gener. Comput. Syst. **40**, 30–43 (2014)

17. Travostino, F., Daspit, P., Gommans, L., Jog, C., De Laat, C., Mambretti, J., Monga, I., Van Oudenaarde, B., Raghunath, S., Yonghui Wang, P.: Seamless live migration of virtual machines over the man/wan. Future Gener. Comput. Syst. **22**(8), 901–907 (2006)

18. Undheim, A., Chilwan, A., Heegaard, P.: Differentiated availability in cloud computing slas. In: Proceedings of the 2011 IEEE/ACM 12th International Conference on Grid Computing, GRID '11, pp. 129–136. IEEE Computer Society (2011)

19. Vallee, G., Engelmann, C., Tikotekar, A., Naughton, T., Charoenpornwattana, K., Leangsuksun, C., Scott, S.: A framework for proactive fault tolerance. In: Third International Conference on Availability, Reliability and Security, (ARES), pp. 659–664. IEEE Press (2008)

20. Vishwanath, K.V., Nagappan, N.: Characterizing cloud computing hardware reliability. In: Proceedings of the 1st ACM Symposium on Cloud Computing, pp. 193–204. ACM Press (2010)

21. Wang, S.S., Wang, S.C.: The consensus problem with dual failure nodes in a cloud computing environment. Inf. Sci. **279**, 213–228 (2014)

# How Do Content Delivery Networks Affect the Economy of the Internet and the Network Neutrality Debate?

Patrick Maillé[1] and Bruno Tuffin[2]([⊠])

[1] Institut Mines-Télécom/Télécom Bretagne, 2, rue de la Châtaigneraie,
35576 Cesson Sévigné Cedex, France
patrick.maille@telecom-bretagne.eu
[2] Inria Rennes Bretagne Atlantique, Campus Universitaire de Beaulieu,
35042 Rennes Cedex, France
Bruno.Tuffin@inria.fr

**Abstract.** This paper investigates the economic impact and strategies of Content Delivery Networks (CDNs), Internet actors that reduce the capacity needs in the backbone network and improve the quality perceived by users. We consider so-called push and pull models where the traffic is paid by the sender or the receiver, respectively, as well as the situation where the CDN is (vertically) integrated to, i.e., owned by, an Internet Service Provider (ISP). We then discuss the implication of CDNs into the network neutrality debate, another issue forgotten by researchers and regulators.

## 1 Introduction

Content delivery networks (CDNs) are large distributed systems of servers deployed within the Internet, aimed at putting data closer to end users to offer better quality of service (QoS) and availability [3]. The role of CDNs is to produce the highest performance for content accessed by users, some typically demanding applications being video delivery or gaming. They are therefore of interest for content/service providers, but also for network providers since reducing the load (congestion) on the network: the most popular pieces of content, being stored at the edge of the network, do not need to be downloaded from their source upon each request.

But the telecommunications economics literature barely addresses the role of CDNs, although they have become major actors of the Internet. While there has been a huge amount of work on CDNs from a technical point of view, the literature on the economics of CDNs is more limited. Existing works focus on the optimal pricing strategies of CDNs [8], or discuss if and how different CDNs within a network should cooperate when setting their caching strategies [1,4, 5,7,9]. But the interactions between CDNs, ISPs, and CPs, have received little attention, while they have a major impact all the different actors.

This paper is a first step in the direction of modeling and analyzing the relations between CDNs and other Internet actors:

© Springer International Publishing Switzerland 2014
J. Altmann et al. (Eds.): GECON 2014, LNCS 8914, pp. 222–230, 2014.
DOI: 10.1007/978-3-319-14609-6_15

- We extend a previous model of ISP competition by including CDNs into the picture, to study how they interact and what their best strategies are.
- We consider both the so-called *pull model* – where the ISP requesting content has to pay the ISP hosting it – and the *push model* – where the transfer fee is paid by the ISP hosting content to the one hosting end users; in addition the CDN can be an independent entity or be owned and managed by an ISP. For each case, we illustrate the impact of CDNs on ISPs' revenues and on fairness between CPs.
- We then discuss the impact of CDNs on the *network neutrality debate* [10–12], in which CDNs have also barely been addressed although they reduce traffic transit, thereby addressing in part the concerns that ISPs express in the debate.

## 2    Model

Extending the model in [6], we consider two ISPs ($A$ and $B$), in competition for end users. We assume a continuum of content, whose total mass normalized to 1 represents the total volume downloaded per time unit (i.e., the mass of each piece of content is proportional to its popularity). Let $x$ (resp., $1 - x$) be the proportion of content that is *directly* connected to the Internet through $A$ (resp., $B$).

At each ISP, we can have a CDN, indexed by the name of its host ISP, caching some of the content rooted at the other ISP to improve QoS and avoid potential transfer fees between ISPs. Each CDN can be an independent actor (ex: Akamai), or a service implemented by the hosting ISP (the CDN is then said *vertically integrated*).

Figure 1 represents the actors and their economic relations. Users are treated too as a continuum (individuals having a negligible impact) of total mass 1. The price $p_A$ (resp. $p_B$) is the *flat-rate* subscription fee of ISP $A$ (resp. $B$), and $t$ is a unit price for the traffic transferred between ISPs: $t = 0$ corresponds to the classical peering agreement with no fee, while $t \neq 0$ means a paid transit.

Finally, only a portion of the downloaded content is cached by the CDNs, we denote those quantities by $y_A \leq 1 - x$ at CDN $A$ and $y_B \leq x$ at CDN $B$.

Users' choice of ISP (if any) is through a standard *attraction model* [2]: the proportion of users choosing Option $i \in \{A, B, 0\}$ –0 meaning no subscription– is

$$\sigma_i(p_A, p_B) \overset{\text{def}}{=} \frac{(x_i/p_i)^\alpha}{(x_A/p_A)^\alpha + (x_B/p_B)^\alpha + 1/p_0^\alpha}, \tag{1}$$

where $\alpha > 0$ is a sensitivity parameter, $p_0$ represents the cost of not benefitting from any content, and $x_i$ is the average perceived quality with ISP $i \in \{A, B\}$. Content is reachable with high quality $\gamma > 1$ (from the local ISP or its host CDN) or low quality 1 (from the distant ISP), yielding

$$x_A = 1 + (x + y_A)(\gamma - 1); \quad x_B = 1 + (1 - x + y_B)(\gamma - 1).$$

Each ISP $i \in \{A, B\}$ focuses on net benefits, stemming from:

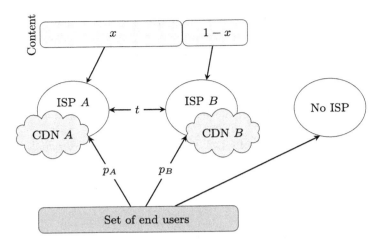

**Fig. 1.** Relations between users, ISPs, and CPs

*(1)* end-users subscriptions, the corresponding incomes being proportional to the market share $\sigma_i$ and the price $p_i$;

*(2)* the potential gains/costs from hosting a CDN:
  - if the CDN is an independent actor (Akamai for instance), we assume the CDN pays a per-unit-of-volume fee $r$ to the ISP for delivering content from the CDN cache servers to the ISP users.
  - If the CDN role is managed by the ISP itself (something increasingly happening), $r$ is the per-unit-of-volume revenue the ISP gets from remote CPs for serving as a CDN. We also add a storing cost $c_i$ depending on $y_i$, that can be considered convex since the most popular contents will be cached in priority.

*(3)* And the potential transit fees between ISPs: content associated to ISP $A$ (resp. $B$) and transferred to $B$ (resp. $A$) being proportional to $x - y_B$ (resp. $1 - x - y_A$) and to ISP B (resp. A) market share, the net (possibly negative) amount $\Delta_{A,B}$ of traffic from $A$ to $B$ is

$$\Delta_{A,B} = (x - y_B)\sigma_B(p_A, p_B) - (1 - x - y_A)\sigma_A(p_A, p_B).$$

- In the *Pull model*, the transfer fee is paid by the ISP hosting end users to the one hosting content, i.e., the service is asked by end users. Let $t$ be the per-unit-of-volume price. This leads to a revenue $t\Delta_{A,B}$ for $A$, from $B$ (and an equal cost for $B$).
- *Push model*: the transfer fee is paid by the ISP hosting content to the one hosting end users, i.e., the service is asked by content providers. The same type of expression can be used with $t < 0$.

Regrouping, the ISP utilities per time unit are:

$$U_A(p_A, p_B) = \sigma_A(p_A, p_B)p_A + t\Delta_{A,B} + ry_A - c_A(y_A),$$
$$U_B(p_A, p_B) = \sigma_B(p_A, p_B)p_B - t\Delta_{A,B} + ry_B - c_B(y_B). \tag{2}$$

We neglect the transfer cost of files from (remote) content providers to CDNs, since that transfer is done only once.

# 3  How Much Content to Cache?

We focus here on the amount of cached content that benefits the most to the ISP hosting the CDN.

## 3.1  Pull Model and Independent CDN

From (2), if ISP $i$ hosts a CDN increasing its cached content: (i) ISP $i$ attracts more users because providing a better QoS (i.e., $\sigma_i$ increases), (ii) ISP $i$ gains more from the CDN ($ry_i$ increases with $y_i$), (iii) ISP $i$ pays less for transit because "pulling" less traffic. $U_i$ thus increases with $y_i$, ISPs should then let CDNs cache as much content as possible.

## 3.2  Push Model and Independent CDN

Now the ISP still gains from CDN payments and increased attractiveness to users, but loses from transfer fees since its competitor will have to "push" less traffic. Figure 2(a) shows the values of $U_A$ when $y_A$ ($\in [0, 1-x]$) varies, for three values of $r$ and with $\alpha = 1.5$, $x = 0.6$, $t = -1$, $y_B = 0.3$, $\gamma = 1.5$, $p_0 = 1$, $p_A = 1.3$, $p_B = 1.7$. Note that $c_A = c_B = 0$, since the storage cost is borne by the CDN. Depending on the parameters, it can be optimal to cache nothing, the whole content, or an intermediate amount, but we expect the optimal cached amount to increase with $r$, because the ISP's revenue from the CDN increases.

## 3.3  Pull Model and Integrated CDN

We take here the same values as for Fig. 2(a), except that now $t = 1$ (pull model) and that the ISP bears storage costs, of the form $c_A(y_A) = (y_A)^{3/2}$. Because of that cost, we end up too with a trade-off. Figure 2(b) displays $U_A$ in terms of $y_A$ ($\in [0, 1-x]$). Note here that because $c'_A(0) = 0$, the derivative of the utility is positive at 0 (the other effects improve revenue), hence there are always incentives to cache some content. Again, when $r$ is large enough, it becomes beneficial to cache all content.

## 3.4  Push Model and Integrated CDN

With the same set of values as for Fig. 2(a), but with the storage costs $c_A(y_A) = (y_A)^{3/2}$, we studied the revenue $U_A$ when $y_A$ varies. The curves have a shape similar to those of Fig. 2(a), we omit them due to space constraints. Even in the push model, an ISP can have an interest in using an integrated CDN if $r$ is large enough.

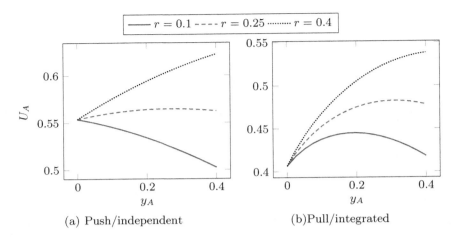

**Fig. 2.** ISP $A$ revenue versus cached amount $y_A$

### 3.5    Caching and Its Impact on Revenues

Figure 3 *(top)* plots the optimal cached amount $y_A$ and the corresponding utility $U_A$ in terms of $x$, for each of the four situations, adding the curve of $U_A$ when no CDN exists. Note it is not relevant to compare the numerical values between integrated and independent: $r$ is taken the same (a cost $c_A$ is added to the integrated case), but it represents a price paid by the CDN in the independent case and a price paid by CPs in the integrated case. Remark in Fig. 3 *(top)* that for the push/integrated case, $y_A$ is 0 or close to 0. In the push/independent case, caching a non-negligible proportion is better for small $x$ but the optimal cached part quickly goes to 0 as $x$ increases. As seen before, all $B$ content (i.e., $y_A = 1-x$) is cached in the pull/independent case. For the pull/integrated model the optimal $y_A$ increases with $x$ when $y_a < 1-x$. Note that $U_A$ increases with $x$ in the pull cases, but the trend is to decrease in the push ones, suggesting there is no interest for ISPs to attract CPs for the latter. Moreover the no-CDN curve is very close to the integrated one in the push case, because $y_A^{opt}$ is close to 0. Caching does not yield a large revenue improvement in the pull/integrated case either (while it does for the independent case), but the gain can be significant with different parameters. Figure 3 *(bottom)* displays the same metrics, but when the price $r$ varies. For small values of $r$, in both push cases there is no incentive to cache content, because gains are not sufficient, but above a threshold caching becomes beneficial. The revenue logically increases in $r$ too (in cases with CDN).

## 4    Fairness Concerns

We now focus on the impact of CDNs on CPs: Is there a difference of treatment among CPs according to the ISP they are attached to? To answer, we use the (aggregated) perceived quality $Q_i$ of content associated to ISP $i$, that is $\gamma$ for

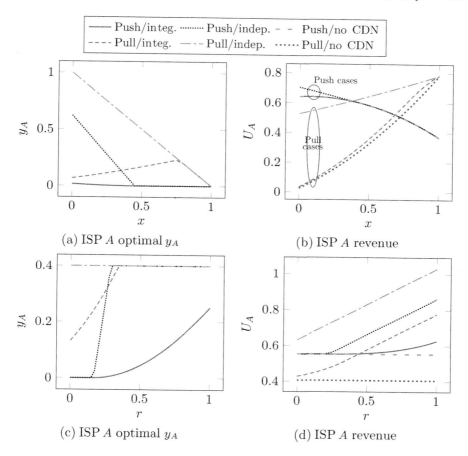

(a) ISP $A$ optimal $y_A$

(b) ISP $A$ revenue

(c) ISP $A$ optimal $y_A$

(d) ISP $A$ revenue

**Fig. 3.** ISP $A$ optimal $y_A$ and utility $U_A$

the customers of ISP $i$ and for those of $j \neq i$ if the content is cached in $j$'s CDN, and 1 otherwise. This gives:

$$Q_A = \gamma\sigma_A + \gamma\sigma_B y_B/x + \sigma_B(1 - y_B/x)$$
$$Q_B = \gamma\sigma_B + \gamma\sigma_A y_A/(1 - x) + \sigma_A(1 - y_A/(1 - x)).$$

Note that for any set of parameters, quality does not depend on the type of model (push/pull, integrated or not). Taking the values (when fixed) of Sect. 3.2 (adding $y_A = 0.2$), we display $Q_A$ and $Q_B$ in Fig. 4 when $x$ and $y_A$ vary.

We observe a difference of treatment depending on the proportion of content hosted by ISPs (note that we have considered heterogeneous parameters). When $x$ is small here, content hosted in $B$ perceived better (because almost all content of $B$ is cached in $A$, the $y_i$ being fixed, while after some point the quality in $A$ becomes better. This illustrates the impact of CDNs on perceived quality, and that CPs may be disadvantaged if associated with a given ISP.

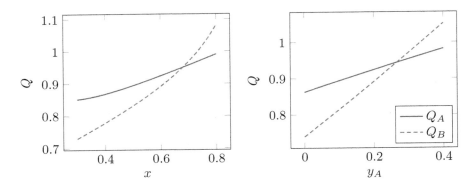

**Fig. 4.** Content quality depending on host ISP

Figure 4 *(right)* shows that as the cached amount in $A$ increases, the quality $Q_B$ of content in $B$ increases, but $Q_A$ also increases (even if to a lesser extent), because $\sigma_A$ increases.

## 5    Discussion: CDN and Neutrality

The question of how CDNs impact the network neutrality debate hasn't been addressed much, but introducing them into the picture reshapes the economic relationships between actors. Several remarks on that matter can be made from our model:

*(1)* For the pull model, the ISP has interest in accepting the operation of an external CDN, even without charging it. In all other cases, there are conditions on the set of parameters for this to occur, but the ISP often has an interest in hosting a CDN (integrated or not).

*(2)* Hosting a CDN induces less traffic within the network, thus reduces the pressure to increase capacities.

*(3)* The CDN operation fees are paid by CPs (to improve their QoS), which somehow is a shift in payment with respect to the side payments requested by ISPs in the neutrality debate. But this fee can hurt innovation exactly as side payments would: can regulators accept that and still prevent ISPs from imposing side payments?

*(4)* Only the most frequently downloaded content is cached by CDNs. If the service is proposed to all (distant) CPs, this makes a differentiation between CPs, which is in a sense against the neutrality principle, because packets are not treated the same. One can also argue that it makes a difference of treatment between local and distant CPs. In any case, the CDN activity requires attention, and its conformity depends on the definition of neutrality.

*(5)* The case $r = 0$ (no payment) would not create any neutrality problem. But as we have seen, this is acceptable for the ISP only for the pull model with an external CDN.

*(6)* But we assumed here that CPs always prefer to use the CDN services, something to be further studied.

We believe that this work highlights the need for CDNs economic modeling in the Internet and for a deeper investigation of their impact on actors, fairness, and neutrality.

## 6    Conclusions and Perspectives

This paper is a first step in the modeling and analysis of CDNs' economics, in interaction with end users, content providers and ISPs, in order to start discussing their influence into the network neutrality debate. We have presented several situations, depending on whether the CDN is vertically integrated with the ISP or not, combined with the so-called push and pull models, where the traffic is paid by the sender or the receiver respectively. We have determined how the CDN can compute the optimal amount data to be cached in each situation (which of course depends on the selected parameters) and the impact on revenue. The impact on the fairness in terms of treatment between the different content providers is then described.

We observed that revenue-oriented CDNs may treat content providers differently, which could go against principles of neutrality and hurt innovation. Again, conclusions are case dependent, since different parameter choices can lead to different conclusions.

As extensions of the work, we would like to investigate the viability of CDNs' business in neutral and non-neutral contexts, and to study the case of more complex topologies involving more ISPs, CDNs in competition, as well as more content providers. The case when ISPs pay for caching will also deserve attention.

## References

1. Atzmon, H., Friedman, R., Vitenberg, R.: Replacement policies for a distributed object caching service. In: Meersman, R., Tari, Z. (eds.) CoopIS/DOA/ODBASE 2002. LNCS, vol. 2519, pp. 661–674. Springer, Heidelberg (2002)
2. Ben-Akiva, M., Lerman, S.: Discrete Choice Analysis. The MIT Press, Cambridge (1985)
3. Buyya, R., Pathan, M., Vakali, A. (eds.): Content Delivery Networks. LNEE, vol. 9. Springer, Heidelberg (2008). http://dx.doi.org/10.1007/978-3-540-77887-5
4. Christin, N., Chuang, J., Grossklags, J.: Economics-informed design of CDNs. In: Buyya, R., Pathan, M., Vakali, A. (eds.) Content Delivery Networks. LNEE, vol. 9, pp. 183–210. Springer, Heidelberg (2008). http://dx.doi.org/10.1007/978-3-540-77887-5_7
5. Chun, B.G., Chaudhuri, K., Wee, H., Barreno, M., Papadimitriou, C.H., Kubiatowicz, J.: Selfish caching in distributed systems: a game-theoretic analysis. In: Proceedings of PODC'04, pp. 21–30. ACM (2004). http://doi.acm.org/10.1145/1011767.1011771

6. Coucheney, P., Maillé, P., Tuffin, B.: Network Neutrality Debate and ISP Inter-Relations: Traffic Exchange, Revenue Sharing, and Disconnection Threat. Rapport de recherche, Inria, January 2012. http://hal.inria.fr/hal-00659278

7. Hosanagar, K.: CDN pricing. In: Buyya, R., Pathan, M., Vakali, A. (eds.) Content Delivery Networks. LNEE, vol. 9, pp. 211–224. Springer, Heidelberg (2008). http://dx.doi.org/10.1007/978-3-540-77887-5_8

8. Hosanagar, K., Chuang, J., Krishnan, R., Smith, M.: Service adoption and pricing of content delivery network (CDN) services. Manag. Sci. 54(9), 1579–1593 (2008). http://pubsonline.informs.org/doi/abs/10.1287/mnsc.1080.0875

9. Hosanagar, K., Krishnan, R., Smith, M., Chuang, J.: Optimal pricing of content delivery network (CDN) services. In: Proceedings of the 37th Annual Hawaii International Conference on System Sciences, January 2004

10. Lenard, T.M., May, R.J. (eds.): Net Neutrality or Net Neutering: Should Broadband Internet Services be Regulated. Springer, New York (2006)

11. Maillé, P., Reichl, P., Tuffin, B.: Internet governance and economics of network neutrality. In: Hadjiantonis, A.M., Stiller, B. (eds.) Telecommunication Economics. LNCS, vol. 7216, pp. 108–116. Springer, Heidelberg (2012)

12. Wu, T.: Network neutrality, broadband discrimination. J. Telecommun. High Technol. 2(1), 141–176 (2003)

# Author Index

Printed in the United States
By Bookmasters